"My friend John Trent has written a truly inspired and important book. *LifeMapping* will provide you with the tools you need to understand those critical events that shaped you. And, more importantly, this book will help you create a plan for 'writing your own future' on purpose! *LifeMapping* works, and now John has made it understandable and wonderfully helpful. I highly recommend this book."

Gary Smalley
President
Today's Family

"Over the past few years, I have had the privilege of getting to know John Trent not only through his writings, but also on a personal level. That's why I'm excited about his new book, *LifeMapping*. The principles you will learn from it will be life-changing. We have already applied some of them to our own lives with very positive results. This book is a must read for those who are serious about 'getting their act together.' "

Dave and Jan Dravecky
Authors of *When You Can't
Come Back*

"When John Trent smiles, it's with unforgettable warmth. Because he knows the Bible, he knows people need encouragement. He knows they were made for relationships. So he deals in smiles, biblical principles, kindnesses, and encouragement—all to the end that you might live better with those you love. *LifeMapping* is a healthy dose of all of these wrapped around some of the most practical, helpful tools for improving your life that you'll ever find."

Stu and Linda Weber
Authors of *Tender Warrior* (Stu)
and *Mom, You're Incredible!* (Linda)

"John Trent is one of America's most innovative and creative 'helpers.' He has assisted thousands of people in the art of determining their destinations and re-examining their directions. When he talks about 'flash points' and 'freeze points,' he makes a contribution of great value. *LifeMapping* will be of enormous help to virtually everyone."

Neil and Marylyn Warren
Author (Neil) of *Finding the
Love of Your Life*

"We all want our lives to be characterized by strong personal character and healthy relationships. With refreshing simplicity, John Trent builds upon the clear teaching of Scripture to give readers a unique and practical tool to help them rebuild, redirect, and strengthen their lives. If you want to move beyond good intentions to growth and change and maturity, *LifeMapping* is must reading for you."

> Gary J. Oliver, Ph.D.
> Daniel W. Trathen, D.Min.
> Co-directors
> Southwest Counseling Associates

"What a thrill it is for us to be able to recommend John Trent's first solo book! We're excited about *LifeMapping* and the hope it offers to heal a hurting past, develop strong, healthy relationships, and move toward maturity as a follower of Jesus Christ. Pro athlete couples love John and are blessed and encouraged by his practical, understandable style. This book will join the others John has co-authored with Gary Smalley that are always on the recommended reading lists we offer to our conferees."

> Norm and Bobbe Evans
> Pro Athletes Outreach

"Whenever we have needed a fresh dose of encouragement, John and Cindy Trent have always been there. Their marriage and ministry are indelibly marked by a deep commitment to the Lord Jesus Christ and a sincere love for others. We count it a privilege to have them as friends."

> John and Teri Nieder
> The Art of Family Living

"*LifeMapping* gives us an incredible hands-on tool that we can use to build our character and develop the healthy, loving relationships for which we all yearn. Sit back and get ready for a journey. This book by John Trent is written in a vulnerable and authentic style that will draw you closer to God and sharpen your insight and vision."

> Gary Rosberg, Ph.D.
> President
> CrossTrainer Ministries

"John Trent's new book, *LifeMapping*, did for me what every book always *hopes* to do—it made me look at my life. But it did something more as well; it made me want to do something about my life in a positive and godly way. I wasn't surprised, though. That always happens when I read something John Trent has written."

Gary Richmond
Author of *A View from the Zoo*
and *The Divorce Decision*

"*LifeMapping* is a long-overdue guide to understanding and dealing with the circumstances of life. Once again, John Trent has made some of life's mountains and valleys much more comprehensible. More importantly, John's book helps map a pathway for our future steps. This is must reading for everyone."

Robert Barnes, Ed.D.
Executive Director
Sheridan House Family Ministries

"In ten years, there will be two groups of Christian adults in this country: those who read *LifeMapping* and are taking the 'high road bound for authentic living,' and those who didn't and need to know about such things as 'image management.' The first group will be saying, 'I'm glad I read it'; the others will be saying, 'I wish I had." Join me as one who has met John and his terrific ideas face to face. I believe your life will be forever the better."

Joe White, Ed.D.
President
Kanakuk-Kanakomo Kamps, Inc.

"We all want to grow and develop in our lives and relationships, but too often, the changes we desire become sidetracked on the roadway of 'good intentions.' Through *LifeMapping*, John Trent has provided a practical, comprehensive, and highly personal road map that allows us to move beyond the frustration of good intentions to the fruitfulness of personal and spiritual maturity."

Dan Bolin, Th.M.
President
Christian Camping International/USA

"Having played for the L.A. Lakers, I appreciate a great guard who will pass the ball inside. *LifeMapping* is a perfect pass from the most encouraging player in the league. Catch it, score, win the game, and become more than a conqueror."

Jay Carty
President
Yes! Ministries

"You don't have to weather a major crisis or near-death experience to get a wide-angle perspective on your life! John Trent's *LifeMapping* keeps you turning pages and nodding your head with recognition. It's kind of like your first ride in an airplane, looking down on familiar landmarks from a new point of view. You can see so clearly where you've been and then gaze out on a wider horizon than you'd ever imagined possible."

Larry Libby
Author of *Someday Heaven*

LifeMapping

John Trent, Ph.D.

PUBLISHING

Colorado Springs, Colorado

LIFEMAPPING

Copyright © 1994 by John Trent, Ph. D. All rights reserved. International copyright secured.

Library of Congress Cataloging-in-Publication Data

Trent, John T.
    LifeMapping / John Trent.
       p.   cm.
    Includes bibliographical references.
    ISBN 1-56179-251-9
      1. Christian life.   2. Intimacy (Psychology)—Religious aspects—Christianity.   3. Change—
Religious aspects—Christianity.
I. Title. II. Title: Life mapping.
BV4501.2.T68   1994
248.4—dc20
                                   94-14106
                                       CIP

Published by Focus on the Family Publishing, Colorado Springs, CO 80995.

Distributed in the U.S.A. and Canada by Word Books, Dallas, Texas.

Unless otherwise noted, Scripture quotations are from the *New American Standard Bible*, © 1960, 1963, 1968, 1971, 1973, 1975, and 1977 by The Lockman Foundation. Used by permission. Scriptures identified as NIV are from the Holy Bible, New International Version, copyright © 1973, 1978, 1984 by the International Bible Society. Used by permission of Zondervan Publishing House. All rights reserved.

People's names and certain details of case studies mentioned in this book have been changed to protect the privacy of the individuals involved. However, the author has attempted to convey the essence of the experience and the underlying principles as accurately as possible.

Editor: Larry K. Weeden
Cover Design: McMonigle and Spooner

Printed in the United States of America
94 95 96 97 98/10 9 8 7 6 5 4 3 2 1

Everyone has dreams, but not everyone gets to live with one.

This book is lovingly dedicated to my wife, Cindy, who has been the main supporting character in my life story for more than 15 years.

Too many times to count, her prayers, love, and support have steered me away from detours and rough roads and kept me focused and on track. I thank God that my LifeMap includes a life's partner who is also my best friend.

Contents

Acknowledgments

Without making this list of acknowledgments as long as an Academy Award acceptance speech, several people deserve special recognition for getting LifeMapping on the map. There's no particular significance to the order in which the names appear, because they all go to the top of my list as incredibly supportive friends and family. My thanks, then, to the following:

Larry Weeden, my editor and special friend who has helped with almost every manuscript I've written, beginning with *The Blessing,* for more than ten years.

Al Janssen, director of book publishing at Focus on the Family. Al is a world-class expert at giving encouragement, and he moved mountains to get this book out in a timely, quality way. Special thanks also go to Nancy Wallace, Beverly Rykerd, and my other friends and consummate professionals in the book and marketing divisions at Focus and Word Books.

Rolf Zettersten, my "piscatorial research" partner and executive vice president at Focus on the Family. His seamless integrity, expertise in publishing, encouragement in launching my new ministry, and personal friendship are invaluable treasures.

Dr. James Dobson, whom I am honored to call friend and who has given such incredible support in the launching of Encouraging Words, and in my publishing with Focus on the Family.

The supportive "Phoenix friends" who make up the board at Encouraging Words and who believed in and supported Cindy and me each step of the way: Doug and Judie Childress; Jim and Pam McGuire; Don and Nancy Schlander; Dan and Kris Stockfisch; and John and Donna Vryhof.

James Fillingame, who deserves a gold medal for shouldering the load at the Encouraging Words office so I could finish this book. Thanks go as well to my mother, Zoa Trent, and older brother, Joe, for taking the registration and shipping loads off me during this time.

Tim Kimmel, another Focus author and consistent lunch buddy, who offered patient suggestions and extremely helpful insights in the development of LifeMapping.

The men of the Scottsdale, Arizona, chapter of CrossTrainers whom I'm honored to lead each Tuesday morning. They have prayed for me nonstop, offered invaluable suggestions and critiques on each aspect of this book, and even acted as if they didn't mind my trying out all these new concepts and messages on them—*as long as I remembered to bring the donuts.*

And not last but saved specially for the end, Gary and Norma Smalley and their team of wonderful friends at Today's Family. Some things don't change when you're writing a book—the months of research, countless hours spent typing on the computer, bottomless cups of bad coffee at all-night restaurants, and that final mad dash at the end. But what did change in writing this book was that I didn't have my great friend and former partner beside me in the process.

I'm honored and very thankful for the ten years God gave Gary and me to team together in helping families. Today, I'm grateful beyond measure for his wholehearted support of my new ministry and solo books. Gary's encouragement to do a great job on this book may be over the phone now instead of over a cup of coffee, but it's just as appreciated and every bit as helpful.

PART 1:

THE BENEFITS, TOOLS, AND PROCESS OF LIFEMAPPING

Creating a Clear Path to Close Relationships

CHAPTER • ONE

Brian was 30 years old, successful, handsome, in shape, in line for a promotion, and now—*in deep trouble.*

It all began when his wife, Susan, opened that letter.

Her teacher's meetings had required only a half day at school. That's why she spontaneously drove to Brian's office to see if she could kidnap him for a late lunch. Bundled up against the cold, she hurried inside through the light snow flurries.

"Hi, Susan!" Brian's secretary greeted her with a warm smile, offering her a cup of hot coffee to help her thaw out. "You missed him by *seconds*. He just went out to lunch by himself. But if you go into his office and call him on his mobile, I'll bet you can find out where he is and join him. I know he'd love to see you."

Buoyed by her words, Susan stepped into Brian's office—and plummeted into a world of emotional hurt.

It's amazing how the smallest acts can sometimes have the most profound effects on a person's life—like making a right turn instead of the usual left and

3

driving straight into a major accident. Or like Susan's glancing down at Brian's desk that day as she picked up the phone. Preparing to punch in the numbers, she saw a letter lying open, obviously written in a woman's hand.

She glanced at the letter . . . then picked it up and began to read more closely. As the phone slipped out of her hand, so, too, did her image of a man who wasn't what he'd claimed to be.

Saving Herself for Trouble

Susan had come from a strong Christian family, and as an only child, she had been the treasured object of her parents' love and attention. She had come to trust in Jesus at an early age, and she stayed close to Him through college and into her teaching career, always saving herself for the husband God would bring to her one day.

She had prayed for a kind man. Someone who loved God. Someone she could trust. Someone like Brian, who showed up at her church one day and swept her off her feet in the following weeks. She had committed her life to him forever on a sunny day on the first of June, but now she discovered he had been lying to her since their first conversation.

From the time they had exchanged vows, they had experienced four years of the normal ups and downs, and now Susan was so close to realizing her American dream. They already had Candy, the golden retriever, a new (to them) house with a manageable payment, and even recent talk of children to fill the halls with love and laughter.

Then she read that letter—written by Brian's *first* wife . . . talking about a business situation with his *second* wife. For the first time, the thundering reality hit Susan that she was Mrs. Brian *the third*.

Brian hadn't realized that tearing open an envelope would rip major holes in his life, but that's exactly what happened. That simple business envelope contained enough emotional explosives to destroy everything he had come to hold most precious.

Susan walked out of his office and right to another phone to call her father for the name of an attorney. Trust torpedoed. Hopes dashed. Dreams of a bright future turned to dust.

Last Call at Your Door

Now picture that three months have gone by, and Brian and Susan are sitting in front of *you*. Anger still flames in Susan's eyes. Guilt and despair line Brian's face. They have two months before their divorce is final, and, prodded (almost dragged) by her pastor, they've agreed to meet with you for six consecutive sessions of counseling before the guillotine drops.

Susan has already purchased a ticket, dated for week seven, to return to her parents' home. *It's a one-way ticket.* And now the clock is ticking. It's session one, and *you* have to pray for guidance, then try to bring them some kind of hope for a relationship that has melted down to ruin.

Of the hundreds of couples I've counseled in more than 15 years, only a handful seemed more out of hope and less likely to experience a positive future. If anyone's hopes and dreams looked like a total loss, Brian's and Susan's did.

But that was then.

Today, nearly two years later, Brian and Susan still have their home, Candy the dog, and each other. In fact, instead of witnessing custody battles and fights over property rights, all Candy has to worry about is their newborn son, Brandon, pulling on "puppy's" tail when he gets older.

What happened that could turn around a tragedy like theirs? When others would have crashed, what enabled them to reverse direction and turn toward happiness instead of heartache?

The same thing that helped Jamie turn the corner on a personal crisis.

Jamie's Story

Jamie was single, unsure of herself, and uncertain about the future. Twice she'd been turned down for promotions, and then she was rejected by a boy she'd dated for two years who had promised repeatedly to marry her.

At an all-time low, Jamie faced another Christmas where everyone else would be living out *It's a Wonderful Life* while her life story felt more like *Nightmare on Elm Street*.

At 26, she felt used up, empty, and worthless to anyone who really mattered—including God. Perhaps it was those feelings, reinforced by 20 straight days of steel gray, Midwestern cloud cover, that blocked all thoughts of the sun's ever coming out again. More as a cry for help than a clear attempt to take her life, she laid the knife alongside her wrist and pulled it across the protruding artery.

But that was then.

Over a year later, Jamie is still single. She's still waiting for a promotion. And she still carries a small scar from that night. But that's about all that's the same.

Today Jamie is nearly 30 pounds lighter, and she has shed twice that amount in the emotional weight she once carried. She has gone from feeling purposeless and stuck to returning to school and being only three semesters from completing her degree. And while she doesn't have a date every night, she has built stronger friendships with both men and women at her church than at any time in her life.

What made such a difference in Jamie's life? What helped her clarify—*and put into action*—plans for a positive future? The same thing that helped Brian and Susan put away significant hurts from their past. It's also the same thing that helped Jim get his spiritual life out of low gear and into overdrive.

Jim's Story

If you looked at Jim's life, you might be tempted to jealousy. His world appeared to come straight off the pages of *Success* magazine, the L.L. Bean catalogue, *Home Beautiful,* and *Christian Parenting.* He had a loving, supportive wife and two children who were so well behaved that their neighbors and church friends all wanted to adopt (or trade for) them. Add a high-paying, nearly recession-proof job, a picture-book home with two practically-new cars in the garage, and he was set . . . *well, almost.*

On the outside, Jim knew others looked up to him. But down deep where it mattered most, he knew he didn't measure up. He was on the deacon board of his church—in fact, the youngest deacon they'd had in their 44-year history. But while he showed all the external signs of spiritual strength, inside he knew he was nursing a weak, unsatisfying faith.

A hundred times, he had dusted off his Bible and made that no-fingers-crossed commitment to get serious and "get into the Word." Yet his determination dissolved quicker than a New Year's resolution to never *ever* eat another dessert.

He had started attending—and stopped—two accountability groups. He kept telling himself he was going to be that Christian leader his kids needed and his wife had patiently waited for. But he kept scolding himself when more months would go by with more of the same.

Jim was a good man, but he knew he wasn't being God's man. He knew he was stuck in first gear.

But that was then.

Over the past 12 months, the gap between who Jim was and who he wanted to be has narrowed considerably. He goes to church and work feeling more authentic and complete than at any time in years. And for the first time since his kids were born, he's actually leading his family instead of playing spiritual catch-up. Best of all, he has rekindled *and maintained* the newness of life and excitement for spiritual things that had been missing since his first few months as a Christian.

In each story above, men and women found a method for turning away from frustration and toward real, positive change. For Brian and Susan, it was rebuilding a troubled marriage. For Jamie, it was reordering her personal life. And for Jim, it was revving up a stalled spiritual life.

All of them made significant, lasting changes when they walked through a process you can apply to your life as well.

Real Change Within Reach

In the pages that follow, you'll learn about one of the most powerful tools I've ever seen for building personal character and developing loving relationships. It's as old and wise as the Hebrew kings, as creative as Leonardo da Vinci and Walt Disney, and as contemporary as our nuclear-warship and space-shuttle programs.

It involves looking at your life—in all its component parts—in a new, fresh way. And it holds the promise of moving away from negative patterns and toward the intimacy, purpose, and direction you've always wanted.

This tool is captured in a personal or small-group process called "LifeMapping." It's a revolutionary way of viewing your life that can help you deal with a difficult past, develop more fulfilling relationships, and pinpoint where you are on the road toward Christlikeness.

> *LifeMapping involves looking at your life—*
> *in all its component parts—*
> *in a new, fresh way.*

Three Wells LifeMapping Draws From

Brian, Susan, Jamie, and Jim could easily have become emotional or spiritual casualties. But instead, all of them did something reserved only for the wise—they sought counsel. For Brian and Susan, it came in a counselor's office, as it did for Jamie. For Jim, it was wrapped around a study in a small group. But for all, an important part of the positive changes they made came as they walked through the same process of LifeMapping you'll learn in this book.

What is LifeMapping? In later chapters, we'll go into more detail and examine the eight major elements that compose a LifeMap. But for now, let's just call it a personal and relational enrichment tool that draws from three life-changing wells:

1. LifeMapping is a strengths-based, future-oriented process.

" 'For I know the plans that I have for you,' declares the LORD, 'plans for welfare and not for calamity to give you a future and a hope' " (Jer. 29:11).

Those encouraging words from the prophet Jeremiah to a group of struggling exiles illustrate a key aspect of LifeMapping. Namely, LifeMapping is a solution-oriented process that seeks to uncover a person's God-given strengths. What's more, while it encourages a person to gain insight from his or her past, it's based on setting clear goals and plans with a strong hope for the future. That's the very thing that helped Brian and Susan swerve away from divorce at the last moment and begin the work of rebuilding a shattered relationship.

That first day they came in for counseling, their cupboards were fresh out of options, and every shelf was clean out of hope. But in the action-oriented, strength-based, solution-focused approach of LifeMapping, they quickly were able to "picture" graphically the relationship strengths they already had. From there, they rapidly began working toward a solution instead of separation. (And with a seven-week clock ticking, *things had to get better quickly.*)

Focusing on strengths, solutions, and a hopeful future even in the midst of trials took them in a far different direction from most traditional counseling approaches. For example, secular counseling has stressed for years that the primary key to changing lives is to discover repressed, buried, or subliminal messages and patterns from our past. Thus, the problems a person faces today are simply "symptoms" and are to be understood and dealt with by focusing one's energies entirely on the past. Yet more and more studies are showing that such a focus isn't all that helpful.[1]

In fact, in several highly publicized, recent court cases, "forgotten" memories somehow resurrected in "regression" sessions have proved unreliable and highly damaging to all involved. No wonder the traditional "recovery" movement that has crowded bookshelves is losing the lion's share of its audience today. *People simply get worn out when the only direction they're told to face is toward the past.*

The problem is not that we can't gain insight and understanding from looking back. We *should* look back in a healthy way. God Himself consistently tells us to "Remember . . . remember . . . remember . . ." But there comes a time when we need to take the insights we've gained from looking back and link them with present actions and a Christ-centered, hope-based future orientation. If we don't, we may step back into recovery—and never recover! Brian and Susan needed more than a look back. And the "picture" they got in the LifeMapping process made a tremendous difference in their reestablishing a positive future (the second well), just as it did for Jamie.

2. *LifeMapping gives a person a graphic "picture" of his or her goals and life story.*

Jamie, in the second story told earlier, was another person who drew a blank when it came to picturing a positive future. Ironically, the dark clouds in her life that drove her to desperation pictured an inner hurt captured by King Solomon in the book of Ecclesiastes: "Remember also your Creator . . . before the evil days come and the years draw near when you will say, 'I have no delight in them'; before the sun, the light, the moon, and the stars are darkened, and clouds return after the rain" (Eccles. 12:1-2).

What a picture of despair and darkness! Like wave after wave of storm clouds, Jamie's discouraging circumstances seemed to drape over her like an endless, once-every-hundred-year winter.

After attending a conference where I spoke about LifeMapping and one element of the process in particular, "memorial markers," she went back home and worked through the process.

"It was really hard at first," she wrote. "I sat there for the longest time looking at the 'strengths' section and drawing nothing but a blank. But I ran out of cards under the 'freeze point' section. As bad as that was, for the first time I *saw* right before me that those negative memories were only one part of me. Apart from them, I could see I did have a future that I could do something about. That day, I made a decision to plan out a direction where I could use my strengths to serve God."

Things began to turn around for Jamie when she finally got a "picture" of her life story. In confronting the good and the bad, her personal triumphs and deferred dreams all laid out before her, she could finally see rays of God's light breaking through. While her trials had clouded the fact, He had been there all the time. The "picture" of her life story helped her see more clearly His presence in her life. And what's more, it ignited a resolve to make positive changes and begin to plan a different, hopeful outcome.

As Gary Smalley and I described in our book on "emotional word pictures," *The Language of Love,* pictures are incredibly powerful tools when employed in our relationships.[2] LifeMapping derives much of its impact from helping people get a "picture" of their life story.

Technically, LifeMapping does this by utilizing something I call "incremental, visual display learning." And while that's a term that may seem long and confusing enough to be in a government form, it's easy to grasp if we break it into its parts.

It's "incremental" because it employs a step-by-step process to help a person put the "pieces" of his or her life story together. And in the actual process of creating a LifeMap, it uses visual reminders to capture key life events, giving people a graphic display of who they are and what they can become.

In addition to tapping into the wells of personal strengths and cloud-clearing pictures, LifeMapping also draws deeply from a third well—biblical optimism.

3. LifeMapping is grounded in authentic, biblical optimism.

Consider the example of Jim, who struggled with an anemic spiritual life. It's not that he didn't want to grow spiritually, but his ups and downs made him feel like a poster child for Romans 7: "For the wishing is present in me, but the doing of the good is not. . . . *Wretched man that I am!*" (vv. 18, 24, emphasis added).

Jim operated the way many people do. His spiritual life was only as good as the last seminar or inspiring message he heard. In fact, even those few spikes of spiritual attention seemed to vanish between the pew and the parking lot—as if he'd had a frontal lobotomy!

Jim felt like a piece of wood in the ocean, carried by currents over which he had no control. That's why the most exciting part of LifeMapping to him was gaining an increased sense of personal control.

Rooted in that growing sense of motivation and self-discipline he experienced was a hearty dose of biblical optimism. Not the kind of optimism that Pollyanna practiced. ("Oh, you broke your leg? *How wonderful!*") Rather, he had *biblical* optimism, a choice of perspective that convinced him he had all the God-given tools he needed to do something positive about his spiritual life.

Genuine optimism always leads to action. It's optimism's opposite, *hopelessness*, that bogs many of us down and robs us of great relationships. In shedding that driftwood syndrome he was stuck in, Jim finally stopped wandering spiritually and set a clear course toward Christlikeness.

Minor Miracles

Your need for change may not be nearly as dramatic as Brian's, Susan's, Jamie's, or Jim's. Perhaps you don't have a marriage on the edge of ruin, seem ready to give up on life, or feel you're floundering in your faith. But you may need those minor miracles that can help you be an even better husband or wife, add more enjoyment and laughter to your life, or reach that next level of spiritual growth and maturity.

Moving forward in your most important relationships doesn't happen by standing still. It takes energy and effort. It takes courage and *old-fashioned character*. And the LifeMapping process begins by stepping *back* . . . to a positive future.

Chapter 2 explains more of the benefits of LifeMapping. However, if you're ready to jump right into the process, feel free to move ahead to chapter 3.

$\mathcal{S}$tepping Back to Your Future

For more than 15 years, I've taken carpenters and corporate leaders, home-makers and newsmakers, professional athletes and prospective parents, pastors and politicians, small groups and large audiences through the LifeMapping process. What's more, the basic elements I'll be describing have worked well with those from all corners of the United States and from countries far beyond.

But what is LifeMapping?

While we'll define terms in more detail in the pages that follow, *a simple definition is this*:

> LifeMapping is a way of looking at your life by displaying its
> component parts so that you see key events, patterns, and your
> potential in a fresh, new way. It involves "storyboarding" your past
> and your future so that you become an active participant in rewrit-
> ing your own life story. And its goal is to move you with clarity
> and conviction toward closer relationships, Christlikeness, and a
> hope-filled future.

13

There are definite reasons this tool has such a dramatic impact on people's lives. In the previous chapter, we saw three wells from which LifeMapping draws: personal strengths, powerful pictures, and biblical optimism. In this chapter, we'll explore five specific ways to use the individual LifeMap you'll create. And while you may be tempted to skip ahead to chapter 3 and jump into the LifeMapping process, I encourage you to take the time to see how this tool can apply specifically to your unique needs and situation.

Five Ways to Use Your Personal LifeMap

1. LifeMapping can help you move away from past hurts.

Would you like to be able to rewrite your life story? Would you like to turn around negative patterns from your past and replace them with a whole new, loving attitude?

If so, you're not alone. All of us have pages or entire chapters in our lives that we'd like to rewrite—even tear out. And many of us fear something even worse. Namely, we're afraid that the pain we've experienced will be etched in stone and we'll never be free of it—a terrible set of chains laid on us that we, in turn, will forge for our children.

The thought of "the sins of the father" being passed down once again to an undeserving generation is something many of us see in our worst dreams. Yet even some nightmares can offer hope.

As you carefully read the words that follow (my paraphrase of a famous story), try to remember where you've heard or seen the tale. It was written nearly two hundred years ago by a man deeply influenced by the Scriptures. And ever since, it has given us a powerful word picture of a biblical truth— *we can change the ultimate outcome of our lives.*[1]

> It's after midnight on a ghastly winter night. The rain comes down in sheets on the shivering form of a broken man. His unwanted companion is not a man but a horrible ghost—a frightening, black-robed monster made more terrible by his unwillingness to speak a single word.
>
> Finally, the spirit points his long skeleton finger at a nondescript headstone, forcing the anguished man to look through the rain at the letters etched in granite.

"Before I draw nearer to that stone to which you point," the man begs, "answer me one question. Are these the shadows of the things that will be, or are they shadows of things that may be only?"

Still the ghost refuses to reply and points menacingly toward the grave by which it stands.

"The course of a man's life will determine its ends; I know that," the man says. "If he perseveres in that direction, that's where it must lead. But if that man changes course, the ends will change, won't they? Won't they?"

Suddenly, an explosion of lightning bathes the graveyard in chalk-white light, illuminating the headstone just long enough for him to read what's written. With a choked scream, the man falls back in uncontrollable terror! It's *his* name on the stone. *His* death recorded. *His* life ended without remorse or regret by anyone who knew him!

"Spirit!" he cries, clutching tightly to the specter's robe. "Hear me! I am not the man I was! Assure me that I yet may change these shadows you have shown me by an altered life!"

For the first time, the cold steel that had been the ghost's demeanor begins to change. Instead of an iron will, the bony hand appears to shake.

Sensing there is still a chance, the man cries out, "I will honor Christmas in my heart and try to keep it all the year. I will live in the past, the present, and the future. The spirits of all three shall strive within me. I will not shut out the lessons that they teach.

"Oh, tell me I may sponge away the writing on this stone!"

Sound familiar? By now, I'm sure you've guessed that this scene comes from Charles Dickens's classic *A Christmas Carol,* featuring Ebeneezer Scrooge. Since it was first published, Scrooge's story has been a holiday favorite performed by Shakespearean troupes, high school drama departments, and even the Muppets!

There's a reason so many are drawn to that story again and again. Namely, Scrooge's cry is often our own. "Oh, tell me that I may sponge away the writing on this stone!"

One powerful element of walking through the LifeMapping process is its ability to help you identify and begin to move past a hurtful history—not by ignoring difficult issues or minimizing their pain or potential consequences, but by appropriating the life-changing power of God's Spirit to redirect a life. To rewrite a life story. To draw a LifeMap to a better tomorrow.

With God's help, we can sponge away the crippling pain of harmful actions and outcomes. Pictures of a negative future that others may have predicted for us can lose their power to be carved in stone. That's because the Lord has already carved words of a special future for each of us, guaranteed by His love: "You are a letter of Christ, . . . written not with ink, but with the Spirit of the living God, not on tablets of stone, but on tablets of human hearts" (2 Cor. 3:3).

Everyone is influenced by his or her past. But as Christians, none of us has to be controlled by it. In the pages that follow, you'll learn specific tools to live a life free of chains, as well as how to free those around you to become all God intends them to be.

> *Everyone is influenced by his or her past. But as Christians, none of us has to be controlled by it.*

2. LifeMapping can move you toward a life-giving, hopeful future.

Have you ever felt that you were "spinning your wheels," that you were merely existing, not contributing something positive to God's kingdom?

Or do you, in contrast, have a clear purpose that gets you up in the morning and inspires you to do your best all day long? Do you have a tangible, written plan, flexible to God's leading but pointing you forward in each major area of your life? Do you have a clearly defined direction that can keep you from seeing failures as final and mistakes as global?

Not only can LifeMapping help you move away from past hurts, but it also holds tremendous power to point you toward a positive, God-honoring future. Everyone needs a clear idea of where he or she is headed. In fact, if you *don't* have a positive plan for your future, you may well be putting your relational and physical health at risk.

> *If you don't have a positive plan for your future,*
> *you may well be putting your relational*
> *and physical health at risk.*

"How?" you may ask.

It may seem that there's no real cost to being aimless, but lack of purpose actually drains energy and life. Since that may sound like an exaggeration, let's look at a dramatic example of what I mean.

In 1944-45, Dr. Viktor Frankl was imprisoned in a Nazi concentration camp. While observing hundreds of fellow prisoners during those terrible years, he made a startling observation: *People could live through even the most deplorable conditions as long as they had a clear purpose to hold onto.* That purpose for living could be anything from planting another garden, to holding a loved one's hand, to finishing a piece of art. As long as the prisoners felt they had some tangible goal to live for, they could tolerate incredible doses of emotional and physical trauma. But once they lost their picture of a positive future, it wasn't long before their lives were at risk.

"It is a peculiarity of man that he can only live by looking to the future," wrote Frankl. "Woe to him who saw no more sense in his life, no aim, no purpose and therefore no point in carrying on. He was soon lost." [2]

Frankl told the story of a fellow prisoner, a well-known composer who had confided to him a particularly vivid dream he'd had. In the dream, the man felt certain that he'd been given a "gift" by a special voice. Namely, that voice had whispered the exact day their camp would be liberated and their sufferings would come to an end. The date: March 30, 1945.

When that man told Frankl about his dream, he was full of hope and conviction that the voice would be right. But as the promised day drew nearer, the war news that reached the camp made it obvious that they *wouldn't* be free on that date.

On March 29, the man suddenly became ill and ran a high temperature.

On March 30, the day his prophecy had told him the war and his suffering would be over, he became delirious and lost consciousness. On March 31, he was dead.

Frankl surmised from that man's case, and countless others he observed as a camp doctor, that a man's clear purpose—or lack of it—were what sustained him through tough times.[3]

"Come on, Trent," you may want to say. "Are you really suggesting that having a clear plan for the future is a life-and-death issue? What about all those couch potatoes whose only 'life plan' is the one found in this week's *TV Guide?*"

In the Scriptures, the word for a couch potato is *sluggard.* And while the lack of purpose, energy, and direction of such people may make it look as though they're enjoying a life of leisure, their lives may actually be full of pain.

" 'A little sleep, a little slumber, a little folding of the hands to rest'—and your poverty will come in like a vagabond, and your need like an armed man" (Prov. 6:10-11).

Sluggards may be wonderful people, but they're storing up potential pain. We need to realize that on a personal level, we're either moving forward or falling back. The same thing is true in our spiritual lives.

A primary key to living a fulfilling, contributing, Christlike life is to focus on the future. We're told to look forward to the "blessed hope" of Christ's future return and the "new heaven and a new earth" God has promised (Rev. 21:1).

Like it or not, how clearly we picture our future, both spiritually and physically, will directly affect our quality of life, and often its length as well!

God has a very real plan for each of us, young and old. And as you "flesh out" that plan in your unique life setting—*and help your older children do so as well*—you'll discover its power to bring important, life-giving changes to your home.

3. LifeMapping can help you increase communication and decrease misunderstandings!

Like Ebeneezer Scrooge's promise to live in the past, present, and future, LifeMapping can help you not only to make changes in your "past" and "future," but also to benefit in the "present"—especially if you'd like to see the current level of communication in your home increase and arguments decrease.

As you practice the LifeMapping process, one side benefit will be an ability to take a difficult issue and break it down into manageable parts.

> *One side benefit of LifeMapping*
> *will be an ability to take a difficult issue*
> *and break it down into manageable parts.*

You'll quickly see how you can focus your energy on mutually shared solutions, not arguing or shouting. (And for those of you who work outside the home, you'll see how the same skills can revolutionize your workplace as well.)

Let's say, for example, that a man just hung up the phone after being presented with a fantastic new job opportunity. It sounds like an exciting position with a brand-new company. That night, he and his wife are faced with a major decision. And along with that decision comes the potential for either closeness or conflict as they discuss it.

From his standpoint, he pictures this new position as having unlimited potential for career advancement. All she sees, however, is his taking a step back with an untested team in a competitive industry. He sees the vision for where they're going; she sees a future that's uncertain and unclear. He sees the personal challenge; she sees the dramatic personal cost to the family of a cross-country move.

At times like that, a major issue can soon become an ever-growing wall, resulting in angry words being tossed over each side. But by applying the storyboarding skills you'll learn in the LifeMapping process, you can see such walls come down and be replaced by healthy communication and closeness. (Look for details of how one couple used the storyboarding process to help solve this "moving" dilemma in Appendix B: Tripling Your Task Effectiveness at Home and at Work.)

If you'd like to focus more of your attention and energy on coming to a mutually agreed-upon solution, not on building up problems, a LifeMapping bonus will be deeper, more meaningful communication.

4. LifeMapping can add intimacy and unstressed hours to your life.

Just before a recent Christmas, Jane rushed into my counseling office ahead of her husband. "I couldn't wait to get here today!" she said, almost out of breath.

"What happened?" I asked, wondering what would get her so excited.

"We did what you asked the last time we met. First we did our LifeMap, and then we storyboarded the holidays . . . *and it worked.* This is the first time in years that I've actually *enjoyed* the holiday season!"

It's sad but true that one of the most wonderful times of the year is also one of the most stressful for many people. But if you'll turn the power of LifeMapping and storyboarding toward what's wrong with the holidays, you can see holiday stress cut almost in half.

That's what Jane found as she gained a new sense of personal control going into the hectic holiday season. Instead of feeling out of control and eventually resenting everything from relatives to crowded malls, she was able to plan in advance for all the known trials—and even leave some room to handle most of the unexpected ones!

In a broad overview, LifeMapping can help you make sense of the years that constitute your past and future. But on a "right now" basis, using the storyboarding technique can help you reduce daily stress—and it can even add hours of intimacy to your week.

That's what I was told by another couple who had nearly drowned in the stress and strain of caring for a two-year-old and newborn twins. At the end of their rope, they found their way into counseling. What they discovered were the same tools you'll learn that helped keep them afloat during those challenging days (and late nights).

"I used to dread the weekends," Mary told me. "I wasn't consciously trying to do so. But I used to build up such incredible expectations of Dan. With his job, I'd have next to no help with the kids during the week. I wanted to enjoy the weekends, but by the time Friday night came, I was tired and stressed out. If Dan did one thing I hadn't planned, I'd explode at him and the kids. By the time the weekend ended, we were both more miserable than ever . . . *and facing another Monday!*

"But we've used your plan," she continued. "Things are still incredibly hectic, but I'm getting more help from Dan and more breathers on the weekend. I've counted it up, and from zero, *you've added three hours of intimacy to our week*—and that's what kept me from going under."

> ## "LifeMapping has added three hours of intimacy to our week!"

With the incredible pace most families maintain today, either we're going to set our schedules or someone else will set them for us. Whether you're faced with raising preschoolers, launching teenagers, or preparing for a major move or transition, LifeMapping can give you an added edge in reducing relational stress. In addition, it can help you gain personal control and even add hours of intimacy to your busy life. But I've saved the most important way to use LifeMapping for last.

5. LifeMapping can provide major motivation toward Christlikeness.

Thus far, we've seen how LifeMapping can help you personally and with your close relationships. But perhaps its greatest value is in freeing you to come closer to your Heavenly Father.

As you look at the component parts of your life and put them into a clearly-laid-out plan, you'll begin to see more than just the individual parts. You'll soon start to see connections and transitions, dead stops and new beginnings, major decisions and potential memorial markers that were all directed by the hand of God. You'll understand that you're on a journey through life so profound and so personal that your daily actions count, and the very hairs on your head are counted.

In the pages that follow, you'll also see that it's the Author of Happy Endings who wants you and me to have fulfilling lives; a purpose that matches His own for us; a plan right out of Scripture that can make our lives into living examples of the love of God.

That's what Rich needed to know in the worst way.

Rich wasn't a Wayne Gretzky or Bobby Hull when it came to hockey, but he had battled for a spot on Canada's national team. What's more, his future seemed unstoppable, as after only two years on pro ice, he was ready to make the jump from AAA hockey to the National Hockey League—that is, until he took just one run on an "off limits" family ski trip, caught an edge, and kissed his left knee good-bye.

Few of us have to face the instantaneous, 180-degree career changes forced upon a wounded warrior. He immediately went from being a pro prospect to being in the also-ran category. And despite his best efforts at rehabilitation, Rich would never get beyond doing well just to keep up with his family at a skating rink.

When life goes from full ahead to dead stop in a matter of moments, it can put tremendous strain on our personal, marital, and spiritual lives. Rich initially responded to that stress by eating his feelings and adding nearly 40 pounds to his body. He struggled daily with self-doubt and often woke up shaking his head (or his fist) at the "stupidity" that caused him to toss away a prestigious and potentially lucrative career.

Part of Rich's healing process came when everyone in his small group at church decided to go through the LifeMapping process. As he looked at the "flash point" that reversed everything in his life, he suddenly saw how God's hand had been an ever-present part of his life story. The Lord hadn't thundered at him that changes were needed, but as he storyboarded the key ups and downs of his life, the sum of the parts took on a whole new shape. In sharing his LifeMap with those in his small group, it suddenly became obvious to him that God was an author of happy endings, even if His wasn't the ending Rich had predicted for himself.

As it was for Jim in the first chapter and for Rich, LifeMapping can be a great aid to your spiritual life.

Time Well Spent
- Dealing effectively with the past
- Gaining a clear plan for the future
- Increasing communication and problem solving
- Adding intimacy as it reduces daily stress
- Deepening our spiritual lives

Sounds like the lead-in to an infomercial or a speech by someone running for elective office, doesn't it? But those are all tangible reasons and results that can go along with your investment of time, energy, and accountability in the LifeMapping process.

Are you ready to look at the LifeMapping tool itself? Good. And remember, you'll never waste one minute of time spent enriching your personal and spiritual life.

Our First Look at LifeMapping

Let's face it, for some of us, beginning the LifeMapping process can be scary. Perhaps we come from a difficult background—even one where no one for generations has had a good LifeMap!

It's my prayer that by the time you finish reading this book and completing the LifeMapping process, you'll find yourself moving closer to your Savior. Closer to your loved ones. And that you'll be even more confident in who you are as a person than ever before.

> *With the right LifeMap, you can begin moving closer to your Savior, closer to your loved ones, and gain more confidence as a person than ever before.*

It can happen! And with that in mind, let's do two things in this chapter on LifeMapping 101.

First, let's take a look at a completed LifeMap to show you a scale model of the process. And while terms like *emotional freeze points, individual flash points, image management, learned hopefulness,* and *memorial markers* may sound new or confusing to you, they'll soon make sense as we get an overview of each of the eight key LifeMapping elements and then add much more detail in subsequent chapters.

Second, I'll introduce you to the tool you'll be using throughout the book to organize, graphically display, and even rewrite your own LifeMap. It's a creative, organizing, and time-lining tool in one package, and it's used extensively in think tanks, movie studios, and advertising agencies across the country. It's called *storyboarding,* and it can help you capture your life story in a way that is fast, insightful, and often life-changing.

With those two goals in mind, let's look at our first LifeMap, mine, which we'll examine in detail throughout the rest of this book. (A blank LifeMap is provided at the back of the book for you to fill out when you're ready.)

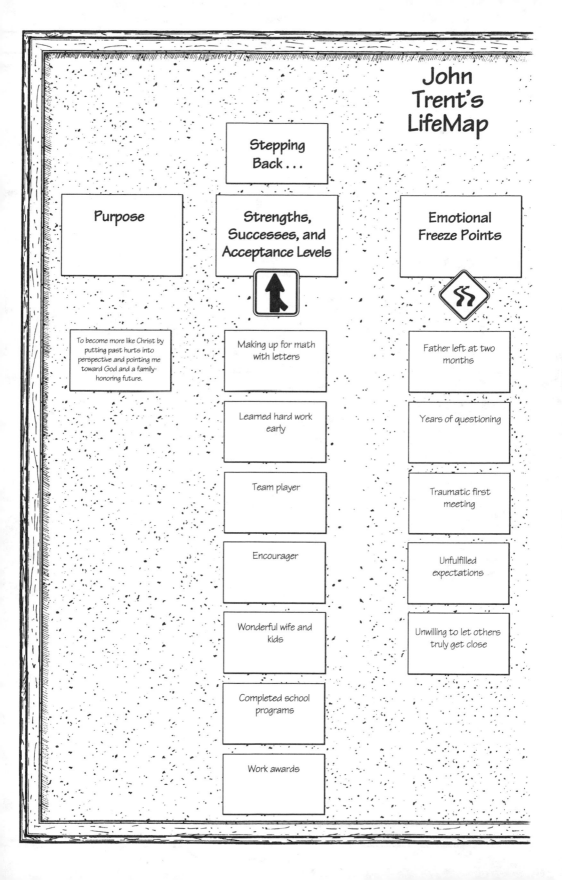

John Trent's LifeMap

Stepping Back . . .

Purpose

Strengths, Successes, and Acceptance Levels

Emotional Freeze Points

To become more like Christ by putting past hurts into perspective and pointing me toward God and a family-honoring future.

Strengths, Successes, and Acceptance Levels	Emotional Freeze Points
Making up for math with letters	Father left at two months
Learned hard work early	Years of questioning
Team player	Traumatic first meeting
Encourager	Unfulfilled expectations
Wonderful wife and kids	Unwilling to let others truly get close
Completed school programs	
Work awards	

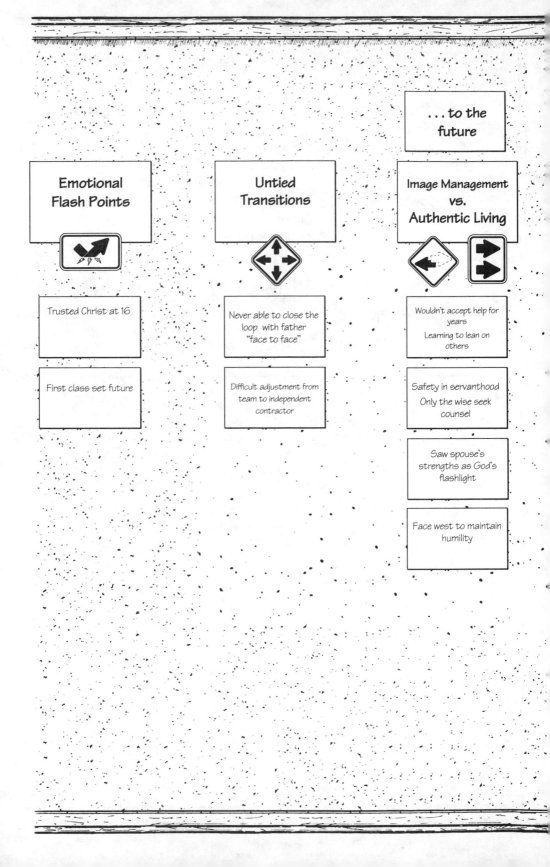

... to the future

Emotional Flash Points

Untied Transitions

Image Management vs. Authentic Living

Trusted Christ at 16

First class set future

Never able to close the loop with father "face to face"

Difficult adjustment from team to independent contractor

Wouldn't accept help for years
Learning to lean on others

Safety in servanthood
Only the wise seek counsel

Saw spouse's strengths as God's flashlight

Face west to maintain humility

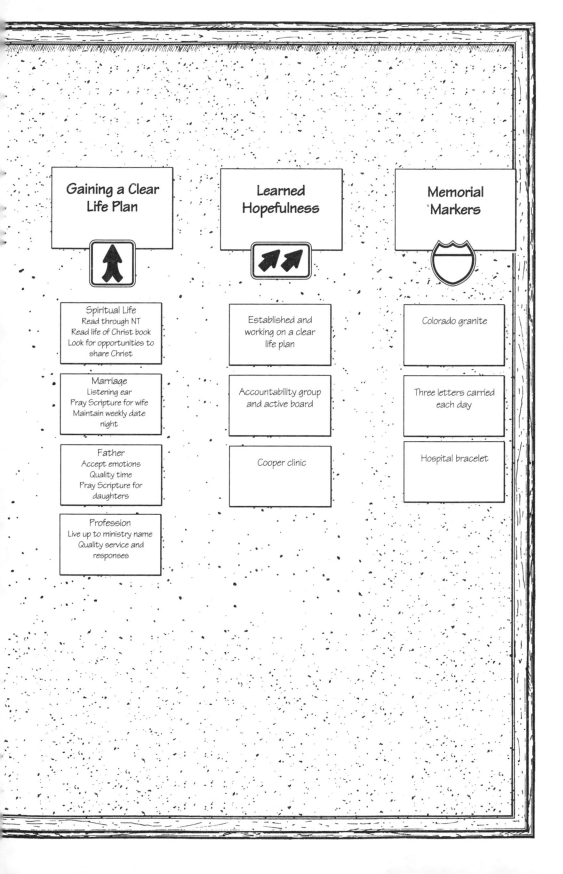

Gaining a Clear Life Plan

Spiritual Life
Read through NT
Read life of Christ book
Look for opportunities to share Christ

Marriage
Listening ear
Pray Scripture for wife
Maintain weekly date night

Father
Accept emotions
Quality time
Pray Scripture for daughters

Profession
Live up to ministry name
Quality service and responses

Learned Hopefulness

Established and working on a clear life plan

Accountability group and active board

Cooper clinic

Memorial Markers

Colorado granite

Three letters carried each day

Hospital bracelet

While my actual LifeMap includes more specifics in each category, this scaled-down example highlights the eight major elements that make up the process: *Remembering strengths, successes, and acceptance levels; uncovering emotional freeze points; understanding individual flash points; dealing with major transitions; choosing authentic living over image management; planning a positive future; practicing learned hopefulness; and picking out tangible memorial markers.*

Eight LifeMapping components may seem like a lot. But before you throw up your hands and say, "I'm just not the creative, organized, reflective type," relax. You've got an ally in pulling the whole process together.

The driving force behind LifeMapping is that powerful tool called *storyboarding*. It's a method that provides the practical means to draw out and capture your thoughts, dreams, hurts, and goals. That way, whether you're so creative you fear your LifeMap will end up as thick as an encyclopedia or so unimaginative that it takes you two weeks to think of something spontaneous, you've got a friend. (And as you can see from my LifeMap, it involves the use of a bulletin board or something similar. More on that in chapter 4.)

Storyboarding captures and directs our thoughts and ideas in a *focused way* that has been used on everything from creating cartoons to launching aircraft carriers. And in the end, it can help us fulfill a clear biblical mandate.

In Matthew 25, the time of Jesus' betrayal was close at hand. While He had told many parables up to that point, now He pictured the challenge and cost of discipleship for His closest followers. And in doing so, He talked about three men who were given different sums to invest.

One man aggressively developed what he'd been given by the master and turned five talents into ten. The second man also stepped out and doubled what he'd been given, bringing his lord four talents where originally there had been only two. Yet one man, who had been given one talent, chose to play it safe, to sit on his talent.

He took no risks. He made no investments of his time or energy. And in the end, he received no "well done" from his master. In fact, his play-it-safe attitude caused him to lose all he had and fail to gain a single reward like the others.

From that passage and others, it's clear that God never intended for us to play it safe. When it comes to investing our lives in His people and service, we're to move ahead, not run and hide.

As difficult as it may be to find the time to complete the LifeMapping process, it's an exercise that can help you "double His investment." Dealing with your past in a positive way and planning out new family and spiritual goals may involve risk. But it won't be without rewards. You'll move forward in a positive way and become a more effective servant for Christ in the process.

With that in mind, let's take an overview of the eight major components of LifeMapping:

Eight Steps to Creating Your Own LifeMap

Stepping back . . .

1. Understanding your strengths, successes, and acceptance levels

2. Identifying emotional freeze points

3. Uncovering individual flash points

4. Dealing with untied transitions

. . . to your future

5. Choosing authentic living over image management

6. Gaining a clear plan for your future

7. Practicing learned hopefulness

8. Picking out memorial markers for lasting change

We'll spend entire chapters on each of those key elements and on the creative storyboarding tool you'll use to gather all your information. But for now, let's begin with a brief introduction.

Stepping Back . . .

LifeMapping begins by looking back in a specific way. Throughout the Old Testament, a consistent theme is pounded into the minds and hearts of God's people. It's wrapped up in the often-repeated word *remember*.

"Remember also your Creator in the days of your youth" (Eccles. 12:1).

"Remember the former things long past, for I am God, and there is no other" (Isa. 46:9).

"Remember . . ."

"Remember . . ."

But what, exactly, is God asking us to do? A key is found in the word picture behind this Old Testament word itself. In Hebrew, one meaning is to make an "imprint" of something. Like an embossed piece of paper or a notary crimping a document with his seal, we're to think back on key events and times and indelibly mark them as special.

That's our goal in the first four elements of LifeMapping—to remember and mark out those successes and failures, key events and important patterns, dreams realized and opportunities missed that have shaped our past. And doing so begins by:

1. Understanding your strengths, successes, and acceptance levels

You wouldn't dream of beginning a cross-country trip without first checking the gas and oil levels of the car (at least if you were serious about arriving at your final destination). And in our journey toward Christlikeness, the same thing ought to be true. We need to check three important internal levels as we begin the LifeMapping process.

First, each person has a deep, heartfelt, legitimate need to be loved and feel valuable, to know he or she is accepted by others. Our search for acceptance begins with our earliest caregivers. Then, as we mature, we look for deeper levels of acceptance in the eyes of a spouse and in the heart of a loving God.

In chapter 5, we'll take a close look at your personal and spiritual acceptance levels. Are you running on empty when it comes to personal acceptance, or is there a deep knowledge of specific positive memories—"imprints" of unquestioned acceptance?

If you've struggled in the area of personal relationships, internal motiva-tion, or in truly feeling loved and forgiven by God, this first step in LifeMapping may help identify the impasse . . . and become the bridge you need to make positive changes.

Just as crucial as assessing our acceptance level is our need to clearly under-stand our God-given strengths and successes. As Christians, we of all people should be aware of our spiritual giftedness and God-given strengths. However, I've found just the opposite to be true.

In talking with hundreds of believers across the country, I've found that many can come up with a list of their greatest weaknesses in seconds. But leap years would pass before they could list their three greatest strengths!

This first aspect of LifeMapping builds on the positive and will help you to focus on the major and minor successes God has given you. In addition, you'll learn about your own personal strengths and how understanding them can be a key factor in defeating your personal weaknesses.

2. Identifying emotional freeze points

Coming to grips with your acceptance level and identi-fying your personal strengths and successes can provide a positive directional sign in your journey toward Christlike-ness. But the first "warning" sign we need to heed in the LifeMapping process is a concept I've called an *emotional freeze point.*

As we'll discuss later in more detail, an emotional freeze point can come out of a difficult *season of time* that we've gone through. While challenging times don't have to produce freeze points, they often do if they remain unprocessed and unexamined. When that happens, those feelings of anger, fear, or worry laid down over time can form an inner layer of emotional ice, effectively slowing down or even stopping completely the growth of mature, Christ-centered love.

A freeze point might have come from a nagging sense of worthlessness after trying and failing five times to get into graduate school. It may be the chilling fear of ever being dominated again by a high-control parent. Or it may be that defensive reflex that comes from three years of reporting to an alcoholic boss—someone who has made every working hour a nightmare.

As we look at emotional freeze points, we'll see how to identify them, as well as ways of moving beyond them. And while a freeze point involves a *season of time*, there are also events in life that can change us for better or worse in the space between heartbeats.

3. Uncovering individual flash points

Some of us have experienced, like a lightning bolt out of a summer sky, a moment in time that has either pushed our lives backward or propelled them forward. Those are emotional flash points, and they can hit with the suddenness of a thunderclap.

In some cases, it may have been a positive sound that rolled over you, such as, "It's triplets!" Or it may have been the sound of tearing metal in a crash that instantly changed your life. In either case, it was an unexpected, unplanned occurrence that tended to dramatically shift the direction of your life.

As you honestly appraise your past, it will be important to see if a flash point has affected the direction you've been heading ever since. In chapter 7, we'll look at a man named Saul whose brief encounter with a blinding light on the road to Damascus changed his life instantaneously and forever.

Then, with a working knowledge of your strengths, successes, and acceptance levels, and having focused on freeze and flash points that may be affecting you, LifeMapping helps in dealing with difficult transitions.

4. Facing untied transitions

While it often goes unnoticed or unappreciated, the way you've dealt with the major transitions in your life can have profound implications for your present and future growth.

For some (like a mother launching her last child out of the nest), *a transition can signal the end of one phase of life*. For others (like the person who received an unexpected promotion with triple the responsibilities), *it signals a new beginning*. Still others (like the spouse who suddenly finds himself or herself a single parent) can find that transitions *instantly force them to take on unexpected or unwanted roles*.

How well you face, process, and *move on* from major transitions is a key to understanding the state of your relationships today. In this section of the LifeMapping process, you'll be able to highlight those expected and unexpected transitions and actually discover how God *designed* us to experience transitions.

Obviously, these first four aspects of LifeMapping all point toward the past. But once you've looked back in a *positive* way, your next step will be to point your LifeMap toward the future—*beginning with a major Y-in-the-road decision.*

> *The way you've dealt with the major transitions in your life can have profound implications for your present and future growth.*

(Stepping Back . . .) to Your Future

5. *Choosing authentic living over image management*

How free are you from what has happened in your past to move toward a positive future? The answer to that question takes each of us to an important Y in the road in our personal lives.

Those who are able to honestly and courageously deal with the past as a learning and shaping tool will take the road that leads to authentic living. That's a way of life that enables us to honestly accept ourselves for who we are— warts, weaknesses, and all.

Yet there's another road we can take. It's a path that starts out wide and inviting but soon turns treacherous. That's the road marked "image management," and it's a certain way to cycle ourselves back into the past and repeat previous unwanted patterns time and again.

In chapter 9, we'll look at how each of us has a "public self" and a "private self." The degree to which these two aspects are in balance will help determine how fulfilling today is and how solid a foundation we're building for the future. Personally, spiritually, and professionally, avoiding image management and taking the road forward to authentic living is a key to a God-honoring future.

How do we choose that road? It begins by . . .

6. Gaining a clear plan for the future

As I mentioned in chapter 2, having a clear picture of where you'd like to be in your faith, family, and work can add quality, health, and length to your life. Using the storyboarding tool that will help you look back at your past, you can also take each important area of your life and lay out goals, dreams, and hopes.

God alone can predict the future. However, a clear plan that is open to His leading and prayerfully seeks to make you a more effective servant can help you do more for Christ and others than you may have ever thought possible.

"But I've made plans before," you may say, "and they never seem to get off the paper and into my everyday life. Something always seems to come up that keeps me from making the changes I really need to make."

What happens when your "clear plan" gets muddied by the unexpected twists and turns life often brings? That's when you focus on another LifeMapping tool filled with everyday encouragement to keep pressing forward.

7. Practicing learned hopefulness

The bumps and jolts of real life can sometimes jog you off course, even when you've taken the time to develop a clear plan. However, in this section, you'll learn a powerful way of staying focused on God's best called *learned hopefulness*. You'll see how to avoid feeling helpless when life seems to take a U-turn and how to maintain a "due north" heading toward the hopeful future God has for you.

8. Lining up memorial markers for lasting change

By the time you get to this point in the book (chapter 13), you'll have your past and future LifeMapped, as well as having applied what you've discovered about image management and learned hopefulness. But while this process can be very motivating, it needs yet another element to make your plans more than just a glorified New Year's resolution.

Here's where the LifeMapping process dips into the Old Testament again and utilizes a concept called *memorial markers* to help you make and maintain positive changes. What's more, these markers can become a powerful, tangible witness to what God has done and is doing in your life.

That's an overview of the eight elements of LifeMapping: four reflections of your past and four building blocks to a special future. Some of you may still feel overwhelmed, however, by the task of displaying a life story. "I'm 55 years old!" you may say. "How in the world can I capture a lifetime of memories and dreams and put them into a format that will made sense?"

How can you tackle something as complicated as a person's life story and make sense out of it? The same way Leonardo da Vinci and Walt Disney created masterpieces and the United States Navy created battleships in World War II! By using storyboarding, the creative tool we'll look at next.

Turning Many Pieces into Masterpieces

When it comes to something as complicated as a person's life story, how do you make sense out of so many component parts? And if LifeMapping involves looking at eight key elements, how do you flesh them out? That's exactly what you'll learn in this chapter as I introduce a powerful way to capture, understand, and rewrite your life story.

Tool Time

In each book I've written individually or jointly with Gary Smalley, while the titles and subjects have changed, one thing has remained constant: Each has sought to provide a tangible tool for the reader to grab hold of—something placed within easy arm's reach that could help heal damaged relationships and bring healthy ones closer than ever.

In *The Blessing,* the tool was a checklist of five biblical aspects of unconditional love that surfaced while I researched my doctoral dissertation. In *The Language of Love,* it was the powerful communication tool Gary uncovered called *emotional word pictures.* In *The Two Sides of Love,* we introduced the "personal strengths survey" that helped a person recognize and develop softness

39

and strength. And in my children's book *There's a Duck in My Closet!* it was a story to change a child's thinking about fear of the dark.

LifeMapping is no exception. Like Tim Taylor's jet-powered lawnmower on the hit TV show *Home Improvement,* LifeMapping is a tool that can blast you forward. But unlike Tim's lawnmower, LifeMapping will propel you in a positive direction!

Storyboarding is a method with a great history and countless present-day applications. I'm confident you'll find it of great worth in planning and organizing tasks around your home, church, and business. But even more, it's the main tool you'll use throughout this book to help you create your own personal LifeMap.

First Steps Toward a Masterpiece

Since storyboarding is so important to the LifeMapping process, let's take a moment to answer a basic question: Where did the technique begin?

While you can't point to one specific person who originated storyboarding, the individual who perhaps comes closest to being the "father" of the method was Leonardo da Vinci (no relation to Donatello, Raphael, and that other Teenage Mutant Ninja Turtle). The process he used to create his masterpieces put him centuries ahead of his time.

Da Vinci was a painter and sculptor who gained worldwide recognition. But while his works are well known, what's less known is the creative process he often used in designing them. Frequently, he would begin a major work by detailing a pencil sketch of the completed project. (Some of them still exist and are on display.)[1] Then, all around the canvas he would place small, pasteboard renderings. Each miniature drawing represented a major step in the creative process. Thus equipped with a sketch of the finished project and with step-by-step pasteboard models pointing the way, he was set to bring incredible beauty out of bare canvas, stone, or clay.

Centuries would pass before another genius remembered his art history studies and drew upon Da Vinci's creative process. That man was an American, and he was trying to accomplish something that had never been done before.

Bringing breath to a famous mouse

The year was 1928, and in a sleepy little cartoon studio in Southern California, Walt Disney was hard at work on the first animated talking cartoon—*Steamboat Willie.*[2]

At the time, the French were doing most of the groundbreaking work in animation. However, the only time a character moved was when he was speaking. That was because of the tremendous number of individual drawings required to manage even that feat.

But Disney wanted to bring *life* to his drawing. He wanted a full range of animation in which the boat would sway, the water would spray, and the characters would walk, talk, and *breathe*. But to do so took a staggering number of drawings—and created a major problem.

With stacks and stacks of drawings collecting at his studio (and without the computer storage technology we have today), how was he to make sense out of all those hundreds of component parts? How could he make a living picture out of hundreds, even thousands, of individual frames?

That's when Disney's art background brought back Da Vinci's system of "mapping out" each step in a complicated process. So Disney borrowed a page from that master artist. Namely, he turned his studio into a wall-to-wall bulletin board!

In Italian, there's a name for those small pasteboards that adorned the edges of Da Vinci's models. That word? *Cartoon*. Those individual "cartoon" art boards pasted up to show each step in the process helped Da Vinci create a masterpiece. Now pinned-up cards and pictures would help Disney create a different kind of cartoon masterpiece generations later.

Walt Disney found that storyboarding could capture the entire sweep and scope of a momentous, even monstrous project. Each time he completed a drawing, it would be pinned up on the wall in sequential order. Soon the individual drawings became a picture that told an expanding story. Almost immediately, his team of animators began to see the incredible benefits of using this system.

Now, instead of nonstop meetings to try to figure out where they were in the sketching process, the picture was out in the open for everyone to see, day or night. It provided a system that generated conversation, discussion, and interaction between illustrators. Accountability, too, became easier as each frame they finished was visually displayed. And if scenes needed to be changed or eliminated, they could be quickly unpinned and discarded.

Steamboat Willie was developed using this creative method, and it rolled out to nationwide acclaim. Storyboards soon branched into many of the creative teams and tasks at the Disney studio. In fact, it was heavily used in the planning of both Disneyland and Disney World, and it can still be found in many Disney offices.[3]

In short order, the storyboarding process moved beyond Disney to many other advertising and creative studios. Then major private and government offices began to see the power of capturing a huge project in storyboard form. For example, since World War II, storyboarding has been used in the design and creation of some of our top warships.[4]

As I was teaching the concept of LifeMapping to a group of men at our church, a retired Naval Academy graduate approached me at the end of a morning meeting. Nearly 40 years before, he said, he had used storyboarding in top-secret Navy planning sessions! At one point during the war, they had a storyboard room at the Naval Shipyard in Norfolk, Virginia. An armed guard was posted outside around the clock. Security clearance was so high that only 12 men on base had access to the final plans and designs being pinned up on the walls. My friend's superior reporting officer grumbled constantly about those "pin stickers" working in his building.

Cartoons and aircraft carriers, okay. *But how does all this relate to building strong relationships and designing a LifeMap?*

Using Storyboarding to Develop Personal Life Plans

When I first learned about storyboarding nearly 15 years ago, I applied it solely to major projects (like when my wife, Cindy, and I storyboarded all the details of our move from Dallas to Phoenix; in planning and developing my doctoral dissertation; in organizing all the details of a family camp for our church; and in writing my first book). But as a counselor, I soon began to see that it offered tremendous benefits to individuals and couples as well.

Many of the men and women I saw in counseling had personal histories so hurtful, confusing, and disjointed that they felt stuck in the past or somehow unable to move toward a positive future. At first just for me to keep track of all the twists and turns, and later because it elicited such positive responses from counselees, I began to bring storyboarding into my counseling sessions.

Soon those same people were gaining a clear picture of their life stories, and LifeMapping was born. We would talk about their experiences, and then together we'd pin up cards to display seemingly unrelated aspects of their past and present.

Once people got a clear look at their life stories, dramatic connections and insights would often emerge. *Instead of continuing to see their lives as a collection of random events, people would make associations and gain insights that led to breakthroughs in stalled or painful relationships.*

Rich, our hockey-playing friend in chapter 2, is a good example of this. As he completed his LifeMap, it was obvious that his world had essentially stopped spinning when he got to the fourth element of LifeMapping—untied transitions. Jamie, mentioned in the first chapter, was another person who had the pieces of the puzzle suddenly come together as she saw her life story mapped out before her. Even with hurtful experiences and memories crowding the freeze point section, she still saw half a board left for building a positive future!

What I found then and see consistently in my office today is the incredible change that takes place when people view their lives as life stories. Suddenly it's easier to see God's hand actively shaping the past and present. They often find underlying themes and patterns that help them put successes and failures in context. What's more, their feelings of self-control go way up as they quickly become focused on solutions (instead of problems) and function as their own "editors." Like Jamie, they see that they can "rewrite" or "remap" the direction in which their stories are headed.

So how exactly does storyboarding help picture a person's life story and create a LifeMap?

To illustrate, I'll teach you the process of storyboarding by applying it to a project, and then we'll see how those same skills can help you develop an individual LifeMap. Next, you can apply the tool to creating your own LifeMap, as well as use it to benefit your family, church, and even business relationships.

Storyboarding an Upcoming Project:

Creating the World's First Stress-Free Camping Trip!

Let's say that my family and our good friends and neighbors, Don and Nancy Schlander, have decided to go on a camping trip together. That's four adults, five kids, two dogs, and a sure way to bond friends and families (particularly with bugs, scrapes, and burnt hotdogs). Now, as anyone who has ever camped knows, heading out for the weekend requires some advance planning. (At least *successful* camping trips do!)

Since Walt Disney isn't around to help us storyboard the trip, how do we do it ourselves? Easy. We just follow a few simple steps.

First, we'd need a few storyboarding necessities. You can get everything necessary at your local office supply store. You'll need several packets of three different-sized index cards (5x7, 4x6, and 3x5 cards), each sized card a different color (e.g., all 5x7 cards red, all 4x6 cards white, and all 3x5 cards blue). You'll also need a cork board, a thin Styrofoam art board, a piece of material stretched onto a large, wooden frame, or other means to pin up the cards. (Basically, you need a "pinnable" surface 3 1/2 feet high by 5 feet long or larger.) Additionally, you'll need a set of wide felt-tipped markers and a large box of push pins.

Before you begin, make sure each person has a marking pen. (By the way, it's always a good idea to give everyone the same color of pen. That way, if you're storyboarding with your boss some day and she's the only one with a red pen, and all her ideas in red get tossed out . . . *you get the picture!*)

In this case, our team consists of John, Cindy, Don, and Nancy, so we'll need four markers. Your situation might require enough markers for your church board, your business team, you and your husband, or your early-morning accountability group. (Obviously, when you're storyboarding by yourself, you cut way down on your Magic Marker expense!)

Storyboarding works wonderfully with individuals, couples, and almost any group. But the key is to have no more than eight people actively involved at one time. Others may look on if you're in a larger group setting, but eight is functionally the largest group you'd want participating.

Now that your group is set, have one person volunteer to be the facilitator and "pinner" who will pin up each idea that will soon be thrown out, and you're ready to begin storyboarding your project. For this example, we've chosen the impossible to show that even it can be attempted. Our task: plan a successful, stress-free camping trip.

Second, follow a specific storyboarding process. Our two couples have gotten together in a comfortable setting. (We decided to let the kids play in the other room after the younger ones sucked all the ink out of two markers and one of the older ones was holding the push pins and looking suspiciously at the cat.) We begin our storyboard by picking up one of our 5x7 cards and a felt marker. From this point on, 5x7 cards are always used as *topic cards*. A topic card is simply a statement of the task you're working on written in big letters on a 5x7 card and pinned at the top center of your cork board. Here's what that would look like:

```
┌─────────────────────────┐
│                         │
│   We're Planning a      │
│     Successful,         │
│     Stress-Free         │
│   Camping Trip!         │
│                         │
└─────────────────────────┘
```

Now we're ready to pick up one of our 4x6 cards. They will always be used as *toppers*. That's because they'll end up going across the top of our story-board. (Clever name.) The first topper is always the *purpose* of what we're designing or creating. It's placed in the top left-hand corner of the board.

The reason the purpose is always the first topper is that someone might actually *ask* some day, "Just what is the purpose of your camping trip?"—and we'd know! Even if they don't ask, having a clear purpose in mind for whatever project we're developing can give us greater clarity and added focus for the task ahead.

So with marker pen in hand, we write "Purpose" in big letters on a 4x6 topper card and pin it to the board. Here's what that would look like:

```
       ┌─────────────────────────┐
       │                         │
       │   We're Planning a      │
       │     Successful,         │
       │     Stress-Free         │
       │   Camping Trip!         │
       │                         │
       └─────────────────────────┘

┌─────────────────────────┐
│                         │
│   Purpose               │
│                         │
│                         │
│                         │
└─────────────────────────┘
```

Once we've got our topic card and first topper in place, we're ready to grab those 3x5 cards and throw out words and ideas to shape our purpose statement.

If the 4x6 cards are called toppers, the 3x5 cards are called *subbers*, because they go beneath the toppers. ("Fox in socks and socks on fox." With topic cards, toppers, and subbers, this may sound as confusing as a Dr. Seuss book, *but hang in there!* You'll quickly see how this makes sense.)

With 3x5 subbers in hand, how do we flesh out the purpose statement? That involves a two-step process. First, we brainstorm the group's thoughts on the purpose—in this case, of going on a camping trip. Brainstorming is a freewheeling process in which as many ideas as possible are generated, collected, and pinned up on the board.

> *Storyboarding can be one of the most fun and "win/win" ways to get a group together on a project.*

During brainstorming, there are four things to remember:

1. No criticism. The brainstorming time is a nonjudgmental setting where creative ideas and thoughts can flow. (Shortly, you'll see where ideas will be critiqued, rearranged, or even thrown out.) So during this part of the story-boarding process, no "She already said that!" "That's not a purpose!" or "You call *that* an idea?"

2. The more ideas the better. Encourage people to express any idea and as many ideas as they'd like when brainstorming. But remember the "popcorn" theory of brainstorming. If you're the facilitator of a storyboard session, throw out the topic, and then let the ideas pop up as God leads. But just like when you're cooking popcorn in a microwave, don't wait until there is dead silence for a long time before moving on. That way you won't burn the popcorn or burn out the people involved.

3. Spelling doesn't count. This is, perhaps, an offshoot of the "no criticism" rule, but it's important to keep in mind (and to tell to your group in advance). As you'll see, storyboarding can be one of the most fun and "win/win" ways to get a group together on a project. That's why you want as much freedom as possible during the brainstorming session to encourage ideas without critique. You'd be surprised how many people feel self-conscious abut their pooor spalling, and comnents about it can shut down creativitie quicklie. (Can you find all the spelling mistakes in the preceding sentence?)

4. Hitchhike. Don't worry. If this book falls into the hands of your children, I'm not advocating hitchhiking on the freeways. What *hitchhike* means in brainstorming is that when you hear someone else's idea and then see it written on a card, it often sparks another idea in your own mind that helps shape the process.

Armed with those four brainstorming rules, our two couples are ready to flesh out the purpose statement, remembering *no criticism, the more ideas the better, spelling doesn't count,* and *hitchhiking is encouraged.*

At the direction of the pinner, each person is asked to (a) offer *one* idea at a time, (b) speak his or her idea *out loud* (so others can hitchhike off what is said), and (c) *write* that idea in big letters on a 3x5 subber card.

Please note: While you may not think it's possible, in the more than 15 years I've been storyboarding with groups and individuals, *I've yet to meet an idea or event that can't be captured in 12 to 15 words or less and put on a card.*

Suppose, for example, that Cindy offers the following purpose for our camping trip: "I think we ought to go camping because it's springtime, and the weather is beautiful, and the birds will be singing, and the little animals are out, and the grass is turning green, and the streams are running, and . . ."

You could just put the word *springtime* on the card, and then everyone would know it captured the grass, birds, animals, running water, chiggers, and so on.

Here's what John, Cindy, Don, and Nancy came up with when they brainstormed their purpose for going camping (*now remember—this is before they've gone to step two and done any editing*):

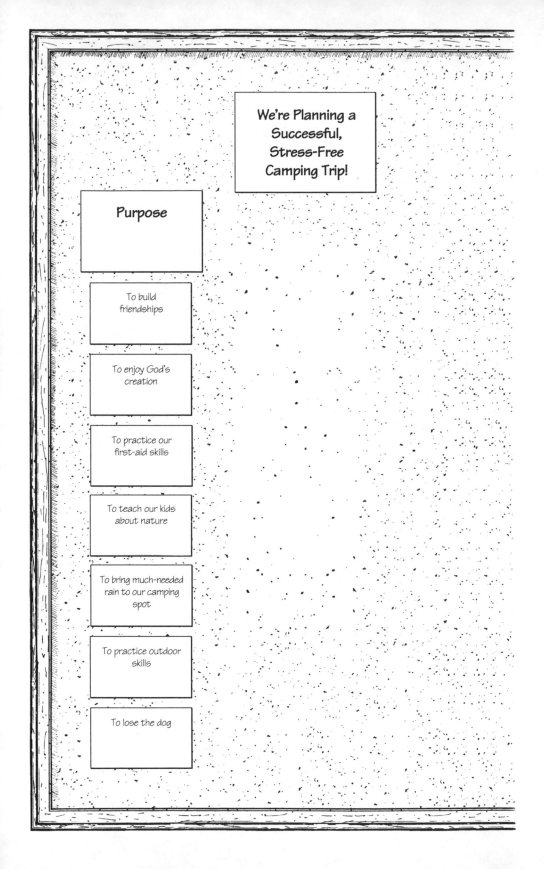

We're Planning a Successful, Stress-Free Camping Trip!

Purpose

To build friendships

To enjoy God's creation

To practice our first-aid skills

To teach our kids about nature

To bring much-needed rain to our camping spot

To practice outdoor skills

To lose the dog

By the time "lose the dog" was said (*remember*—no criticism at this point), it was obvious that the popcorn was beginning to burn, so we went on to step two of the storyboarding process. After you've brainstormed and gathered all your ideas, the second step is called *sharpening*.

Sharpening is when you cut, question, and rearrange the cards you've collected. If the "creative" people get to shine during the brainstorming part, the "critical thinkers" get the spotlight during the sharpening process. Here's where you can openly question, discuss, and toss out responses to end up with what your storyboard team (or yourself if you're doing it alone) feels best represents your thoughts. For our two couples, here are the process illustrated and the final subbers we left intact:

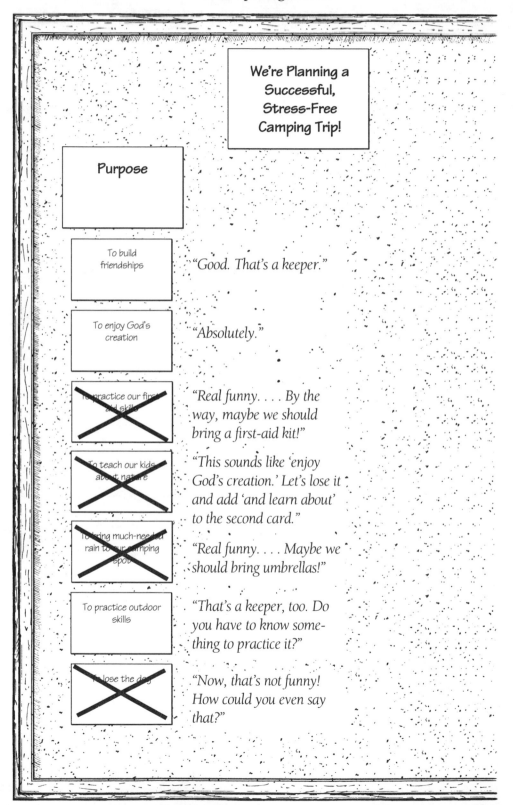

We're Planning a Successful, Stress-Free Camping Trip!

Purpose

To build friendships

"Good. That's a keeper."

To enjoy God's creation

"Absolutely."

To practice our first aid skills

"Real funny. . . . By the way, maybe we should bring a first-aid kit!"

To teach our kids about nature

"This sounds like 'enjoy God's creation.' Let's lose it and add 'and learn about' to the second card."

To bring much-needed rain to our camping spot

"Real funny. . . . Maybe we should bring umbrellas!"

To practice outdoor skills

"That's a keeper, too. Do you have to know something to practice it?"

To lose the dog

"Now, that's not funny! How could you even say that?"

How did the purpose look after we had brainstormed and sharpened it? Like this:

The Purpose Refined After Sharpening

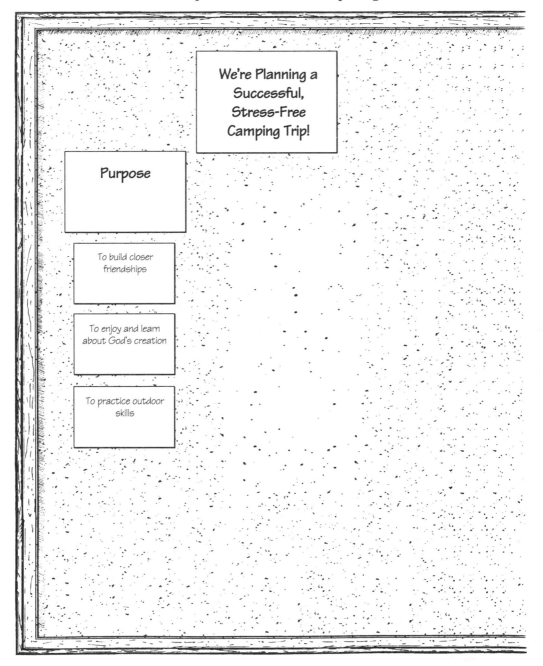

Then we took our sharpened purpose and turned it into a run-on sentence, and we had a storyboarded purpose for the camping trip: "We want to organize a successful, stress-free camping trip so that we can build friendships, enjoy and learn about God's creation, and practice our outdoor skills."

It's that easy!

Once you've got your purpose clearly in view (like Da Vinci's completed pencil sketch that showed him the *end* of a project as he started work on the beginning), you're ready to storyboard all the toppers. To do that, you use the same two-step method of brainstorming and sharpening.

The story the toppers tell captures the main categories and factors needed to pull off your purpose. So alert your group, grab your 4x6 topper cards, and get ready to brainstorm. Here's the result of the two couples brainstorming the toppers for our camping trip:

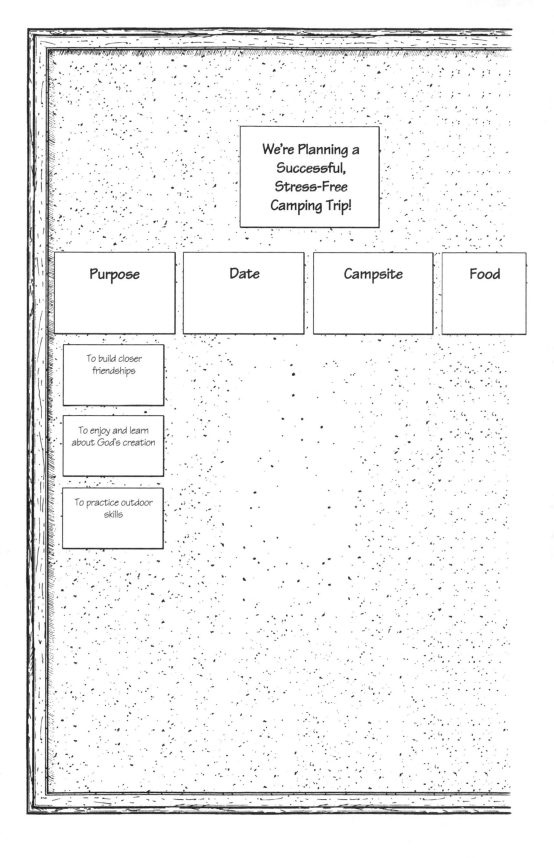

We're Planning a Successful, Stress-Free Camping Trip!

Purpose	Date	Campsite	Food

To build closer friendships

To enjoy and learn about God's creation

To practice outdoor skills

Activities and Games	Transportation	Equipment	Food

Once we ran out of brainstorming ideas for the major aspects of a successful camping trip, we turned to sharpening and cut, rearranged, and reworked the toppers to capture the major categories.

The next two pages show what that process might look like:

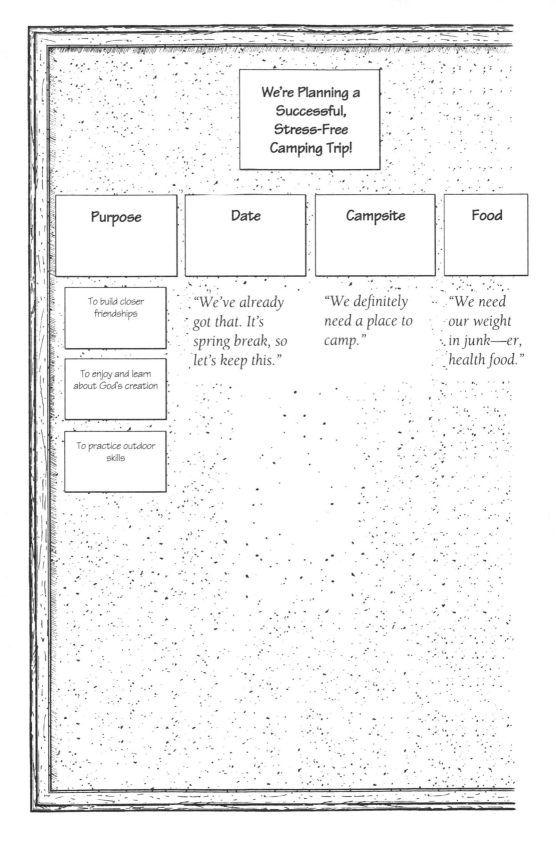

We're Planning a Successful, Stress-Free Camping Trip!

Purpose	Date	Campsite	Food

To build closer friendships

To enjoy and learn about God's creation

To practice outdoor skills

"We've already got that. It's spring break, so let's keep this."

"We definitely need a place to camp."

"We need our weight in junk—er, health food."

Activities and Games	Transportation Cars	Equipment	Food

"There's more than just fish-ing? Okay, we'll keep it. Is cleaning fish a game?"

"That's a keeper. Let's put CB's under equipment, good buddy."

"Absolutely. Should I buy new equipment or just unpack that wet tent I folded up last year?"

"Again? We've already got it."

What do our sharpened toppers look like? Turn to the next page.

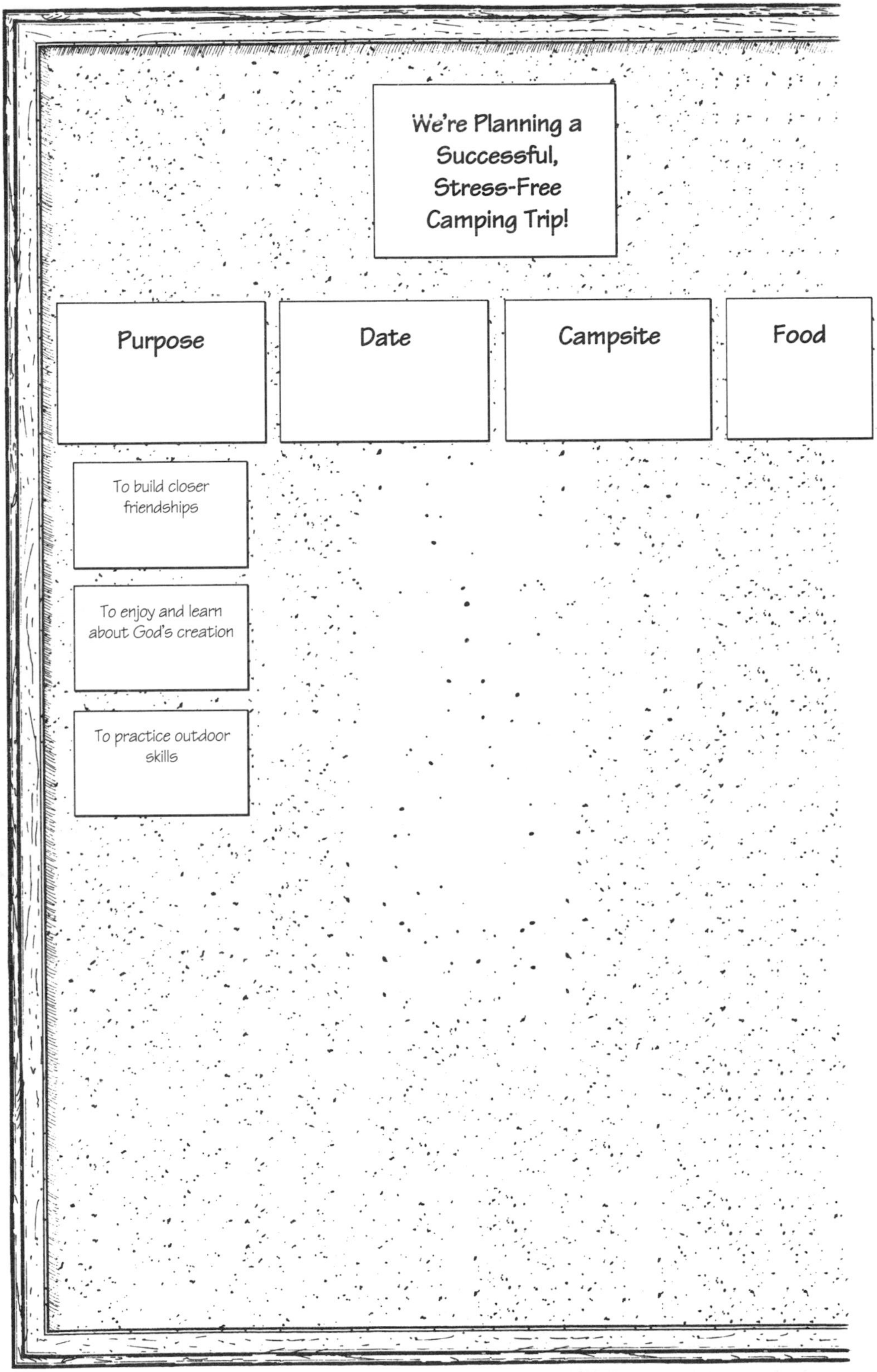

We're Planning a
Successful,
Stress-Free
Camping Trip!

Purpose	Date	Campsite	Food

To build closer
friendships

To enjoy and learn
about God's creation

To practice outdoor
skills

Activities and Games	Cars	Equipment

Once you've storyboarded your purpose and toppers, you just take each topper card and develop the subbers under it. For example, let's say you were developing the last topper, "Equipment." You'd just do the same thing we've done so far: brainstorm and then sharpen. For example, here's how the two couples might brainstorm "Equipment":

Activities and Games	Cars	Equipment
		Radio to listen to ballgame
		Tents
		Lantern
		Cookstove and utensils
		Water jugs
		First-aid kit
		Portable TV and generator to watch game

After brainstorming the subbers, you do what? That's right, sharpen.

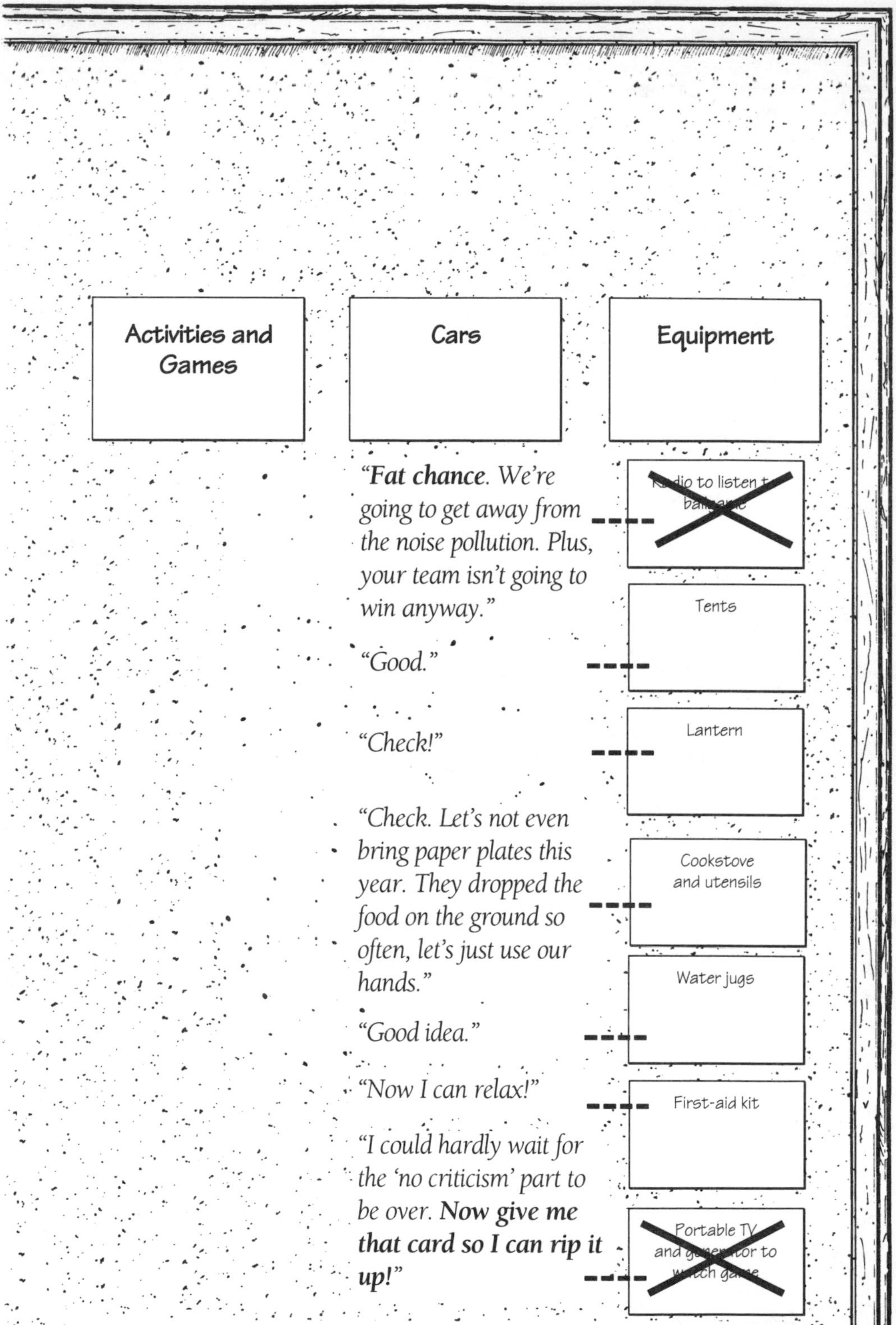

Activities and Games	Cars	Equipment

"**Fat chance**. We're going to get away from the noise pollution. Plus, your team isn't going to win anyway."

~~Radio to listen to ballgame~~

"Good."

Tents

"Check!"

Lantern

"Check. Let's not even bring paper plates this year. They dropped the food on the ground so often, let's just use our hands."

Cookstove and utensils

"Good idea."

Water jugs

"Now I can relax!"

First-aid kit

"I could hardly wait for the 'no criticism' part to be over. **Now give me that card so I can rip it up!**"

~~Portable TV and generator to watch game~~

The result of brainstorming and sharpening the topper "Equipment"?

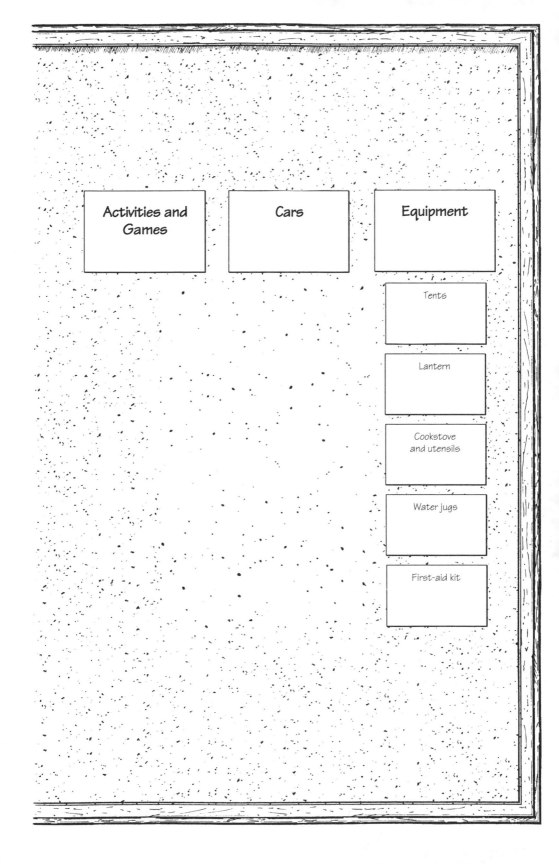

Activities and Games

Cars

Equipment

Tents

Lantern

Cookstove and utensils

Water jugs

First-aid kit

Then you just go through the remaining topper cards and storyboard (brainstorm and sharpen) the subbers under each one until you've got a completed storyboard. And here it is (in abbreviated form, of course), a clear plan for creating a "successful, stress-free camping trip!"

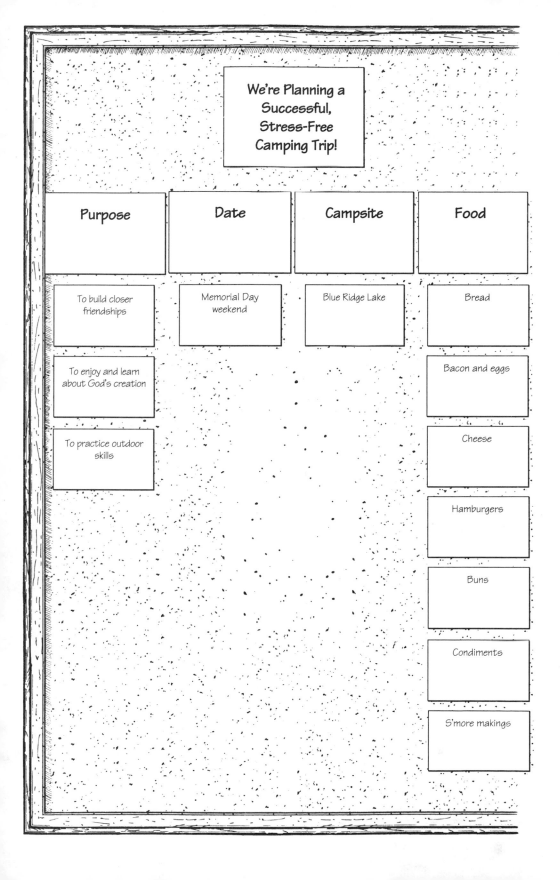

We're Planning a Successful, Stress-Free Camping Trip!

Purpose	Date	Campsite	Food
To build closer friendships	Memorial Day weekend	Blue Ridge Lake	Bread
To enjoy and learn about God's creation			Bacon and eggs
To practice outdoor skills			Cheese
			Hamburgers
			Buns
			Condiments
			S'more makings

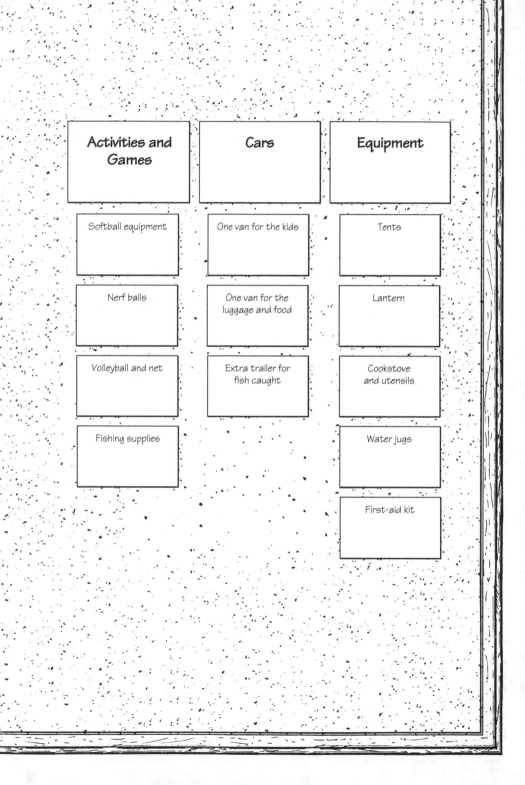

Activities and Games	Cars	Equipment
Softball equipment	One van for the kids	Tents
Nerf balls	One van for the luggage and food	Lantern
Volleyball and net	Extra trailer for fish caught	Cookstove and utensils
Fishing supplies		Water jugs
		First-aid kit

By now, perhaps you've thought of that pet project in your family, church, or work setting that is dying to be storyboarded. Perhaps you're getting ready to build a room addition on your house, and you want to storyboard that task to include each family member's thoughts and feelings. Maybe you're head of the Christian education committee at your church, and you can hardly wait to see a topic card with the words "Create an effective teacher training and recruitment program" on it at your next meeting. Or you might be a businessman, and having your employees storyboard how to "Provide excellent service to our customers" would build teamwork and ownership of something you've had a hard time selling yourself.

Projects of all sizes and shapes, from cartoons to camping trips, from award-winning books to successful bake sales, were *made* for storyboarding. As you'll recall from chapter 2, one couple I counseled storyboarded all their Christmas activities and found the season less hectic and more enjoyable than any holiday in years. Another couple storyboarded a "less-stress-filled week," and they're the ones who rushed in with the words, "LifeMapping has added three hours of intimacy to our week!"

As much help as storyboarding can be with home and work projects, it's also a tremendous help in capturing and making sense of a person's life story.

Turning Now to LifeMapping

"That's great, John," you may be saying, "but it's ten o'clock at night, and there's no storyboarding group standing around me as I read this book. *Can I do this all by myself?*"

Absolutely! Now that you know the basics of storyboarding with a group, that "group" can be one person—*you*—as you map out your life story. In fact, in developing LifeMapping with scores of individuals and couples over the years, I've made it even more "user friendly" than ever. *That's because you've already got your list of eight toppers in place* (the eight elements of LifeMapping).

With those eight parts of LifeMapping as your main toppers, all you've got to do (once you've gone through the rest of the book and understood each element) is to personalize your purpose (again, just in case somebody ever asked you, "Why'd you come up with a LifeMap?") and then fill in the subbers.

That's the process you'll be using to complete a storyboard that captures your LifeMap!

Let's look again at my LifeMap that we saw at the beginning of chapter 3. And as you look at a scale copy of my personal life story, you'll see my personalized purpose statement and the subbers that went under the eight LifeMapping toppers.

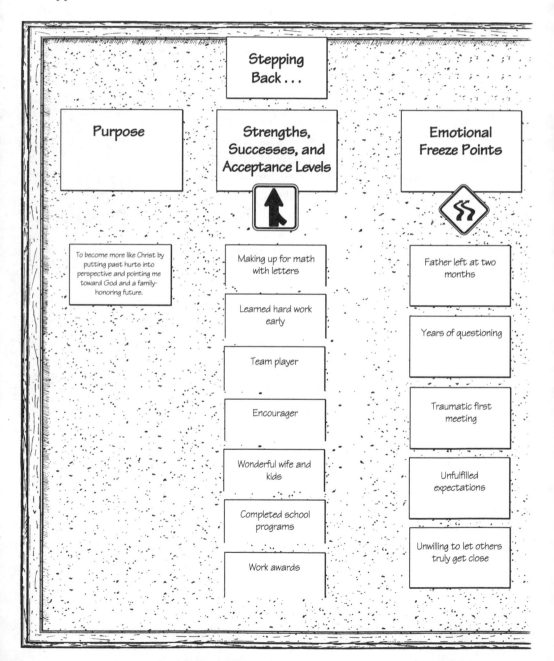

Stepping Back . . .

Purpose	Strengths, Successes, and Acceptance Levels	Emotional Freeze Points
To become more like Christ by putting past hurts into perspective and pointing me toward God and a family-honoring future.	Making up for math with letters	Father left at two months
	Learned hard work early	Years of questioning
	Team player	Traumatic first meeting
	Encourager	Unfulfilled expectations
	Wonderful wife and kids	Unwilling to let others truly get close
	Completed school programs	
	Work awards	

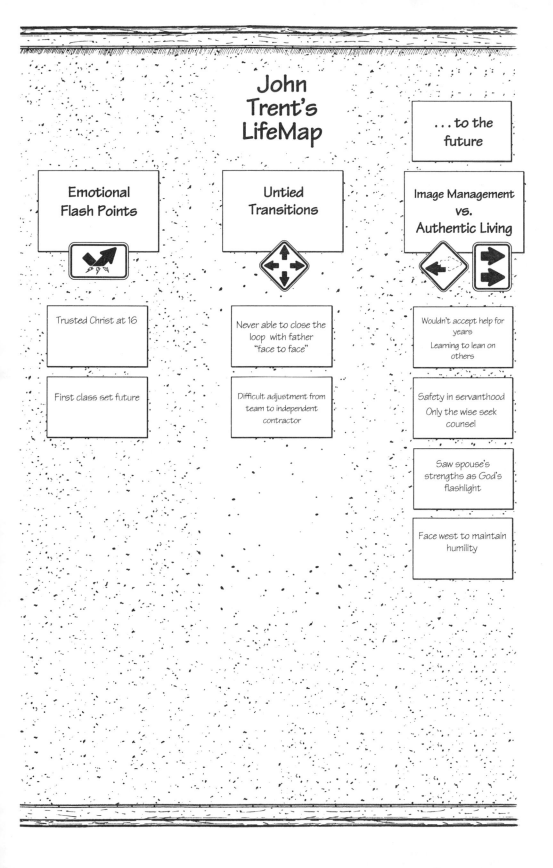

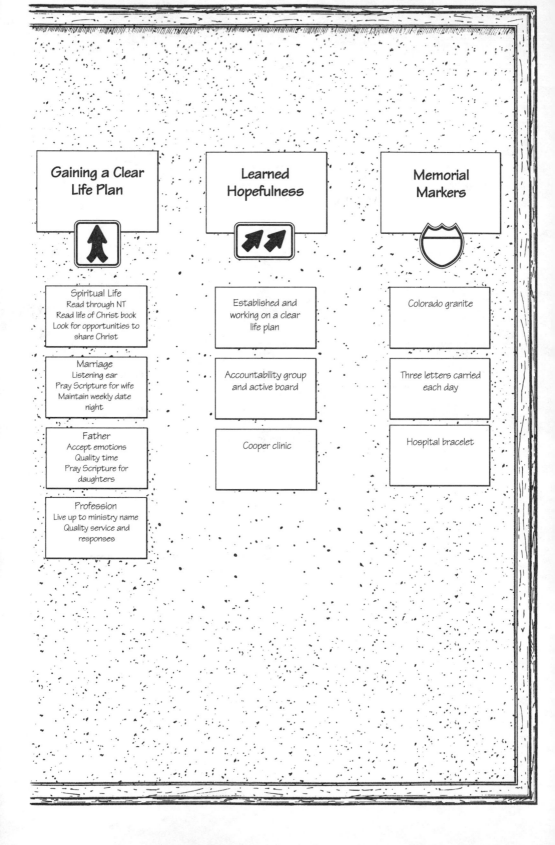

Gaining a Clear Life Plan	Learned Hopefulness	Memorial Markers
Spiritual Life Read through NT Read life of Christ book Look for opportunities to share Christ	Established and working on a clear life plan	Colorado granite
Marriage Listening ear Pray Scripture for wife Maintain weekly date night	Accountability group and active board	Three letters carried each day
Father Accept emotions Quality time Pray Scripture for daughters	Cooper clinic	Hospital bracelet
Profession Live up to ministry name Quality service and responses		

When I first sat down (or actually stood up) to storyboard my LifeMap, I did just what I'm asking you to do. First, I focused on personalizing a purpose statement, and then I started at the front and filled in the subbers under the eight elements of LifeMapping.

And while initially I did it individually, using my best thoughts and recollections, I later showed my LifeMap to my wife, Cindy, who was a great help in confirming and suggesting other key issues, developmental factors, and important goals. Then I showed it to my older brother for his input, and finally to my accountability group.

Each time I showed it, it took better form, and I gained more of a picture of the key factors that had helped to shape who I was and who I could become. In particular, the responsibility, closeness, and insight I gained from showing my LifeMap to my small accountability group was tremendous. *All four of us* ended up completing our LifeMaps and then showing them to each other. Talk about a bonding experience as we each saw through a window, as it were, into the other people's goals, dreams, struggles, and histories!

To paraphrase Jesus' disciple Thomas, if "seeing is believing," let's look at another man's LifeMap to illustrate again how you can use the process to capture a life story. In this case, it's a picture of a man who could teach us much about godly living. Since he has already gone to be with the Lord, I've filled out what I think his LifeMap would have looked like. After reading it over, see if you can identify whom I've described. Then I'll give you his name.

_____'s LifeMap

Purpose	Strengths, Successes, and Acceptance Levels	Freeze Points

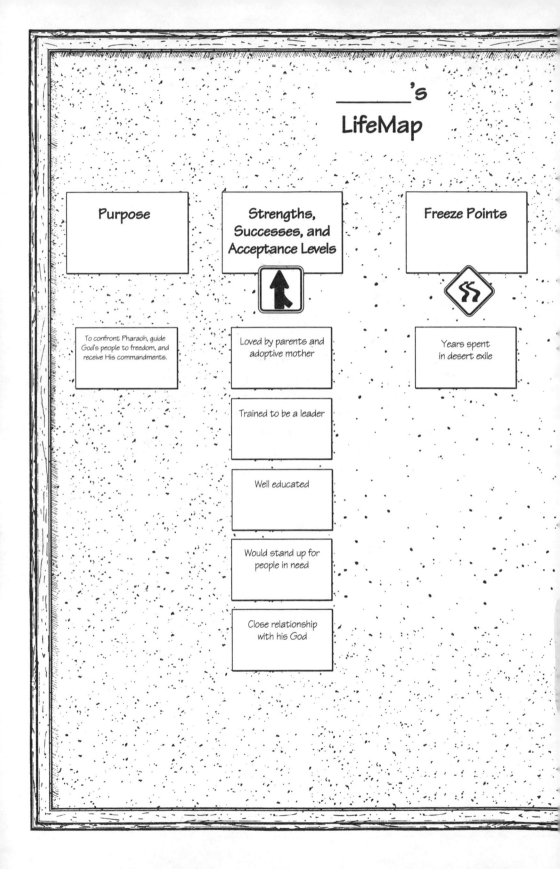

Purpose

To confront Pharaoh, guide God's people to freedom, and receive His commandments.

Strengths, Successes, and Acceptance Levels

Loved by parents and adoptive mother

Trained to be a leader

Well educated

Would stand up for people in need

Close relationship with his God

Freeze Points

Years spent in desert exile

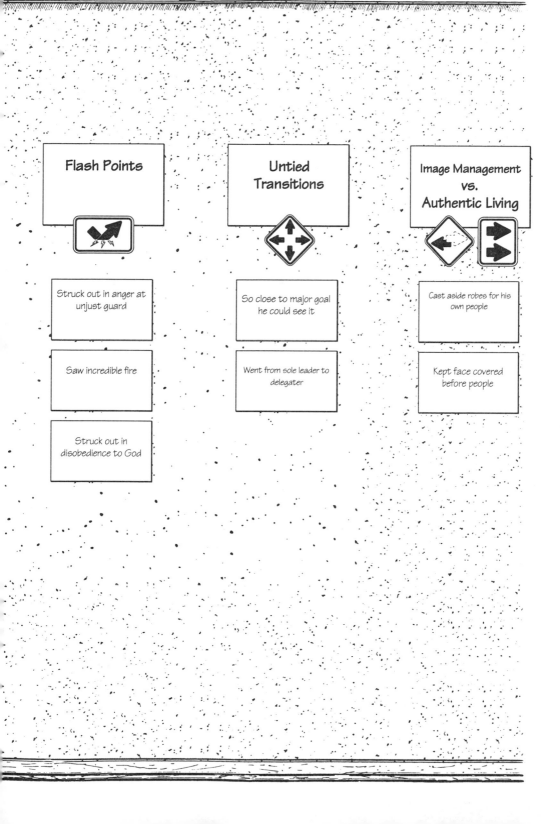

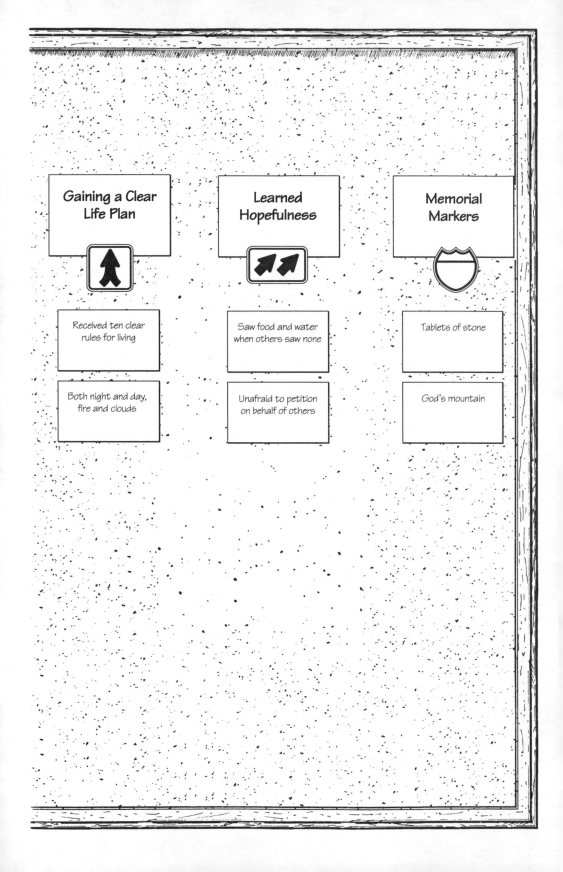

Gaining a Clear Life Plan

Received ten clear rules for living

Both night and day, fire and clouds

Learned Hopefulness

Saw food and water when others saw none

Unafraid to petition on behalf of others

Memorial Markers

Tablets of stone

God's mountain

Which biblical personality's LifeMap is pictured on the preceding pages? If you guessed Charlton Heston, you get half credit. If you guessed Moses, congratulations!

Let's suppose you're standing with Moses near the end of his life, looking across the Jordan at the Promised Land. If you reviewed the highlights of his life story from that vantage point, you'd see that his life clearly reflects each of the eight elements of LifeMapping.

First, he was a man with great personal strengths of leadership and conviction. Second, he went through an extremely difficult season of time that could easily have created an emotional freeze point if he had let it. Third, his life held several individual flash points, from his need to drop everything and flee Egypt, to the burning bush, to the Red Sea parting, to receiving the Ten Commandments.

Fourth, he certainly had many major transitions, moving from Pharaoh's palace to being a refugee on the run, finally ending up as God's anointed ruler, standing again before Egypt's royalty. Fifth, while he could have hidden his faith and heritage in image management, he chose authentic living instead and experienced the consequences and rewards of a life of faith.

Sixth, in Moses' case, God helped him gain a "clear plan" for his life and His people. And while Moses certainly went through enough disappointments to have felt helpless at times, he chose instead to exercise learned hopefulness. Finally, from the Ark of the Covenant to the pillar of cloud by day and fire by night, to the tablets of stone themselves, Moses had ample memorial markers to confirm his walk of faith to the last day of his life.

From Theory to Practice

By this point, I hope you're beginning to see that creating a personal LifeMap becomes much more manageable and insightful when you use storyboarding to flesh it out. And now that you've read why LifeMapping can be so powerful, gotten a glimpse of two LifeMaps, and been briefly introduced to the eight elements, *you're ready to begin creating your own LifeMap, one element at a time*.

As the following chapters unfold, you'll see more clearly what each of the eight elements of LifeMapping entails. So it's time to get that storyboard kit ready, grab your marking pen, blow the dust off your old memories (even enlisting a supportive friend, small group, or spouse if you'd like), and then get set to polish up a bright, shining future. All this will happen as we walk step by step through a process that I pray will change your life as much as it has helped to encourage and redirect mine.

First stop—creating a clearly defined purpose statement for your LifeMap, and then a closer look at the first element of LifeMapping. That's where you'll see three crucial factors—your strengths, successes, and acceptance level.

PART 2:
STEPPING BACK . . .

Recognizing Your Strengths, Successes, and Acceptance Levels

CHAPTER • FIVE

You may not be ready to graduate from Disney University when it comes to your storyboarding skills, but I'm certain you remember the first step that begins the process. *That's right!* You develop a clear purpose for what you're doing before you start filling in all the blanks. (I know that for some readers, stopping to ask for directions is a sign of weakness. But if you're not clear on the storyboarding process, it's perfectly acceptable to review chapter 4 before launching into this chapter.)

To illustrate, here's how the first part of my LifeMap looked after I had brainstormed, sharpened, and then reorganized the purpose.

John Trent's LifeMap

Purpose
first topper card

To draw closer to Christ

To gain insight and healing
from past hurts

To gain a clear
spiritual growth plan

To strengthen my marriage
and parenting skills

To reflect Christ's love and
character in my work

Your list of purposes may look very different. You may want to move past a difficult time of transition, focus on healing a specific past relationship, or make personal acceptance a stated goal. Again, the key is to flesh out the subbers under this first topper card. Then, once they're sharpened and rearranged in the order you like them, take all your cards and turn them into a run-on sentence.

Here are my subber cards put into a purpose statement for my LifeMap: *Purpose:* To become more like Christ by putting past hurts into perspective and pointing me toward God and a family-honoring future.

Take the time to toss around some 3x5 subber cards now, and come up with your own purpose statement that is unique to you. Once you've got that personalized goal in mind, copy it to your LifeMap. Like Da Vinci, you've now got a picture of the "finished" work in mind. Then you're ready to begin working on the masterpiece! And you do that by developing the second topper card (the first being the purpose), which is the first key element in the LifeMapping process.

Stepping Back . . . to Your Strengths

LifeMapping starts by looking at your past, but not in a negative way. In fact, it begins by looking back in a way that might surprise you.

No matter how positive or difficult a background you came from, LifeMapping starts by focusing on your *strengths* and recounting times of success. What's more, we'll look at how well your successes were *celebrated* by those close to you and the personal acceptance level you carry forward as a result.

But why strengths and successes? Why start there? After all, for many of us, a look back simply brings to mind dark shadows of failure or icy patches of pain, neglect, or regret. While it ought to be just the opposite, *even Christians* often have an easier time coming up with a list of weaknesses than they do clearly recounting strengths. *I know that for a fact.*

A guaranteed test of success

The year was 1974, and I was as nervous as a cat in a room full of rocking chairs (as my grandfather used to say). While I had struggled through summer-school Greek, this was my first day of regular classes at Dallas Theological Seminary. Deep inside, I knew God wanted me in seminary, but emotionally, I felt awkward and very out of place.

There I was, a relatively new Christian tossed in with the best and the brightest. I knew the admissions officers at Dallas had turned down nearly three students for every applicant they'd accepted. I also knew that I'd gotten in on academic probation just days before the summer semester started. (I've always wanted to meet the person who didn't show up, creating a spot for me to attend.)

It didn't help when I introduced myself to the man sitting on my right. I discovered he was a pastor's son *and* an honors graduate from Columbia University. Looking left made it worse—the guy there was a Wheaton honors student. He'd been to Christian grade school, high school, and college. And there I sat never having been to Sunday school!

We were waiting for class to start when I caught a first glimpse of a man I'd heard much about. It was Dr. Howard Hendricks, a noted Christian educator and a man who, I'm honored to say, would become a mentor and special friend. "Prof" stepped up to the podium right on time.

After opening the class in prayer, Dr. Hendricks said in his booming voice, "People, I've got a test for you as we begin this class."

I didn't hear a single groan except my own.

Oh, great, I thought as I fumbled for my Bible. *Here comes one of those "Name the Old Testament Kings" tests that I feared would happen.*

"If you pass this test," Prof said, "I can almost guarantee that you'll be a success here at seminary and in your ministry. But if you fail this test, I can almost assure you that you won't be successful in either area."

Let's see, there was Hezekiah, Ahab, Saul, David . . . or was Hezekiah a judge?

"Now take out a 3x5 card and write down your three greatest weaknesses."

Weaknesses? Did he say, "Write down your weaknesses"? If that's what it took to be a success in seminary and ministry, I was going to be *incredibly* successful! *Move over, Chuck Swindoll!* I thought. I forgot all about the 3x5 card and reached for a legal pad instead.

I was just filling up my second sheet of weaknesses when Prof's voice cut in: "Okay, men, that was just the warm-up. Here's the *real* test."

I knew it! I thought, shaking my head. *That guy from Wheaton probably lived in a dorm named after one of those Hebrew kings!*

"Turn your 3x5 card over and write down your three greatest *strengths.*"

Strengths? I thought. *Strengths???*

I'd had no trouble listing weaknesses. Yet suddenly I saw that my pen had stopped dead still in my hand. And from my position in the back row, I noticed that almost everyone else's pen had stopped, too.

Why is it so hard for us to see our strengths?

A second national pastime

If baseball is our national pastime, being critical has got to come in a close second. And that's not just true of the Washington press corps. As a country, we have a national obsession with looking at what's wrong.

When was the last time a positive, redeeming story led off the nightly news? Why isn't our credit rating based on the years we've *paid* the mortgage on time rather than on those two payments we missed? Why do studies of both male *and* female bosses have them pointing out failures four times more often than offering praise?[1]

While there may be some merit in chronicling our failures, I'm convinced that is not where God would have us focus. In fact, it's His desire that we look at a marvelous mirror that can tell us what's *right* with us, not what's wrong.

Mirror, mirror on the wall . . .

Did you know that there's a miraculous mirror you can go to anytime that will reflect the brightest and best part of you? It's a mirror not of make-believe, like the talking mirror in *Snow White,* but one of rock-solid reality. Just open your Bible to 2 Corinthians 3:18 and you'll find a mirror that can reveal your strengths and point you toward the person you'd most like to become.

The apostle Paul put it this way: "But we all, with unveiled face beholding as in a mirror the glory of the Lord, are being transformed into the same image from glory to glory, just as from the Lord, the Spirit."

The miraculous mirror Paul described is a picture of all your positive potential and capacity for love. That's because it's a reflection of His Son and Holy Spirit inside you and the promise of all He can help you to become.

There's actually a double miracle described here. First, you can see the Almighty God face to face in the mirror (in Jesus, the "image of the invisible God" [Col. 1:15]). And second, God Himself is committed to transforming— literally *transfiguring*—you into His glorious image.

Remember Da Vinci's masterpieces? They started with a sketch of the finished product—*beginning with the end in sight*. The same thing should be true of you.

It's easy to look at your failures and defeats. (And as we'll see in the next element of LifeMapping, emotional freeze points, it may be necessary as well.) But it's extremely important that you recount and *believe* that you also have God-given strengths and high personal value—strengths you can develop today and tomorrow that can increase "glory by glory" to reflect His love all the more.

Once you've identified your strengths, you can more easily look at those times when you've exercised them. It's the exercising of your strengths that leads to your *successes*. And finally, we'll look at whether your strengths were *celebrated*—whether they were ever *verbally, tangibly* acknowledged by your parents, spouse, or others. That acknowledgment of your personal strengths and successes is a key factor in forming the *level of acceptance* you carry forward each day of your life.

But before we get into chronicling successes and times your strengths were celebrated, let's look at one roadblock that can keep you from ever seeing them. That roadblock can effectively block out anything positive from your past and ultimately will lead you down a bumpy, dead-end road.

A Potential Roadblock

What's the roadblock I'm talking about? *Legalism.* I agree with my friend Chuck Swindoll that perhaps the greatest danger facing the church today isn't unbridled license but legalism.

In the verses leading up to 2 Corinthians 3:18, Paul pointed out that we must turn from gazing only at rules and look instead at the giver of life. If the focus of our lives becomes a performance-oriented scorecard handed to us by a modern Pharisee, we'll never see our strengths. That's because focusing on the rules serves a major purpose—namely, to condemn us because we can't keep them! As Romans 3:23 says, "For all have sinned and fall short of the glory of God."

However, when we look at Christ, His Spirit takes the veil of blindness from our eyes; we accept the forgiveness and newness of life He offers; and we find that the rules of God's way of life that were once outside us become mysteriously written on our hearts (see 2 Cor. 3:4-11). Then we're free from the condemnation of basing our lives on a set of enslaving rules and daily drill-sergeant inspections, and we're free to love and serve Him in righteousness from a place of refreshing acceptance.

If all that sounds too technical, let me put it another way. A relationship with Jesus is based on what we can *become* in Him—not what we've failed to measure up to. When we become that "new creature" in Christ as God promises (see 2 Cor. 5:17), we inherit a relationship with Someone who forever will look at and develop our *strengths*—not focus on our weaknesses.

Our teachers may grade us on the curve, our bosses may judge us by how much work we get done, and the IRS may force us to account for each penny we earn, but God judges us by a different standard—the cross. And when we accept Jesus as our Savior and Lord, we've got a secure base on which to build and grow a fulfilling life.

Let's face it, we've all made mistakes, and to some extent, we're all damaged goods. But in Jesus, we don't have to focus on what's wrong. Now we're free to focus on our strengths, our "spiritual gifts," and the God-given value we have in Him.

So how do we look back at the past and come up with our strengths and successes? And how do they tie in with acceptance levels?

Four Faces of Our Strengths

First, let's clarify what we mean by looking for our strengths and examine what successes represent. Then we'll look at how you can capture them for use on your LifeMap.

For LifeMapping purposes, our strengths are those God-given abilities, talents, desires, and sensitivities that He has chosen to make a part of our lives. In some cases (like a spiritual gift), it's something that comes with our spiritual birth.[2] In others, it's a general tendency or enjoyable habit or skill with which we were born.

If our *strengths* are the talents, abilities, or gifts we've been given, then *successes* are those special times when we've used our strengths to enrich God's kingdom or the lives of others.

Notice that the way I've defined success isn't necessarily in terms of personal accomplishment. For example, if we've used our God-given strength of overseeing or directing others to push, shove, or bully them on our way to the top, that's not success. Rather, it's when we use our strengths and talents to empower and benefit others that we can claim genuine success.

For example, consider Eric Liddle, the Scottish runner whose life story inspired the wonderful movie *Chariots of Fire*. In one particularly poignant scene, Liddle was debating with his sister whether he should continue his running toward the Olympics or head straight to the mission field. She seemed crestfallen when he announced his intention to put off missions temporarily for the chance at a medal. But instead of shaming or arguing with her, he comforted her with the words, "Jenny, Jenny. I know God created me for His service. But He also made me *fast*. And when I run, I feel His pleasure."

That's one way to look at our strengths. In this case, God had given Liddle a special ability to run. And in exercising that talent, he felt God's approval. The use of that talent not only blessed him, but it also provided a platform to encourage many, many others.

I'm not saying that all strengths are physical talents like running, typing, or skating. Nor do our strengths have to win us a gold medal or become the basis of an Academy Award-winning movie. Instead, more often God gives us everyday strengths that often fall into one of four areas. See if you can recognize some of your strengths in one, two, or even all four of the following areas.

The Four Primary Areas of God-Given Strengths
A. Verbal strengths
B. Analytical strengths
C. Sensing strengths
D. Directing strengths

Verbal strengths
For some of us, the thing we do best is talk! Believe it or not, that can be a real strength. As you think back on your past, perhaps you can identify some special verbal skills God has given you to encourage others.

You may sing in the church choir, use your voice to sell insurance that protects people from catastrophe, or stand up front as a teacher. Perhaps you're good at writing down your words in notes of encouragement, or at speaking out in public to protect biblical values or the unborn.

Is this an area where you've been gifted? Those verbal skills don't have to be so unique that they win a blue ribbon at a debate contest. Rather, they may be as soft as a grandmother's quiet lullaby that calms a colicky child's tummy.

Take a moment to go through this checklist and see if you enjoy any of these activities or situations:

Verbal Skills Self-Test

- Do you enjoy meeting new people without feeling shy or awkward?
- When a conversation hits a lull, are you usually the first one to say something to get it restarted?
- Would you rather have somebody "talk you through" a new skill instead of watching a demonstration on video?
- Do you enjoy talking on the telephone and do it frequently?
- Can you recall times when someone has specifically told you, "Your [written or spoken] words really helped me"?

If you said yes to two or more of the statements above, you most likely gain real enjoyment in using words. Think about how your verbal strengths have developed or been used to help others, and those are things that you may want to put on your LifeMap. But verbal strengths aren't the only ones God gives.

Analytical strengths

For some of us, our God-given strengths are in the ability to take things or problems apart and see key ways to refine a process. Perhaps you're a high-school coach who has drawn up successful plays since you were a child on the sandlots. You may be an accomplished typist or data processor. Or you might be a church business administrator who, after 20 years of keeping the Navy in line, now keeps the church records shipshape.

See if any of these statements are things you could check off:

Analytical Strengths Self-Test

- Do you enjoy setting something up right out of the box—and following directions?
- Do you like to do things right, in order, and in a logical way?
- Do you look forward to times when you can "get things squared away," like uncluttering an overfull garage?
- Do people sometimes tell you you're good at following maps or instructions?
- Are you the type of person who enjoys making up lists for yourself and others?

Again, if you answer yes to two or more of those questions, you might look more closely at whether God has gifted you in an analytical way. All those orderly traits can reflect a special ability to make the lives of others better and less cluttered. As with any strength, this one can sometimes be pushed too far and become a weakness (like the organized person who becomes enslaved to an unbendable schedule). If you get personal satisfaction, however, and "feel God's pleasure" in a job well organized and well planned, this could very well go on your LifeMap.

Sensing strengths

Sensing strengths are just what they sound like—that special ability to feel the hurts of others, to perceive what that person in front of you is really like, and to communicate warmth and encouragement to meet another person's need.

An example of this skill showed up in a study of excellent nurses. They discovered that patients who interacted regularly with nurses who were "warm, sensitive, and likable" took less medicine for pain and discomfort! In other words, by sensing and empathizing with their patients' pain, those nurses actually helped relieve the aches.[3]

I'm not suggesting that those with sensing strengths are human aspirin bottles, but that's one way to look at their God-given skills. Have you ever been around someone who seemed to make you feel better just by listening to you? Have you had others comment to you that you're a "loyal" or "sensitive" friend? Do you get particular pleasure out of simply "being there" for a friend who is working through a problem—even if you don't get up-front credit for doing so?

If that sounds like you, take a moment to go through this checklist:

Sensing Strengths Self-Test

- Since the time you were young, have you always had an ability to "size up" a person or situation?
- Do you tend to bond to people and even things around you (like giving your car a name or looking at your pets as major parts of your family)?
- Do you find yourself changing channels or quickly flipping the page if there's a particularly gruesome story in the news?
- Do you enjoy helping others become successful, even if you don't get credit?
- Do you seem to have more patience than others to hang in there with people and situations?

Push sensing strengths to an extreme and you may run into hypersensitivity. But the compassion, attention, and insight held in balance that make up sensing skills are great assets and should go on your LifeMap. So, too, should the fourth area of strength.

Directing strengths

As you look at your past, perhaps you see that the times you've felt most fulfilled and "alive" are when you've been directing something to a purposeful conclusion. It may have been anything from producing the second-grade play, to leading a recon platoon in combat, to running for public office, to making sure things work smoothly in your home. But the common denominator is that from your position as "point man" or "point woman," you were leading the parade and enjoying it.

If that description sounds like you, you'll probably check off several of the following items:

Directing Strengths Self-Test

- Can you think of projects that wouldn't have been done if your direction hadn't "pulled the ox out of the ditch"?
- Have there been times when your leadership made the difference in keeping or pulling a business deal together?
- Would you prefer to take an active role in shaping a project rather than being assigned a task by others?
- Do you often look for challenges or get bored if there are none to face?
- Does your communication tend to be brief, focused, and to the point?

If statements like those are characteristic of you, you've got directing strengths that you can thank God for and that can go on your LifeMap.

Now that you have a better idea of what's meant by *strengths*, you're ready to begin capturing them on your LifeMap.

> *No matter how positive or difficult a background you came from, LifeMapping starts by focusing on your strengths and recounting times of success.*

Storyboarding Your Strengths and Successes

It's time to pull out your LifeMap and begin putting cards under the topper labeled "Strengths, Successes, and Acceptance Levels." And to show you how that's done, let's go back to my LifeMap as an illustration of what you can do with your own.

John Trent's LifeMap

Strengths, Successes, and Acceptance Levels

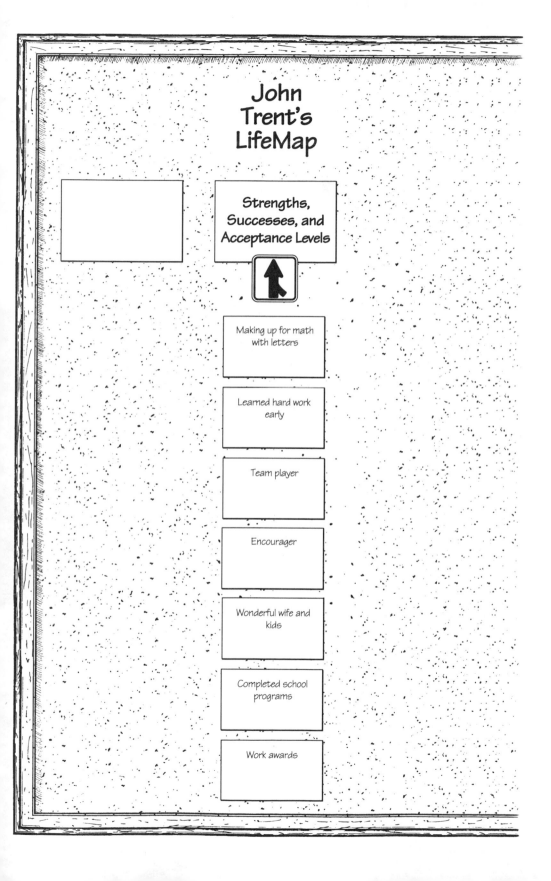

Making up for math with letters

Learned hard work early

Team player

Encourager

Wonderful wife and kids

Completed school programs

Work awards

As I thought back on the strengths and successes in my life story, I found seven things that went up on cards. The first I wrote down was "Making up for math with letters." Let me tell you the story behind that.

I remember sitting in a doctoral class one day where we were studying how to construct, conduct, and interpret various types of tests. Each of us students had to take numerous kinds of tests. And when it came time to dissect an IQ test, mine was randomly chosen by the professor as the class example.

I had never actually seen the results of one of my IQ tests before, and I didn't mind at all that I was the class illustration . . . at first.

"Now, John," the professor said, looking over my results. "This shows that you scored extremely high in the verbal and writing portions of the test."

I humbly nodded and tried not to act too proud in front of the other, less-gifted students.

Then my bubble burst. The professor went on, "But I need to ask you, *Did you go through a very difficult birth experience, or were you ever held underwater for a long period of time?*"

"What?" I asked, not understanding where his question was coming from. "No, sir," I managed to get out. "I can't say as either thing has happened to me. Why?"

"Well," he said, gazing intently at my test scores, "you're very high in the verbal and writing section—but you're four points away from *brain damage* when it comes to the mathematical and spatial orientation sections!"

Brain damage?

For each semester thereafter, you can guess how many jokes I endured from my fellow classmates. (Many of them showed great insensitivity by asking if I had my handicapped parking sticker yet or if I needed some other type of specialized care.)

While that particular day was quite humiliating, upon reflection I realized what God had done in giving me a few extra points in the verbal and writing area. He had helped make up for my poor math and spatial skills by allowing me to compensate with words! I would need every bit of those verbal skills to talk my way through the one and only math class I took in college. It was a course on "elementary sets." (Remember sets and subsets?) As simple as that class was, I would have flunked if the teacher hadn't let me *write* an extra-credit paper to pull out a passing grade.

So verbal strengths went on my LifeMap. And if you'll look closer, you'll also see that I've listed some sensing strengths like "Team player" and "Encourager." Those are reflections of the enjoyment I get in encouraging and serving others.

While some of my cards point to God-given strengths and abilities, others reflect *applications* of those strengths, or "successes." For example, I've been blessed with a wonderful wife and two daughters, and I work hard at being a good husband and father. Also, by using my writing skills, God has allowed me to gain a few awards along the way ("Work awards" on the LifeMap) that have highlighted those skills.

I explain these not as a way to pat myself on the back but to do what God asked us repeatedly to do—*remember* His faithfulness in giving us our strengths, and in their use to help and serve others. We need to chronicle our strengths, thank God for them, and thank Him that He has used us, whether it's in volunteering at the hospital or manning a space station.

But what about our weaknesses? I hear some of you saying, "Focusing on strengths may be great for Pollyanna or for you, John, but I've never written a book or led a conference. In fact, I can't think of a *single* strength God has given me."

If you can't think of even one strength out of the four categories mentioned above, nor of a single time when you used personal strengths to benefit or encourage others—*then almost certainly, one of two things has happened.*

First, you may have drunk *way* too many diet thirst busters, which can give you short-term memory loss . . . and it can give you short-term memory loss. Or, on a more serious note, you've missed out on something vital, and that has blinded you to recognizing your strengths. If legalism is a wooden roadblock that can keep you from seeing your strengths, this other problem can become a brick wall. It can make the pen freeze in your hand when it comes to listing strengths on your storyboarding cards.

This second reason some people can't think of a single strength is that they can't remember even one time when their abilities were *celebrated*. And it's the degree to which our strengths are celebrated that primarily determines the acceptance level we live with every day.

Opening Our Eyes to See Our Strengths

Let's say you grew up in a home that wasn't perfect, but you did consistently and *verbally* hear your strengths praised by loved ones. That's a home where your strengths were *celebrated*, and while it shocked me to learn it, that's the kind of home an old friend named Roger came from.

Roger and I went to grade school and high school together. I felt I knew him well, but there was something about him that confused me. He always seemed so confident and quick to encourage others. He has since gone on to do well in his vocation, and he married and has a wonderful, loving family. Yet as I watched him growing up in a troubled household, I would never have guessed that he would turn out so well.

I remember being at his house when his dad would stumble in drunk and all us kids would be ordered outside by his mom. I also recall that at age 15, on the day before a major game we were to play, Roger was called out of practice and informed that his father had died.

I'd seen firsthand the effects of an alcoholic father, and I was always impressed by the way Roger had coped and grown through it. But it wasn't until recently, when I brought this up to him, that he told me something that floored me.

I had congratulated him on "beating the odds" and building a strong family from such a tough background. He responded, "But John, you don't realize something. It's true that my dad drank. Sometimes way too much. And when he died, it really hurt. *But I had something to hang onto.*

"You wouldn't know it," he continued, "but every single day of my life that I can remember, my father would come into my room before bedtime. And every night, he'd tell me how proud he was of me for what I'd done that day in school or sports. I must have heard hundreds of times how special I was to him and how much he loved me. Even after those nights when he'd been drinking, when he would sober up he'd ask me to forgive him. And he always told me I had a wonderful future ahead of me—*one without alcohol.*"

While it didn't show to those of us *outside* his family, Roger had a hidden source of inner strength given to him by his father. In those bedtime visits, he heard his strengths celebrated repeatedly by a loving dad. And that's what has helped in filling up his need for acceptance over the years.

Acceptance Levels

We've looked at God-given strengths and successes. We've also seen that when those strengths are celebrated, it can fill a life with positives that can help a person outlast and overcome many negatives. Unfortunately, some of us come from homes where we never heard our strengths celebrated. As a result, "the dipstick isn't touching oil" when it comes to measuring a positive acceptance level.

Look at 16-year-old Darren, for example. His father was an angry alcoholic who had left him and his mother and sister six years before. But now that Darren was the captain of his small-town basketball team, his father wanted to use him for bragging rights with his drinking buddies.

Darren remembers the last time he saw his father. His dad was standing inside a raunchy saloon, demanding that Darren come inside and have a drink with him to "celebrate the big game." But mindful of a mother who had warned him to never step inside a bar, Darren told his father, "If you want to talk to me, sober up and come to one of my games."

As Darren walked away, the old man screamed at him, "Don't walk away from me! You're worthless! You're nothing but scum! You'll never amount to anything!"

That was hardly a celebration of Darren's strengths. And it was particularly hard to swallow when his dad died a few months later and those scorching words were the last he would ever hear from him.

Perhaps you came from a home where your strengths were never mentioned, never appreciated, never celebrated. If so, don't be surprised if you can't think of a single thing to put on cards in this column—at least until you deal with the next element of LifeMapping, emotional freeze points. As you'll see in the next chapter, you can begin to "thaw out" from those difficult seasons of life when your strengths weren't celebrated and find God's strength to go on.

Overcoming Evil with Good

We've seen that God invites us to look into His mirror and see all the good things we can become in His Son. What's more, we've seen that God has gifted each of us with valuable strengths, be they verbal, analytical, sensing, or directing.

For all of us, recognizing and building on our strengths is an important place to begin, not only in the LifeMapping process, but in building a fulfilling life as well.

For some, however, a nagging question might remain: Do I just ignore my weaknesses and focus on my strengths? To a certain extent, the answer is yes!

In the book *Soaring with Our Strengths,* the story is told of a conversation the authors had with the coach of the Chinese men's table tennis team. At the time of the interview, the Chinese had never failed to capture an Olympic gold medal in this sport, and the 1984 games were no exception. The authors asked the coach, "Tell us about your team's daily training regimen."

"We practice eight hours a day perfecting our strengths," he said.

"Could you be a little more specific?"

"Here is our philosophy: If you develop your strengths to the maximum, the strength becomes so great it overwhelms the weaknesses. Our winning player, you see, plays only his forehand. Even though he cannot play backhand and his competition know he cannot play backhand, his forehand is so invincible that it cannot be beaten."[4]

Get the picture? Focusing on your strengths—*and on the application of those strengths, which produces your successes*—will often reduce or eliminate your weaknesses. You get so focused on the positive goal in front of you (helping, serving, leading, encouraging) that you cut down on the time, energy, and desire to maintain the negative. And when your strengths get celebrated, you're in the best possible position to turn around and fill up the acceptance level of others.

A reminder to build and bless the strengths of others

We need to be people who recognize and thank God for the strengths He's given us. And we also need to point out the strengths in others' lives.

You may be a parent who can celebrate your child's strengths. You might be a neighbor like Tim Taylor's "backyard friend" Wilson on TV's *Home Improvement,* offering encouragement across a fence. You may be a coach who builds a positive legacy like John Wooden at UCLA (unlike a certain Midwestern coach who built a dynasty by tearing down players). You might be a pastor who can change lives by acknowledging and affirming people's strengths.

Or maybe you're just an everyday person with an everyday job who can make a life-changing difference by pointing out others' gifts and abilities. Sister Helen Mrosla was such a person.

She remembers her first teaching experience. There were 34 third-graders in her class in Morris, Minnesota, all of them filled with youthful bounce.

Sister Mrosla vividly recalls one young man named Mark who talked incessantly. He was handsome, and in every way except that constant chattering, he was well behaved. Finally, in total frustration one afternoon, Sister Mrosla issued an ultimatum she instantly wished she'd left unsaid: "If you open your mouth one more time, Mark, I'm going to tape it closed!"

As you can imagine, it wasn't two minutes later before another student shouted out, "Mark's talking! Mark's talking!"

Since the punishment had been stated in front of the class, Sister Mrosla was stuck. So, too, were Mark's lips when she very purposefully (and with the room falling into a deep hush) proceeded to Mark's desk, tore off two pieces of tape, and made a big X over his mouth. Then she returned to her desk.

As she glanced at Mark to see how he was doing, he winked at her, and soon she was chuckling and then laughing out loud. The entire class cheered as she walked back to Mark's desk and removed the tape. His first words after the tape came off were, "Thank you for correcting me, Sister."

Several years passed, and Mark found himself in Sister Mrosla's class again. Now it was junior high, and she had gone on to teaching math. At one point, she could sense that it was the time of year when students were getting on each others' nerves. The frustration increased as they were trying and failing to understand a difficult concept all week, and friction seemed to permeate the room.

"Take out a sheet of paper," she told the class at the end of that trying week, "and write down the names of each student in the room on two sheets of paper, leaving a space between each name. Now I want you to think of the nicest thing you can say about each of your classmates, and write that down beneath their name."

Sister Mrosla had the class take the rest of the period to finish the assignment, and that weekend, she listed each child's name on a separate sheet of paper, then compiled everything positive that everyone else had said about that individual. On Monday, she gave each child his or her list. And while everyone seemed pleased, no one ever mentioned those papers in class again.

Years passed, and one day Sister Mrosla was returning from a vacation. Her parents met her at the airport. As they were driving home, her father cleared his throat and said, "Mark Eklund's family called last night. You know, he was in your class."

"Really?" she said. "I haven't heard from them in several years. I wonder how Mark is?"

He father responded quietly, "Mark was killed in Vietnam. The funeral is tomorrow, and his parents would like it if you could attend."

The church was packed, and the service was a tribute to a fallen hero. But afterward, something totally unexpected happened. Mark's mother and father came up to Sister Mrosla and said, "We want to show you something." Opening his wallet, the father pulled out a wad of papers to show her.

"They found this on Mark when he was killed," he said. "We thought you might recognize it."

He carefully revealed two worn pieces of notebook paper that had obviously been taped, folded, and refolded many times. The papers were the ones on which Sister Mrosla had listed all the good things each of Mark's classmates had said about him that day in junior high school.

"Thank you so much for doing that," Mark's mother said. "As you can see, Mark treasured it."[5]

When you point out another person's strengths, you may be creating a memory he or she carries for a lifetime—or into the next. You might do something as simple as picking up the phone and making "double sure" your grown children know they're special and deeply loved, possessing strengths you can celebrate. It may involve something as easy as turning off the television and sitting beside your son who is such a good reader, making sure he knows you appreciate that gift. Or it might be something as minor as showing up at a practice—not even a game—and pointing out your daughter's persistence in her team sport.

We've looked now at the first element of LifeMapping—recognizing your strengths, successes, and acceptance level. Next, it's time to turn our attention to the second element. For if this first element can get you off on a positive start in life, the second—emotional freeze points—can slow your growth down to a crawl unless you learn how to recognize and deal with it.

$\mathcal{E}$motional Freeze Points

Novelist Willa Cather wrote, "Most of the basic material a writer works with is acquired before the age of 15." And if you think about it, that's often true.

Most of Mark Twain's adventure stories, like *Tom Sawyer* and *The Adventures of Huckleberry Finn,* came from remembrances of his early boyhood. Much of Harper Lee's novel *To Kill a Mockingbird* was based on reflections of her days before age 15. And on the dark side, both Edgar Allan Poe and Stephen King have said that childhood fears and traumas greatly influenced their horror writings.

Those who write stories—or live them—are all surrounded and shaped by their early memories. One author, Morris Massey, has built an entire system of values formation around this tenet: "You are who you were when you were ten years old."

When it comes to the past, whether key events happened when we were ten, 15, or pushing 50, we all can be affected by memories. Unfortunately, some of us are also controlled by them.

As you seek to map out your life, you need to look back honestly and see

97

if there were any dark, treacherous, "black ice" patches in your past—cold seasons of hurt— especially if they came before age 15—that can cause you to skid off the road toward Christlikeness and plow right into an emotional freeze point.

In the last chapter, we focused on our strengths by looking back. In this chapter, we need to look at those rocky roads in your LifeMap that may have taken you through the shadowlands. For I'm convinced that if you can face the hurt and put those difficult times in context, you're in the best position to move past those often-gripping memories and on toward your high calling in Christ.

Our look at emotional freeze points will begin with a definition, and then we'll consider several ways to understand and begin to overcome those challenging times and get back on the high road. But one thing we can't do is ignore those icy patches. That's something Jamie tried (the woman introduced in the first chapter), and she carries the scar to prove it.

A View of Jamie's LifeMap

I met Jamie at a conference where I spoke about memorial markers, the eighth element of LifeMapping. The seminar had been recommended to her by her counselor, who felt she needed to hear its message.

As Jamie learned about LifeMapping and memorial markers, then reflected on what she had been learning in counseling, two things fell into place for her. See if you can find them in this brief, edited excerpt of her LifeMap:

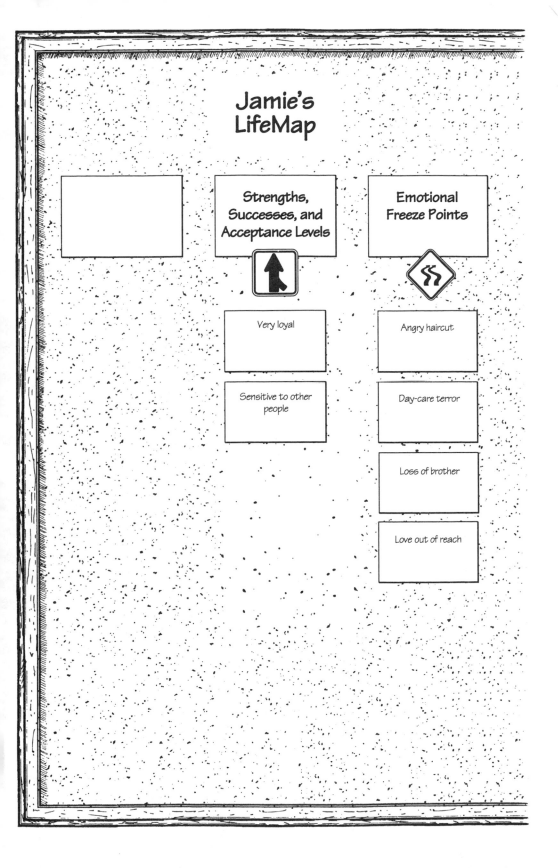

Jamie's LifeMap

Strengths, Successes, and Acceptance Levels	Emotional Freeze Points
Very loyal	Angry haircut
Sensitive to other people	Day-care terror
	Loss of brother
	Love out of reach

Jamie's life story was one of strengths in the sensing area that were never recognized or celebrated, and of her hand being slapped away by everyone she reached out to love.

One of her earliest memories was of playing with scissors and cutting off several snippets of a baby doll's hair. She remembers her mother thundering at her about what a "horrible" child she was to "destroy" such an expensive toy, and then proceeding to slam her into a chair and cut off her hair in huge clumps so she could "see what it feels like" (as if a doll could really *feel*).

Regular traumatic trials like that one were replicated in a day-care setting that was also a living nightmare. While most day-care settings are warm and supportive environments, Jamie was placed in an overcrowded room with an overworked, uncaring staff. Being separated from her mother brought tears to her eyes and contempt from busy teachers. She was labeled a "cry baby" and pushed aside until she could "grow up."

Can you see the faulty path that began to develop in Jamie's life story? She started with God-given skills of sensing, relating, and desiring to help and encourage others. She was a young girl with a deep need for love and an equally deep longing to love others. Yet it seemed that each turn of life took her toward a painful dead end.

Her father had left the home when Jamie was young, and he never looked back. Her mother was too busy and too preoccupied with work and other children to bother with her. Her older brother, whom she adored, would stand up for her at home and at school. He also was the brother who lay upstairs in his room for months, finally dying of Hodgkin's disease when she was still in grade school.

Years passed and Jamie grew up, but even the men she dated treated her terribly. It was always the same story—her tying to please them in a vain attempt to receive their love, and their taking advantage of and finally rejecting her instead.

As I said in chapter 1, after breaking up with a man who for two years used and abused her, Jamie came to a conclusion as dark as the winter clouds. If all roads in her life led to pain, what use was it to keep trying? That's when she picked up the knife and slid it across her wrist.

She wasn't serious about killing herself, though. It was more a gesture of frustration and a cry for help. But the pain and small cut she caused acted like a wake-up call that shocked her into realizing how depressed she'd become and pushed her into a counselor's office. And in the days and weeks that followed, her supportive Christian counselor became both her coach and her friend.[1]

As I said in an earlier chapter, when Jamie got to this part of the LifeMapping process, she almost quit. She had only come up with two cards in the strengths column, and she had far more than 20 that described freeze points. But looking at all that blank space to the right of her freeze points convinced her that her life story didn't have to end in a freeze point.

"I still have a small scar on my hand and wrist," she wrote. "It's not real noticeable, but it's there. But God is healing my wounds. In fact, now every time I look at that scar, it has become a memorial marker of God's love to me, saying, 'Jamie, I already carry scars on My hands for all your sorrow and pain. You don't have to hurt yourself again.'"

Whether you've got one card or 20 under the freeze point topper on your LifeMap, writing them down is one way to begin removing them from your everyday memory. As to how you do that, let's gain a clear definition of what I mean by a freeze point and how you can begin to break free.

What Exactly Is an Emotional Freeze Point?

An emotional freeze point is a *season of time* over which *unexamined* and *unprocessed* layers of hurt are laid down, restricting or blocking personal and spiritual growth.

> *A freeze point is most likely to occur when you've never "processed" a trial, when you've left it unexamined.*

You'll notice several important distinctions in the definition. *First, freeze points are linked with a progression of time.* In the next element of LifeMapping, we'll look at those things that instantaneously break upon us (flash points) and can result in good or bad. But freeze points are more like the creeping of winter on a northern lake. First the sun moves farther away and the days become shorter. Then the frost on the water begins to sheet. And finally, layers of cold rain and snow can add inches to an icy, immovable cover.

Second, not all seasons of hurt cause a freeze point. A freeze point is most likely to occur when you've never "processed" a trial, when you've left it unexamined. If you've never been willing to talk about past hurts with the Lord, a pastor, or a close friend, then just like that frozen lake, it's likely that you're adding layers of emotional ice with the passage of time. But if you can honestly take what has happened to you and turn it toward the warming light of God's love, you can see even difficult times draw you closer to Him.

Consider Joe, for example. Here's a picture of his LifeMap under "freeze points"; the events listed there should have left him with three feet of ice, yet they didn't.

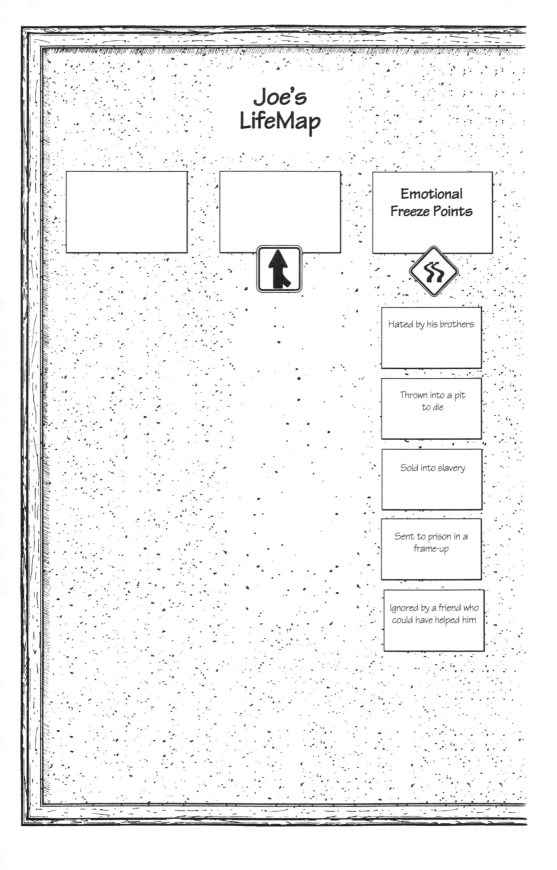

Joe's
LifeMap

Emotional
Freeze Points

Hated by his brothers

Thrown into a pit
to die

Sold into slavery

Sent to prison in a
frame-up

Ignored by a friend who
could have helped him

If anyone could have been a model for emotional freeze points, it had to be Joe—that is, Joseph in the Old Testament. He got the multicolored robe from his father, and his brothers got ticked off—so angry, in fact, that they tricked him, tied him up, and threw him in a pit in order to kill him. Only by God's grace and an older brother's conscience was Joseph allowed to live instead of becoming food for the wolves.

But if being hated and rejected by his brothers didn't create a freeze point, what happened next should have. He was sold into slavery and drew a cushy assignment in the house of Potiphar, a wealthy aristocrat. But that man's adulterous wife repeatedly tried to get him to sleep with her. And in a true instance of sexual harassment, Joseph ran from her lust and was rewarded by being framed and thrown into prison!

Being behind bars would cause a freeze point in almost anyone's life, but here again, Joseph decided to keep moving forward, not freezing inside. He soon worked hard enough to become the manager of the entire prison, and he was even able to offer help to two friends.

Joseph endured poor family relationships, being plucked out of a well and sold into slavery, suffering the consequences of being unjustly accused of attempted rape after weeks of harassment, and finally being tossed into prison. Those four seasons of pain should have provided enough ice for an Alaskan ice-fishing tournament! And there was more to come.

After turning to God to interpret a dream for a prison friend and seeing that man released, Joseph was promised help and a hearing to clear him of wrongdoing. But what he got instead was a *fifth* instance in which a protracted, painful experience could have produced a freeze point. In this case, it was a "friend" who forgot to put in a good word for him and left Joseph to toil in prison for many more weeks and months.

If you'd been betrayed that often and that dramatically by family, employers, and friends, don't you think you'd be suffering from a freeze point by now? But Joseph had a secret weapon that worked better than electric socks in a cold, Chicago winter. He had a God who allowed him to carry his own weather inside him—Someone whose love was so warm, whose character was so bright, that even cold nights in a dark prison cell couldn't keep spring from erupting in Joseph's commitment and spirit.

Joseph did many things right. But what about us mortals? What *didn't* happen in Joseph's life that normally occurs when we experience a season of pain and leave it unexamined and unprocessed? *Actually, there were* three things *he didn't do that make all the difference between staying warm and free or being frozen solid emotionally.*

Three Marks of an Emotional Freeze Point

Read carefully in the next few pages the three characteristics of a freeze point. Take particular note if you find yourself living as if they are there (poor at commitment and communication, and either extremely defensive or overly sensitive) but you can't think of anything obvious that constituted a freeze point. If that's the case, it's time to go back through your personal history, and this time look for the *less obvious.*

Perhaps you grew up in a home where Mom and Dad stayed together. You were never beaten. No one forced you to clean chimneys or denied you permission to go to the king's ball (or play sports or join the band). It may even have been a home where you were taken to church on Sundays and celebrated Christmas at a midnight candlelight service. But outward looks can be deceiving.

Take a closer look. Perhaps you came from a home where image was put above true intent and actions. (We'll take an entire chapter to talk about homes that practice image management in the fifth element of LifeMapping.) Or you may have come from a home that looked harmless but conveyed one of the most damaging messages of all, the double message that says, *"I'm always here . . . but you can never come to me."*

That's the kind of home where a father is simply a shadow that slips in and out, or a mother is far too busy with "important" or "grown-up" things to spend time with the children. Like looking at a broken candy machine, the kids can see what they want but are never able to get to it.

If you felt like an emotional orphan in your home, even though your parents stayed together, face the facts. *The lack of positives from an unattached parent can be just as damaging as the presence of obvious negatives* (like yelling, fighting, or divorce).

So if you search your heart (and perhaps even ask your spouse or a close friend) and find that you exhibit all three of the following characteristics, you're almost certainly suffering the aftereffects of an emotional freeze point.

1. Freeze points can cause us to make pessimism a life-style choice.

A life-style of pessimism is a common indicator of one or more freeze points. I'm not talking about being a critical thinker or one who thinks things through from all sides. Nor am I talking about that analytically gifted person in the previous chapter who can come up with a long list of hard questions before making a decision.

Pessimism is more than that. It's a deep-seated layer of emotional ice that refuses to see hope on the horizon. It's like the man who went to a psychiatrist because he was depressed. "What's the matter?" the doctor asked.

"Two months ago, my cousin died and left me $100,000," the man said. "Then last month, a great-aunt passed away and left me $500,000."

"Then why are you depressed?"

"This month . . . *nothing!*"

That's what pessimism does to us. It's not a character trait of cautiousness but an unattractive callus that develops over our ability to have faith and hope. And this pessimism growing out of seasons of hurt can literally be killing us.

The high cost of choosing pessimism

People have often dismissed optimism as silliness or even mental illness. Consider these examples:

"Optimism is a mania for maintaining that all is well when things are going badly" (Voltaire, 1759).

"The place where optimism most flourishes is a lunatic asylum" (Havelock Ellis, 1923).

"Pessimism is only the name that men of weak nerves give to wisdom" (Bernard de Voto, 1935).[2]

But clinical research and biblical truth show they're wrong. True optimism is formed when we see life as having meaning; when our life story has a purpose; when we see our LifeMap heading ultimately in a positive direction, even in the midst of trials.

Furthermore, genuine optimism always moves people to positive action. It moved Joseph to action, not apathy, when he worked his way to the top in Potiphar's household and in prison. And it was surely protecting his health as well.

While no Egyptian tablets have yet been unearthed from Joseph's day showing the positive medical effects of being optimistic, we can be sure he bene-fited from a biblically positive attitude nonetheless. Today we have multiple studies linking health and optimism, and one of the best came from the Harvard Study of Adult Development program headed most recently by Dr. George E. Vaillant at the Dartmouth Medical School.

The study began with a group of physically and mentally healthy members of the Harvard classes of 1942 through 1944. In all, 268 young men were included. The study has continued unabated until today and has provided invaluable insights into those men's lives and health. (In fact, only ten men withdrew from the study during college, and two more since graduation.)

Each year, the men have voluntarily taken health and psychological tests to gather data across their life span. Now that they've reached their sixties, one finding stands out loud and clear: Overall, *those men who were classified as "optimists" at age 25 are far healthier than those who viewed life and its circumstances pessimistically at that age.* In other words, *optimism early in life is associated with good health later in life.*[3]

And that's not just a finding reserved for Harvard students. In a major study done at the University of Michigan on those in the workplace, researchers found that the more optimistic people were, the fewer sick days they reported and the fewer times they reported being ill at all.[4] Even cancer patients have been shown to live longer and go into remission more often and for longer periods if they have a more optimistic view of their circumstances and future.[5]

But why?

A doctor might chalk it up to the effects of "immunocompetence," and specifically T4 (helper) cells and T8 (suppresser) cells. The "helper" and "suppresser" labels reflect the roles those cells play in turning on and off the body's fight against infections. A high ratio (where helper cells outnumber suppresser cells) means a robust, on-the-attack immune system. A low ratio means a weak immune system, with fewer helper cells and relatively more suppresser cells.[6]

As you might have guessed by now, even the blood work done on optimists and pessimists shows a difference in their immunocompetence. Optimists tend to have higher levels of helper cells, and pessimists tend to have more suppresser cells—just as Vaillant's study and many others would suggest.

But clinical studies are only part of the picture. If you're suffering from an emotional freeze point, you're *probably* putting your physical health at risk. But you're *certainly* putting your relational health at risk.

When pain and pessimism walk down the aisle

Dr. John Gottman at the University of Washington studied more than two thousand married couples over two decades. What he discovered about how wives and husbands relate to one another is so remarkable that he could predict, with 94 percent accuracy, which marriages would succeed and which would fail![7]

In his landmark research, he found that *for a marriage to last, there must be at least five positive interactions for every negative one between partners.* What happens when one person has a trapped layer of emotional hurt that produces a critical, negative attitude? He calls it a "cycle of negativity" that can literally cave in on a couple and end their marriage.

That's when the four relationship "killers" he isolated—criticism, contempt, defensiveness, and rigidity—form a deepening spiral that leads to more criticism, greater contempt, increasing defensiveness, and stone-wall rigidity.

Who displays such attitudes? In his studies, it was often people who come into marriage with a history of emotional hurt (i.e., periods when there were freeze points) and who have become critical pessimists in their marriages. And such people are not found only in secular circles. They're also scattered throughout the church.

Coming home to a hug

One day several years ago, when we were living in Texas, my wife, Cindy, came home from a Bible study group. Although we're an affectionate couple anyway, this day she threw her arms around me the moment she saw me, and for the longest time she refused to let go.

"What have you been studying at your Bible study?" I asked. "Song of Solomon? If this is the homework, why don't you all meet twice a week!"

"No," she assured me, they hadn't been studying the romantic Song of Songs. "We've been studying what the Scriptures say about a 'critical spirit.' And the reason I hugged you was that out of the five women in my group, I'm the only one who doesn't live with a critical husband."

Granted, her group was overloaded with women living with pessimists, but many men and women face that challenge. And as it says in the book of Proverbs, "It is better to live in a corner of the roof than in a house shared with a contentious woman [or man]" (Prov. 25:24).

"But I'm not a critical pessimist!" you might say. Well, to help you get a better idea of whether you are or aren't, ask yourself if you've said or thought anything like these statements in the past six months of your marriage:

"I'm Not Critical or a Pessimist!"

- I feel it's important to determine whose fault it is when there's an argument.
- He (she) always comes at things from his (her) side only.
- I don't censor my complaints when I'm angry. I just let it rip.
- Sure I'm negative at times, but that gets things off my chest.
- I don't start an argument unless I know I'm right.
- I don't have to take this kind of treatment from anybody.
- We've tried and tried to change. Nothing works.
- This is just one more area of my life where another person has killed my dreams.

Studies of pessimists reveal that they make a great number of critical comments—criticizing both themselves and those with whom they live. And often without realizing it, they do so at high cost to both their personal and their marital health.

You didn't see Joseph being pessimistic about the setting God had him in. Nor did you see him being critical. Even when family scorned him and friends walked out and forgot him, or when he was railroaded into a wrongful conviction, he kept his eyes focused forward on a living God who loved him and had a future for him.

That's not because he was a pacifist or didn't actively try to change his circumstances. (He fought the accusation that he had attempted to sleep with Potiphar's wife and sought help from a friend in prison to get him out.) But during those seasons of pain, he kept a crucial perspective. *Joseph felt so strongly that God was directing his outward circumstances that he was free to concentrate on his internal state.* Joseph's faith in Almighty God allowed him not only to avoid pessimism, but also to avoid another mark of emotional freeze points.

2. Freeze points can produce procrastination.

Some people have looked at unbridled optimism as an enemy of productivity. It's the pessimist who supposedly brings serious thought to a task, the pie-in-the-sky optimist who doesn't care enough about outcomes to make a difference.

Want to bet?

Clinical studies show just the opposite to be true. Genuine optimism—the kind that Joseph displayed every day—leads to *action*, not inaction. It's pessimism that leads to procrastination.

For example, take confirmed gamblers. As a general rule, wouldn't you think they'd be a very optimistic lot? Here they are, pulling the handle "one more time" after they've lost for the two hundredth time, or cheering for Lightning Bolt to win in the twelfth race when all 11 of their previous picks stumbled in dead last.

I was shocked when I discovered that the opposite is true. Heavy gamblers *aren't* overly optimistic. ("I know it'll work this time!") Actually, they're highly *fatalistic*. ("You never know when *luck* is going to change. What happens to you is out of your hands, so just keep pulling the handle!")

For a pessimist, the inner message is, *I really can't change things, so I'll just rely on chance to get me through.* (More about this in chapter 11 on learned hopefulness.) If whatever you do doesn't matter, why not just act like much of the world and "eat, drink, and be merry, for tomorrow we die"?

The truly optimistic person is empowered by the future and actively seeks to move and look toward it. And for the Christian, the future is our calling! "In My Father's house are many dwelling places. . . . 'For I know the plans that I have for you,' declares the LORD, 'plans . . . to give you a future and a hope.' . . . Reaching forward to what lies ahead . . ." (John 14:2; Jer. 29:11; Phil. 3:13).

We can be active in moving toward the future because it's a positive place when Christ is in the picture—even if today we're in prison as Joseph was.

That's the healthy perspective we ought to have. But emotional freeze points result in fear of the future and push us toward procrastination. Why is that?

As we've seen, the more pessimistic you are about having a positive future, the lower your motivation to make changes today. And the greater *fear* you have trapped inside you that things will never change, the more you'll put off working your way out of problems and toward helpful goals.

Drs. Burka and Yuen have written a helpful book on this subject called *Procrastination: Why You Do It, What to Do About It.* While I didn't actually finish the book, the parts I did read were very helpful. (Just kidding—I did finish the book . . . finally.)

In their studies of confirmed procrastinators, the authors saw this consistent fact: *Procrastination is purposeful.* In other words, while people may not realize it or want to admit it, when they slow down or avoid doing even the most necessary things—like taking their high-blood-pressure medicine or depositing their paychecks so checks don't bounce—there's a purposeful decision to "not" do those things. And where does that decision to "not" step forward come from? It grows out of one of four types of fear: *fear of failure, fear of success, fear of being controlled,* or *fear of intimacy.*

Think back to those cards that are under "freeze points" on your LifeMap. Did any of those events lead you to experience any one of those types of fear?

Like Jamie, did a fear of failure keep you hanging on to a destructive relationship when you should have let go? Has the fear of success, with its elevated expectations, kept you from finishing the school degree that is all that stands between you and a big promotion? Many of us fear being controlled by others—especially if we've felt the cold steel boot of being in an overcontrolling situation. And still others grow up fearing intimacy, particularly if they've regularly experienced distance, not closeness.

Emotional freeze points can damage your health and ruin important relationships by making you a pessimist. Then when you add fear to that toxic mix, it can make you a pessimistic procrastinator. But Joseph was neither, nor did he suffer from the third malady commonly linked with emotional freeze points.

3. Freeze points can cause us to play God.

This indication of an emotional freeze point means taking it upon yourself to be judge, jury, and executioner rather than leaving that to God.

Not long ago, I counseled with a woman named Linda. Her freeze point was created in the years she put up with a sometimes physically abusive father. A great sheet of emotional ice had made her so hard and impenetrable that her husband had recently left her, and even her lucrative job was teetering on the rocks.

Finally, during a counseling session, I confronted her about the venom that poured forth when the issue of her father came up. I asked if she had ever forgiven him.

"Forgive him?" she almost screamed at me. "I will never forgive my father. I will overcome him. Do you hear me? *I will overcome him!*"

With that, she walked out of the office, and she never came back.

What a tragedy! And what an example of an emotional freeze point! She had decided that her layer of hurt couldn't be thawed out by love, only beaten to pieces by hate. But in every case—no exceptions—we're the ones who end up broken when we try to out-hate others.

There's a reason the Scriptures tell us to love our enemies, not hate them. Namely, when we hold on to anger and hurts, we don't diminish our enemies' power over us—*we increase it.* We actually empower their hold on our lives when we try to play God and take judgment in our own hands.

Not that it wouldn't feel good to execute "righteous indignation" on an abusive father or someone who harmed our spouse or children. But God has established institutions like governments and civil authorities to carry out His punishment, for otherwise we carry their sentence within ourselves as well.

If you find that you can't forgive someone who laid down a layer of hurt in your life, then like it or not, you're playing God. Not following God—playing God. And our God is a jealous God. He refuses to share His prerogatives with you, just as He refused to share them with an angel named Satan, who was infinitely more qualified than you or me to play the part.

There was just one person who could get away with playing God with others. Picture the following scene.

A rowdy crowd was working its way down the street, pushing a young woman in front of it. She was scantily clad, which in itself, in this culture that prided itself on covering up, caused a stir among the many gathering to watch the boisterous procession.

Then, of all things, they cast this woman in front of a carpenter from Nazareth. "Teacher," they told Him, "this woman has been caught in adultery, in the very act. Now in the Law Moses commanded us to stone such women; what then do You say?" (John 8:4-5).

We don't know if her actions were the result of a pharisaic setup or just her individual lust. But either way, the religious leaders certainly felt her actions provided them with a great opportunity to trap Jesus. If He rejected Moses' words, as they anticipated, they could brand Him as a lawbreaker and have Him written off.

That's when the same hands that worked in a wood shop as a young man and crafted the heavens ages before began to write on the ground. We don't know what words Jesus wrote. Perhaps He spelled out *envy, lust, lying, hypocrisy.*

The Bible says they "persisted" in pressing Him for an answer. They kept taunting Him: "What do You say? What's Your reply?" We don't know how long they kept at Him, but we do know what Jesus did when He stood up. He spoke words that rang out like thunder in their ears.

Here was a band of angry, intense, intelligent men who felt they had Jesus trapped as tightly as a chess master traps a novice. Bishop to king 2. But with one move, Jesus showed who was King, and He went from checked to checkmate.

"He who is without sin among you, let him be the first to throw a stone at her" (John 8:7).

With that, He stooped down and went back to His writing.

Most of us are familiar with this New Testament story. The Scriptures record that beginning with the oldest (who had had the most time to accumulate sins) on down to the youngest, they all left. Every one of them.

While this is a great story of Christ's compassion and mastery of the moment, what's it got to do with our discussion? A lot. Namely, it's what happened *after* the people had all left that illustrates the third aspect of an emotional freeze point.

Jesus straightened up for a second time and said to the woman, " 'Woman, where are they? Did no one condemn you?' And she said, 'No one, Lord.' And Jesus said, 'Neither do I condemn you; go your way. From now on sin no more' " (John 8:10-11).

Do you hear the clear message behind His words?

She wasn't safe when the crowd left. There was still someone left standing who could have picked up a rock. One person who was without sin and could have crushed her skull as the angry mob had wanted to do. But He didn't. As God, He had the authority, purity, and right. But He chose to forgive her and send her on her way with the challenge to live a pure life.

One of the lessons from this passage is that judgment is best left to God. There have been times (as at Sodom and Gomorrah) when God would pick up flaming rocks and strike down entire cities. But in this case, God Himself in human form suspended judgment and issued forgiveness.

Can we do less? Forgiveness isn't the easy way of melting a freeze point, but it's essential in doing so.[8] How, then, can you deal with freeze points if you see them in your life?

Turning a Blow Torch on Emotional Freeze Points

If you've experienced a season of hurt that has frozen your emotions, it does no good to slip into pessimism, procrastination, and playing God. Rather, like Joseph, you need to maintain an optimism rooted in the knowledge that God is in control of all circumstances—even the ones you have on cards on your storyboard.

You throw rock salt on a freeze point when you face your fear of failure, success, being controlled, or intimacy and have your life marked by responsibility and accountability, not procrastination. (More on this in chapters 9 and 10.) And finally, you turn a blow torch on that layer of ice when you can actually do the godly thing and forgive those who have wronged you.

Sound easy? It couldn't have been for Joseph, particularly on a day when he had those same brothers, who had sold him down the river, up a creek without a paddle.

The strength to drop the stone

Joseph's father, Israel, had just died, and his brothers' guilty con-sciences began working overtime. "What if Joseph should bear a grudge against us and pay us back in full for all the wrong we did to him!" they asked themselves. So they groveled before Joseph and asked him to forgive them for their transgression against him.

Joseph's response? Up to that point, he had done everything just the way Jesus would have done—but now could have been an exception.

If there was one man who deserved to throw stones at his brothers—the same ones who were willing to stone him and sentence him to the rock pile of slavery—it was Joseph. Yet when it came time to pick up a rock (or to call for the palace guards and have his brothers slain, which he certainly had the power to do), he chose the harder path—the one Christ would take Himself ("Father forgive them, for they know not what they do").

" 'Do not be afraid,' " Joseph said to them, " 'for am I in God's place? And as for you, you meant evil against me, but God meant it for good in order to bring about this present result, to preserve many people alive. So therefore, do not be afraid; I will provide for you and your little ones.' So he comforted them and spoke kindly to them" (Gen. 50:19-21).

Wow! What an example of someone who had every right to blame an emotional freeze point for an unfulfilled life! What a temptation to put himself in God's place and become an agent of judgment rather than offer an act of healing!

As his brothers stood before him, it was Joseph who had been the prisoner for years. But that day, he was freer inside than any of them, even to the point of being willing to provide for their little ones.

The hardest cards to put up . . . or take down

I know how hard it is to put cards on a storyboard that identify emotional freeze points. Do you remember those things I put on my LifeMap?

John Trent's LifeMap

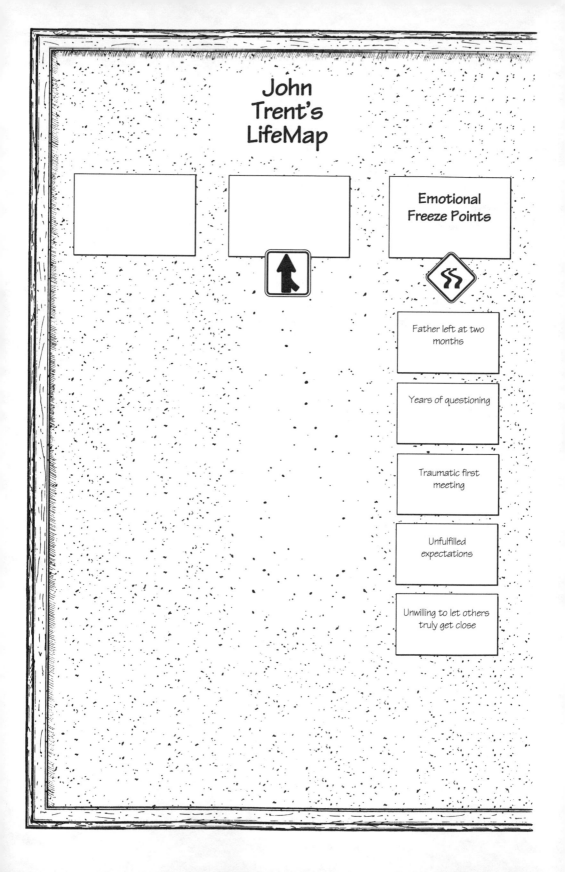

Emotional Freeze Points

Father left at two months

Years of questioning

Traumatic first meeting

Unfulfilled expectations

Unwilling to let others truly get close

I also know that it's possible to take them down. To extend forgiveness when what you've wanted to do is extend a left hook. To let God be the judge and take the higher road of forgiveness—and freedom.

I wish I hadn't had an unfaithful father who left a wife and three children under the age of three (when I was an infant). I'd love to have back all the time I spent questioning why he left. I would gladly have traded in being stood up by him the first time I was to meet him as a teenager (the "Traumatic first meeting" card on my LifeMap). It still hurts to think that for more than 30 years, I prayed, worked, and hoped for a positive relationship, only to have him die angry and indifferent, not knowing my younger daughter's name and not caring. The pain of those experiences led, in turn, to the card at the bottom of my freeze-points column: "Unwilling to let others truly get close."

I wish I didn't have a single card under this category in my LifeMap. These cards are not fresh and clean like the ones charting a positive future, nor are they filled with happy memories like those picturing strengths and successes. But they're a part of my LifeMap, and you may have similar ones.

However, they're not all there is to our LifeMaps.

We can move on to look at other aspects of our past and to build a positive future. Through our own growth, we can even influence the next generation so they won't have to put rows of cards under "Emotional Freeze Points" on their LifeMaps years from now.

We've looked at acceptance levels, successes and strengths, and now emotional freeze points. Next up—*individual flash points,* the third element of LifeMapping.

*I*ndividual
Flash Points

Our God-given strengths can be with us from birth. Emotional freeze points typically develop over a season of time. But this third LifeMapping element doesn't measure time in decades or even days. Individual flash points can arrive with the suddenness of a sonic boom. In fact, that's one of their characteristics. A flash point is often a lightning-bolt occurrence that happens instantly, yet it carves out a new direction we may end up traveling in for years—or a lifetime.

In this chapter, we'll look at the four characteristics individual flash points share, and at the incredible power they have to rocket your life story forward or backward. And while individual flash points can pop up as suddenly as a Texas tornado, they can also be captured and recorded on a LifeMap.

For some people, flash points may involve a traumatic event with tragic consequences, like the sudden loss of a loved one. For others, they may be something positive, like the moment a friendship turns into real love and you realize that person sitting next to you is the one you're going to marry.

Let's start with a glimpse of the life-changing power of flash points. In the true story I'm about to tell, the flash point wasn't as exciting as an explosion or lightning bolt from the sky. It was just a few simple words, quietly spoken by a casual friend. But when they arrived suddenly and unexpectedly, they had an immediate, life-long impact on my mother's life, and indirectly on my own.

Keeping a Friend from Falling through the Cracks

The year was 1952. For my mother, it was a time of heartache, pain, and transition. Less than six months earlier, my father had walked out the door, leaving her to raise and support a two-year-old (my older brother, Joe) and a set of two-month-old twins (my brother Jeff and me).

It's tough being a single parent today, but it was just as challenging in the 1950s. The new world she faced didn't look at divorce the way today's society does, as an acceptable option. There were no displaced-homemaker programs, no alimony, no family money to lessen the blow. And this was long before anyone got serious about holding deadbeat dads accountable, so no court-directed child support would ever come from my father.

Without a college degree or any job experience, Mom was suddenly required to raise three rambunctious boys while holding down a full-time clerical job. But if she had to work (and in her case she did), she knew she needed more than the pittance she received for filing papers to keep four mouths fed. That's why she felt so strongly that if she were to make ends meet or ever move us ahead, she had to attend business school.

During her first days there, she had a horrible time mastering the fundamental business skill of typing. She had an even more difficult time with her typing teacher. Recently retired from the army, he grilled and pushed his students like a drill sergeant with a sore tooth. And it seemed to my mother that he particularly delighted in tormenting her.

He relished pulling wadded papers from her trash can. He'd glance at the crumpled papers filled with errors. Then he'd thunder at her that she'd never be a good typist and how she ought to spare everyone the trouble, especially him, and just quit the class.

His teaching method, intimidation, might have worked in boot camp. But added to all the pressures of work and home, his scare tactics only made Mom's efforts *more* error prone. *And what made it worse was that typing was a required part of her curriculum.*

She couldn't skip over the class. She couldn't avoid his barrages. And she couldn't seem to make her fingers work fast enough to ever please him. That's why one night, after a particularly vicious outburst at the end of class, she was left with her head down, fighting back tears.

Everyone else had left the room when the pressure finally overwhelmed her. *It's just not working,* she said to herself, hot tears falling on her sweater. *Maybe I should quit.* And that's when a classmate suddenly appeared at her side.

The woman was just a casual acquaintance who had walked back by the class and saw my mother sitting there. Mom had said hi to her in the hall but didn't even know her last name. This kindhearted friend gently put her hand on my mother's shoulder. And then she said something that would lift the gloom and set the course of Mom's life for the next 30 years.

"Honey," came a soft, southern voice from a round, pretty face, "you just hang in there, ya hear? He's just putting on airs.

"You remember this, Zoa . . . *You're going to make it. You're special.*

"And starting tomorrow, you *fold* those papers you're throwing away before you put them in the basket. That way they don't stack up so much, and he won't bother you—just watch."

With that she was gone. But that evening—with Mom at the end of her rope—God had brought a friend's words at just the right time. Simple words. Quietly spoken. But seven words that surely came from God's heart: *"You're going to make it. You're special."*

No one in the building heard a lightning bolt strike that night . . . except my mother. Her friend's words were a heavenly shot of encouragement at the very moment she was running up the white flag and ready to surrender.

With renewed hope (and now *folding* each paper she threw away), Mom came back for one more day. She worked harder than ever at the speed and accuracy tests the teacher barked out. Then came the moment of reckoning when she knew she was turning into harm's way.

There was her teacher, slowly moving down each row and finally rumbling to a stop at her desk like a Sherman tank. But this time, instead of turning the turret and blasting away at her, he paused—and gave her his first backhanded compliment. After grudgingly inspecting her wastebasket, he said, "I guess Zoa is finally getting with things."

Then he walked away to torment some other paper wadder.

Sometimes the smallest things become huge levers that shift the balance and direction of our lives—like a friend taking the time to walk over and offer brief words of hope and a simple suggestion like folding error-filled papers.

I'm proud to say that my mother graduated from business school with flying colors, and besides being a great mom, she went on to have a wonderful career in the savings and loan field (long before its fall). In fact, she became so accomplished that in 1959, *she became the first businesswoman to ever grace the ink sketch on* The Wall Street Journal's *front page!*

But by her own account, none of that would have happened if she'd quit that night in 1952. What she realized in looking back on her life was that she had been hit by an individual flash point made up of seven simple words that changed her life forever.

That's the power of a flash point. In some cases, it may be bold and brassy, like a row of French horns or the clash of the timpani. In other cases, it's as muted as the flute section or as quiet as a single touch of a triangle.

But flash points do have four things in common. Let's look at those characteristics now.

A Flash Point Can Move You from Darkness to Light

To illustrate the four traits, let's turn to a dramatic section of Scripture. There we find a man named Saul who felt he was on a mission from God. His orders: Track down, arrest, and kill those naming the name of Christ, those "Christians" who were followers of the "Way" (see Acts 9:2).

He had gone to the authorities to obtain permission to make a "list" of those in Damascus who belonged to this sect. And being on Saul's list didn't hold out the hope that being on "Schindler's List" would hold for another group of Jews centuries later. The names Saul collected were of people he was convinced were a plague and that he had already sentenced to die.

But a funny thing happened on his way to exterminate more "heretics." He was hit by an individual flash point—and a blinding heavenly light.

"And it came about that as he journeyed, he was approaching Damascus, and suddenly a light from heaven flashed around him; and he fell to the ground, and heard a voice saying to him, 'Saul, Saul, why are you persecuting Me?' And he said, 'Who art Thou, Lord?' And He said, 'I am Jesus whom you are persecuting, but rise, and enter the city, and it shall be told you what you must do' " (Acts 9:3-6).

What happened to Paul and what happened to my mother were worlds apart in scope and importance. Yet they do share and underscore those four things that characterize individual flash points.

1. A flash point happens suddenly.

The book of Acts is the account of the founding of the early church. As such, it chronicles the workings of God's Spirit in launching the gospel world-wide. What's more, it highlights the "suddenness" with which God often broke into people's lives.

There was the "sudden" sound that filled the room at Pentecost.

The "sudden" appearance of the blinding light with Saul.

The "sudden" appearance of an angel who freed Peter from prison and led him to safety.

The "sudden" earthquake that again freed Peter and Silas.

And there's a reason for the many "sudden" occurrences in the book of Acts: It's a history of God at work in the lives of His people, *and He often works in decisive and dramatic ways.*

That's the first aspect of an individual flash point. It usually doesn't come after 20 warm-up pitches or a long preseason. It comes suddenly, like the unexpected swing of a baton that smashed Nancy Kerrigan's knee. Silver medal aside, her life will never be quite the same after that event. And neither will Tonya Harding's. That's the nature of a flash point. It often catches you off guard.

2. A flash point is unplanned.

Two years ago, Mike was a critical player in a major San Diego management firm. He was told over and over how indispensable he was because he was the only in-house person handling the entire firm's pension work.

Two days later, Mike just knew that when they brought his name up at the annual partners' meeting, it would be to recommend him for partnership. Little did he know that instead of facing up to fourth-quarter losses and cutting partnership shares, they would decide to cut staff instead. And in a matter of minutes, Mike went from essential to expendable. When 9:00 A.M. rolled around the next business day, instead of working on his pension fund, he needed to draw on it after being let go.

Without a doubt, that was the most sudden and dramatic personal and vocational change Mike has gone through. Today, several years later, Mike owns and runs a fast-food establishment in a local mall.

Who'd have thought it? Four years of college. Three times struggling with and finally passing the CPA exam. He was trained to do books, not dishes. And now, he isn't even the one doing the accounting. He's the one selling sushi and wonderful wok-cooked food.

If a flash point is marked by suddenness, it's also characterized by unexpectedness. It's something that leaves us saying, "Can you believe that happened?" "I never would have expected it in a million years!" "That's the last thing I'd have chosen."

I'm sure more heads were turning in Damascus at Paul's sudden conversion than is the case at a tennis tournament. From exterminator to evangelist. From a committed Pharisee to a preacher of the cross. Who'd have expected it? And yet it's so like God.

Who would have sent a young boy with a slingshot to face a giant except God? Who could have come up with a huge fish submarine to transport Jonah where he needed to be but God? Who else would have expected the King of kings and Lord of lords to be born in a manger and looked over by shepherds?

Dennis Byrd was a tremendous professional football player and is a marvelous person. But one play, one crushing collision, and he was not only sidelined, but also immobilized. His dramatic struggle to recover is chronicled in his outstanding book, *Rise and Walk,* but his experience is a dramatic example of the unexpected nature of life.

It's sudden. It's unplanned. And there's a third aspect of a flash point.

3. A flash point is often unexplainable.

Why did my friend Dave Dravecky work so hard to come back from cancer and end up not only losing a career, but also his arm? Why did that radio operator on Oahu fail to heed the warnings on December 7, 1941, that a mass of unidentified airplanes was coming toward Pearl Harbor?

There's an element of God's dealing in our lives that remains unexplainable, unfathomable. But that doesn't mean He's erratic or unprincipled like the gods of Olympus. Rather, Almighty God reserves the right to alter any life story in the blink of an eye, no matter how carefully we've planned it out.

My twin brother, Jeff, and his family were at Candlestick Park in San Francisco the night baseball pitcher Dave Dravecky made his incredible comeback from cancer. They have the ticket stub he signed after winning the game and a picture he sent them with a verse he treasures. But in spite of his courage and his wife, Jan's, love and support, his arm snapped in a split-second's time a few weeks later.

It's hard to understand the dramatic nature of some individual flash points. But in the message of Dave and Jan's outstanding book *When You Can't Come Back*, it's clear that we can trust God even if all the logical reasons don't add up.

4. A flash point is individual.

When Saul was driven to the ground by the heavenly light that surrounded the risen Christ he persecuted, others stood "hearing the voice, but seeing no one" (Acts 9:7). While millions of viewers might have seen the play that broke Dennis Byrd's spine or the one that snapped Dave Dravecky's arm, there was an element of even those public experiences reserved only for the individuals.

To some other person, in some other setting, the words my mother heard might have meant little or nothing. For her, they held tremendous individual encouragement.

> *A flash point may or may not be something remarkable to another person who observes it, but from a personal standpoint, you know deep inside that life has made a pivotal change.*

While others often participate in the flash-point experience, it's what goes on personally that defines a flash point. It may or may not be something remarkable to another person who observes it, but from a personal standpoint, you know deep inside that life has made a pivotal change.

Sudden. Unplanned. Unexplainable. Individual.

Those are four marks of a flash point. And like the three LifeMapping elements before this, you can capture them as part of your life story. As you look at your life, however, you may be thinking, *The others I can see, but this one I'm sure is a blank. I've never been visited by angels, won a medal on TV, or had anything dramatic happen to me.*

But remember. The operative word with a flash point isn't necessarily *drama* but *direction*.

Can you think of a time when someone said or did something and it challenged or changed the direction of your life? Did a single event, or perhaps even several, come ringing through that pushed aside all your priorities at the time and suddenly gave you a new set of hurdles to face?

Let's look at several other examples of flash points that might help you identify some cards for your storyboard. For some, a flash point will come out of a first-time experience. For others, it will be something incredibly positive. And for still others, it may be the most shameful thing they've ever faced.

Where to Look for Individual Flash Points

Sometimes, your first experience at something can become a flash point for you. That's what happened to TV star Bill Cosby years ago. He realized he wanted to be a comedian in the eighth grade. It happened when he got laughs telling his classmates what it was like growing up with his brothers in a poor part of Philadelphia.

Says Cosby, "With my teacher's permission, I walked to the front of the classroom and faced my first audience.

" 'I share a bed with my little brother,' I began, 'but he's not little enough.'

"The laughter hit me like a drug.

"In a stronger voice, I said, 'Y'see, he keeps touching me, and I don't like a bed that feels like a bus.'

"More laughter.

" 'And sometimes he thinks the bed is a boxing ring, but he never goes to a neutral corner.'

"Their laughter was even a sweeter sound than the tinkle of change in my father's pants. It was the only vocational guidance I would ever need." [1]

Was there a time you can remember when something happened so you "just knew" the direction you wanted to head in life? If Bill Cosby found that standing in front of an audience brought out the best in him, it was just the opposite experience for another much-loved celebrity, Dr. Seuss.

Born Theodore Seuss Geisel in 1904, as a young man he was witty and outgoing with friends. Such verbal strengths might have led him into business, sales, or even drama—but not after an incident that happened when he was 13.

During World War I, Geisel's Boy Scout troop sold a record number of war bonds, and the boys were to be presented with medals by former President Theodore Roosevelt. Geisel's troop sat on the stage as Roosevelt praised them and called out their names one by one.

Finally, young Theodore was left alone on the stage with Roosevelt. The former president searched his list and then glared at the embarrassed boy. "What is this little boy doing here?" he said.

Unfortunately, Geisel's name had been inadvertently omitted from the list. Years later, explaining why he felt insecure in crowds and seldom gave speeches, he recalled the shame: "I can still hear people saying, 'What is *he* doing here?'"[2]

Facing a crowd caused Bill Cosby to move forward, while it caused Dr. Seuss to retreat from public speaking and teaching. But both benefited from those flash-point experiences. Cosby went on to entertainment fame, and Geisel's redirected efforts went into writing and illustrating children's books, bringing joy to millions of fans. (All this from a man whose high-school art teacher told him, "You will never learn to draw!" and whose Dartmouth College fraternity voted him "least likely to succeed"!)

For me personally, both cards on my LifeMap are connected to a first experience I had in seminary. In fact, one card came out of the same class where Dr. Hendricks gave us the "strengths test" I mentioned in chapter 5.

First class . . . lifelong direction

During registration the week before school started, I was wading through lines of students who, like me, were scurrying to fill their class schedules. That's when a friend grabbed me and said, "Hey, they're switching to the auditorium for Dr. Hendricks's class on the Christian home, so more seats have opened up. Come on and sign up with me."

My friend was married, and he and his wife were expecting their second child any day. I was single and so broke and busy, just getting a date would have been exciting. Why in the world did I need to sign up for "Christian Home"?

But I needed an elective, and I'd heard how hard it was to get into Dr. Hendricks's classes. So I followed my friend to register and unexpectedly found the direction God wanted for my ministry from that point forward.

An individual flash point for me was my first day in that class. I was a relatively new Christian, out of a difficult family background, and uncertain about what God wanted me to do. I had ended up at seminary instead of law school, but I didn't go in with the clear picture of becoming a senior pastor like many of my friends. In fact, I didn't know exactly *why* I'd gone to seminary . . . until that first day in class.

After Prof had given us our "name your strengths" test, he said something that hit me so hard, it blocked out most of the rest of what he said that morning. (And since that class took place more than 15 years ago, you can tell it had a major impact on me!)

This is what he said: "Men, this class isn't just for your family. With all the hurt that's out there, I'm convinced that one of the greatest tools for winning people to Christ is a distinctively Christian home."

Suddenly I discovered why I'd gone to seminary. I was working with Young Life as a club leader at the time, and I saw kids every day from backgrounds like mine. I'd work with them. Love them. Lead them to Christ. And then see them go back into a highly dysfunctional home and often have their light for Christ dim and come close to flickering out.

Prof was right. The thing I'd seen and personally experienced that kept me from dimming my light as a new Christian was the "shining light" of loving Christian homes.

As Dr. Hendricks continued to talk, I thought about a home God used dramatically in my life. In fact, it was a "distinctively Christian home" that led me to Christ when I was in high school (and, if you'll notice, caused the card to go up on my LifeMap under flash points).

Doug Barram, then a Young Life area director, showed up at our football practice one day. Soon I started hearing about "Young Life Clubs" and even began attending. But for all the fun and skits, and even the clear messages on receiving Christ, they're not what led me to Christ. *Doug's life and the love he had for his wife, Loretta, and his two boys convinced me that all he said was real.*

Without a doubt, it was Doug's home that drew me to Christ. That's where, for the first time, I saw what a loving father looked like. What a committed husband acted like. What a godly man who stayed put talked about. During high school, there were times when I wanted so much to see a picture of the love they had as a family that I'd go to their home and mow the yard just to be around them!

As I heard Dr. Hendricks talk about the Christian home that day, I knew I'd found my life's calling. If I could help families "keep the light on" in this world of darkness—that was a ministry to which I could give my life! In 1974, there were only a few "family pastors" across the country, and at the time I'd never heard of any or talked to one. But like Saul being struck with a light from above, I graphically felt that God had directed, or "called," me to a ministry to families that day.

I walked out of his class and right to a phone to call my mother and tell her what I'd be doing with the rest of my life. (Unlike my friend, I didn't have a wife at home to call!) At the time of this writing, it's pushing 20 years since that day in class, but I remember it as if it were yesterday. And I've never once doubted that encouraging couples and families is exactly what God has called me to do.

That class was a flash point for me. It redirected my life and reoriented the compass that would lead me.

How about you? Has your life taken pivotal turns that have shaped your future?

God Does Pivotal Things in Everyday People's Lives

I'm not sure what cards will go under your list of individual flash points. My friend Stu Weber describes two of his cards in his excellent book, *Tender Warrior*. One flash point came when he was a Green Beret in Vietnam, and one time he jumped out of a plane and his parachute didn't open! The other was the day his wife, Lindy (author of a wonderful book every mom ought to read called *Mom, You're Incredible!*), told him he wasn't measuring up as a husband and father.

Your flash point may be something as dramatic as the sound the wind makes when you're falling at 80 miles an hour and your parachute won't open, or as quiet as words of correction that shake you to your very core. But it's likely that you have some watershed events in your life that your LifeMap can capture. And once you have those on your map, you're ready to make one more stop to "tie up" loose ends from your past.

$\mathcal{U}$ntied Transitions

We face all kinds of transitions in life—going from grade school to high school; from single to married; from parent to grandparent. And in each transition, there is great potential for positive change or for being unable to make needed changes.

All the positive potential *and* potential problems that transitions bring constitute this fourth element of the LifeMapping process. That's why in this chapter, we'll take a close look at the four major types of transitions we all face, and at the three phases we must go through when they happen. We'll see how God designed us to deal with transitions and how we can gain an edge on many of them by anticipating and preparing for their often-telegraphed arrival.

Let's begin by examining a picture of someone who faced incredible transitions in an exemplary way.

Losing a War . . . Rebuilding a Nation

No period in our nation's history has been so divisive as the Civil War. And while there was absolutely nothing good about slavery, there were men of honor dressed in both blue and gray from whom we can learn. When it comes to dealing with transitions, one of the most remarkable was General Robert E. Lee.

Ralph Waldo Emerson was quoted as saying, "Not in his goals but in his transitions is a man shown to be great." Lee certainly fit that definition. (I'm grateful for much of what I've learned about Lee to Lt. Col. Michael Parker, a gerontologist and leading expert on life's transitions.)

General Lee was the ranking commander of the Army of Northern Virginia. He left his home a wealthy man, commanding a mighty army, committed to victory. He would return in defeat, paroled as a prisoner of war, to a country-side mired in economic depression. At home he would find an invalid wife, five unemployed adult children, and another son missing in action.

Lee's leadership in battle was recognized on both sides of the line. But it was how he handled himself as a civilian after the war that truly showed his character.

For example, there came a time when a visiting minister, a diehard Confederate, took the pulpit of Lee's home church. His sermon topic that morning: drumming up hatred against the North. His message was full of old animosities, dripping with bitterness over the destruction of Southern homes and railing against the bonds of Reconstruction. Yet that preacher didn't know that Lee fought as hard for reconciliation after the war with letters and words as he had fought for victory with cold steel and cannon at Gettysburg and Bull Run.

Confronting the man in private, Lee said to him, "Doctor, there is a good old book which I read and you preach from, which says, 'Love your enemies, bless them that curse you, do good to them that hate you, and pray for them which despitefully use you and persecute you.' Do you think your remarks this evening were quite in the spirit of that teaching?"

And then came words you'd least expect from a man who had seen thousands of his own men die and his homeland devastated: "I have never cherished toward them bitter or vindictive feelings, and have never seen the day when I did not pray for them." [1]

Pray daily for men who only months before had been his mortal enemies?

Talk about a man who made a transition from soldier to servant, from warrior to healer! In fact, he was so committed to reconciliation that one historian would say of Lee, he did "more than any other American to heal the wounds of war."

Lee dedicated his later life to writing hundreds of letters, urging his fellow Southerners to put away their anger and focus on Christ and rebuilding the Union. In doing so, he provided a guiding light to thousands of Southerners who followed his example and pounded their swords into plowshares.

General Lee showed an incredible ability to bend with transitions, and he did so by believing that changes large and small come from the hand of God. But some people are broken by times of change and crushed by an inability to accept even minor movements of life over which they have no control.

I doubt if many of us reading this book have gone through as many twists and transitions as General Lee did. But all of us face our own brand of changes that can either cripple us or empower us to move forward. So get those 3x5 cards ready as you learn more about transitions and how they can make up an important part of your LifeMap.

Essentially Different from a Flash Point

"But wait a minute, John," you may want to say. "Aren't we talking about the same thing as in the last chapter? Isn't a flash point the same as a transition?"

It's true that a flash point can forcibly evict you from one season of life, ushering you into times of significant transition. But while some transitions come with the suddenness of a flash point, many arrive with glacial speed. There's hardly a "flash" between turning 20 and turning 40, but both occasions can signal major changes that need to be accepted and processed in a person's life.

In many ways, flash points could be likened to a wedding, marking off the start of a transition. But the quality of the marriage that results would reflect how you handle that transition. So while there may be some overlap, let's look at a definition of a transition that might further clarify what is meant.

Defining a Time of Transition

Transitions, as I'm defining them, are major movements in your life, often outside your control, that usher in a new season of life or a new way of relating, and close off the old. A good way to look at major transitions is to view them as "mini rites of passage." A flash point may take you to a point of transition, but how successfully you deal with the new set of rules will determine if you pass through it successfully or remain stuck and stymied by it. Let me illustrate with an example from one of the most beautiful places in the United States.

A few years ago, I had the chance to meet a precious family who live on Kodiak Island, Alaska. (I'll admit that doing a conference in Alaska is a tough job, but somebody's got to do it!) Craig and Terrie Johnson were our seminar coordinators for the "Love Is a Decision" seminar Gary Smalley and I held there. (They were also our fishing guides five minutes after the seminar ended!)

I'll never forget flying in on a seaplane to a smaller island called Afognac and fishing for salmon up and down a beautiful river. Salmon fishing is serious business in Alaska, and at one point along the river, we came across a cabin next to a salmon gate (called a *weir*).

There in the middle of the wilderness, a state game and fish employee was manning this gate, accompanied by his wife and three small children. (The gatekeeper and his wife, Cort and Katrina Neff, turned out to be members of Craig and Terrie's home church.) I'd never seen a salmon gate before, but essentially, it represents a transition point for a migrating salmon. It also provides a picture of what transitions can mean to you.

When salmon are hatched in those beautiful mountain streams, they stay in the shallows until they grow big enough, and then they travel downstream to the bay and finally out into the ocean. After they grow large and fearsome in the rough, cold Arctic waters, God turns on an internal homing signal that points them back to Afognac. "Back" in some cases means beginning a journey of two thousand miles or more to end up in the very stream where they were born, and where they now seek to lay their eggs.

The salmon gate provides two services for the fish and the fish managers. First, it allows the game and fish employee to count the number of salmon heading upstream (an incredible feat with the hundreds of salmon that congregate below the gate). That allows a forecast to be made of the amount of salmon they expect to harvest that year. But the gate also provides a breathing place for the salmon to rest and gather strength before continuing the arduous journey upstream.

It was astounding to stand above the gate and look at the hundreds of salmon waiting for it to open. Milling around. Darting back and forth. Looking like carbon copies of those huge fish you see on the walls at Red

Lobster. And finally when the gate opened, they shot through the opening and on toward their goal.

When the gates are wide open during the peak of their run, at times hundreds of fish will be jumping ahead, pushing forward . . . and yet some never do. For reasons as varied as sickness or choice, they stay right at the entrance to the gate, never taking that next step in their journey.

The same thing is true for all of us who face transitions in life.

Some people shoot through each gate marking a passage into another phase of life with reckless abandon. Others do well with the first two or three gates, but then they can't seem to get beyond the fourth.

To help you determine some of those "gates" in your life, take a moment to write down the answers to four questions that might help you identify transitions in your life:

- As you look at your life story, at what point would you say a "new chapter" opened up for you?
- When would you say childhood ended for you?
- When was the first time you said to yourself, *I'm really on my own?*
- What was it that made you ready to say, "It's time to settle down"?

Questions like those can help you picture the key transitions in your life. How well you're able to deal with those changes and the positive or negative marks they leave on your life often comes down to one thing—your ability to adapt to events not under your personal control. For you see, it's often someone besides you who opens and closes the "gates" you seek to go through. And each of the four major types of transitions can seem to have a life and mind of its own.

The Four Major Transitions That Can Shape Your LifeMap

If you're a serious storyboarder by this point, you might want to get four different-colored sets of 3x5 subber cards to highlight the four areas of transition on your LifeMap. The first cards could be red, because they reflect changes in your *core relationships*.

1. Core relationships

Put your memory on rewind, and think about your most important relationships since childhood. Certainly there would be a mother and father.

Often siblings, aunts, uncles, and grandparents come to mind.

Then there are those core relationships you develop apart from your family. Perhaps it's that first teacher who became a mentor or friend. Maybe it's your first boss or first employee. And of special note are those long-term dating relationships or a marriage that established another person as a central part of your life.

As you can imagine, transitions that involve these core individuals can have an incredible impact. I remember my grandfather's passing away when I was just a boy. He died so quickly of a brain aneurysm that one minute he was standing with us in the living room, and the next he was gone. Years later, I would travel the same back roads to where we'd laid him to rest in Cloverdale, Indiana, to attend funeral services for my grandmother and then for a much-loved aunt. Notably for me, there was also that incredibly hot day in August when I spent morning to night holding my father's hand, praying for him and finally watching his life literally slip away.[2]

It's not just death that can change our core relationships and force us into a time of transition, however. Sometimes it's brought on by a change in the *quality* of a person's life.

My mother is a wonderful person with an irrepressible spirit and contagious trust in God. Yet that pillar of strength that I have leaned on all my life occasionally gets tired now at age 74. She has battled arthritis for almost four decades, and the struggle has taken its toll. There are times now when our roles get reversed. She needs someone to be strong for her and hold her hand when the shadows grow long.

God stands at the gate of our core relationships. At times, the gate is open and changes take place rapidly. And then there are times of quiet and waiting, periods when the gate is closed and it seems things will never change. But deep inside, we know they will.

We're never really safe from a shifting in core relationships in any season of life. It might mean losing a parent as a child; gaining a spouse in our twenties; ending a friendship in our forties; or laying a brother to rest in our sixties. And that's just one type of transition.

2. Physical changes

Changes can be physical in two senses of the word. First, there are those inevitable physiological changes you face with aging. On a basketball court, for example, those changes make you go from unstoppable at driving to the basket at 19 to shooting from the outside at age 35 and letting those "young guys" crash the boards. They result in having more hair growing out of your ears than on your head in your forties (if you're a man). And they make necessary that first serious visit to a doctor in your late fifties.

We all wear out. That's a reality that's tough to face. But I learned it the hard way on my birthday two years ago when I was thrown headlong.

I was out in the rugged mountain preserve where I regularly ride my mountain bike. It was the crack of dawn on a beautiful June morning. It was also my fortieth birthday, and I was feeling great. I was bombing down steep hills and cranking through the uphill parts without breaking a sweat.

I have a favorite course I've laid out, and I'd already made it through the steep, life-threatening part in record time. Now I was flying down a wide, perfectly level trail on my way out of the preserve and toward the paved road home.

I had just thought *I'm in great shape for a 40-year-old!* when somehow, either a rock or a patch of gravel pushed my front tire slightly off the trail—and straight into trouble. With incredible timing, my tire slid right between two rocks that were half buried and formed a perfect V.

As you can imagine, when my front tire hit that solid-rock V, the bike went from full speed to full stop instantly—only I didn't. I flew over my handlebars, crashed into the rocky ground, and rolled into a cholla cactus. (For those of you unfamiliar with the Sonoran Desert, cholla, or "jumping," cacti are the Arnold Schwarzeneggers of cacti! They're the mean ones you really don't want to mess with!)

That day, mortality stared me right in the face. Or at least it put a dent in my helmet and filled my arms with cactus spines. Even today, whenever I "respectfully" pass that part of my course, I always think about the living example God gave me of "Pride cometh before a fall."

No matter how fast you ride right now, the day will come when you take a fall. Your health, vitality, or eyesight will gradually fail, and when it does, it brings on unquestioned transitions. But while *physical* here may mean a health-related change, it has other meanings as well.

Physical can also refer to those major geographic or standard-of-living changes that can jar you as much as a poor EKG reading. I think of the lady I heard of recently who won $10 million in a state lottery, and within a single year she had lost all her money and her marriage as well. For her, physical changes meant going from a lower-middle-class home, to life at the Ritz, to ending up in a suitcase—all in one year!

I also think of Dane, who spent the first 13 years of his life in 18 different grade schools because of a father who "liked to move around." For him, physical transitions reflected the ever-changing landscape of his youth and the lack of "roots" he struggles with setting down even today in spiritual and personal relationships.

Core relationships and physical changes may show up as cards on your LifeMap. So, too, may the third type of transition.

3. Vocational changes

For both men and women, vocational changes can be particularly dramatic and traumatic. But for men in particular, job changes often cause major adjustment problems.

For example, did you know that insurance actuarial tables show that the average man lives only three years beyond retirement? That is, unless you happen to be George "Bear" Bryant of Alabama football fame and you die three *weeks* after you stop coaching.

What about all the Winnebago trips those men talked about at work? What about those cries for days when there was nothing to do but bowl and go fishing?

For many men, *retirement can mean a loss of a vocational definition of who they are*—and that unprocessed vacuum can spell trouble with their life and health.

Perhaps in the past year or two, you've been hired or fired from a job. That shuffling of the bread-and-butter role can play havoc with your life—and may need to be represented on your LifeMap. And there's one further area of transition that should show up as well.

4. Spiritual changes

Each of us experiences spiritual transitions as well as relational and physical ones. Initially, we move from lost to found; from immature to mature;

from milk to solid food. But some of us also move backward from mature to immature, like Dan.

Dan and his family were founding members of a small church with five other couples who first met in each other's homes. Today, only 12 years later, that same church sits on 14 acres. With eight buildings, it carries over *two thousand* families on its rolls.

Dan was the first elder. The first *chairman* of the elder board. The first building committee chairman. And the first board member to leave his wife of 30 years and move in with a woman one year *younger* than his oldest daughter.

Talk about a spiritual transition for him, his family, *and* his church family![3]

Negative changes in our spiritual life can significantly affect us and set off changes in others as well. But thankfully, many more people make positive spiritual changes instead.

Think back to Jim's story in the first chapter of this book—he was the man who saw his spiritual vitality draining away. He found himself going through the motions and reaching for a close relationship with Christ, but never taking hold of it.

But that has changed, in part because he went through the LifeMapping process with his small group at church. For the first time, Jim saw how much work dominated his life. And in a pivotal way, he saw several freeze-point cards that pointed out an unwelcome pattern he'd never faced—fear of letting others truly get close.

As a good leader, Jim had risen to the top by hard work and self-reliance. But once he'd "arrived," while he was friendly with everyone, he was close to no one. And in his case, "no one" included God.

Deep inside, Jim was truly afraid of giving God direct access to his LifeMap. While he knew that trying to resist God was as futile as Jonah's trying to run from God's will, he still feared that if he really turned over his life to the Lord, God would somehow "mess it up."

He didn't mean to be blasphemous. But in everything from sports to the office to his position at church, he was always in control. And after he did his LifeMap, he realized that he was also the young boy who had grown up with so many fears from being controlled by a dominating father.

In the process of looking at his life story—the entire LifeMap—he finally saw what was holding him back. As he looked at his Heavenly Father, visions of a powerful, uninvited earthly father took their toll—an earthly father who would barge into his room without ever knocking, dominate his Saturdays by using him as unpaid labor, and deny appropriate privileges like getting his driver's license at 16 or going out for contact sports.

> *Core relationships, physical changes, vocational shifts, and spiritual growth—these are four major areas in which transitions hit us.*

As long as Jim stayed "independent," he felt safe. But let someone, particularly someone as powerful as his father, get close and he felt powerless and depressed. No wonder every time he moved close to his Heavenly Father, his spiritual relationship dried up! He'd never made a transition between an earthly father who used authority without love and a gracious God who linked love with His power.

It took time, *and it took linking his insights with accountability* (more on that in the next chapter on image management), but in the past year Jim has made the greatest changes ever in his spiritual life. He's made a transition from being driven to seeking God's direction; from being a controller to being a servant. And far from losing anything by letting God and others get close, he's gained love and respect from his wife, family, and even business associates who have marveled at the way his leadership style has changed. He was always effective, but like the Tin Man in *The Wizard of Oz,* now he has a heart.

Spiritual transitions often force changes in the lives of others as well. I'm sure the Pharisees weren't thrilled when Saul's "spotlight" experience changed his name to Paul and his heart toward Christ. But the power of God is available to redirect our priorities, and the Word of God is sharp enough to cut away negative patterns and behaviors.

Core relationships, physical changes, vocational shifts, and spiritual growth—these are four major areas in which transitions hit us. And when they do, they frequently bring with them a three-part challenge.

Three Challenges That Come with Each Transition

As you think back over your life story and some of the transitions you've already experienced, you'll quickly see the three steps that come as an inescapable part of each turning point. It's as my old boss on the construction site used to say, "If you order Chinese, you're going to get a fortune cookie." And if you experience a transition, you're inevitably going to face the following three challenges.

1. The phase of endings

While it may sound contradictory, transitions always begin with an ending. The apostle Paul said, "When I was a child, I used to . . . think as a child . . .; when I became a man, I did away with childish things" (1 Cor. 13:11).

Adulthood begins with the ending of youth. Marriage marks off the end of single life. Parenting signals the end of sleeping in. In each case, coming to grips with the fact that one way of life is ending and being replaced by another isn't always easy. (But take heart. If endings were easy, there would be no country music!)

Can you remember when your children were young and you would throw them high up in the air? While they'd scream bloody murder on the way up, what's the first thing they'd say after they landed safely back on earth? *"Do it again! Do it again!"*

No matter how often we ask, there are things in life that we can't do again, pages in life we can't turn back to except in our minds.

Can you imagine what it would have been like living in the last generation of ancient Romans before the fall of the empire? With the barbarians at the gates, I'm sure they wondered why history had to change with them. Why *they* couldn't pass down a culture that had been the world leader to their children. But there wasn't to be a handoff for that last generation. They had outlived their season of glory, and there was no way they could revive it.

There comes a time when we have to put things down and admit that a particular period of time has passed.

I once heard the story of two monks who started on a long journey. It had rained hard the day before they had left, and they rounded a corner and saw where the river had washed away a bridge. Standing beside the river was a beautiful woman dressed in an exquisite gown.

Cheerfully, one of the monks offered to carry her across the river so as not to have her dress ruined. Lifting her into his arms, he waded across and deposited her safe and dry on the other side. With a polite word of thanks, the woman went her way, and the monks continued their journey in a different direction.

They had just gotten out of earshot of the woman when the monk who had *not* carried the woman turned in anger on his companion. "How could you do that?" he spat. "You know our order forbids interaction with women, and you held one close and carried her across the river!"

"Yes," said the other monk, "I carried her across and set her down. But it appears that you carry her still."

Many of us have things in our past that we can't seem to "put down." They stay lodged in our minds or held in our arms. But the fact is, while we may try to put an old title on a new book, it simply doesn't fit anymore. There are endings that need to be processed . . . and sometimes even grieved.

Last farewells

I remember an "ending" I had to face up to. The year was 1970. I'd been up almost all night, first saying good-bye to high-school friends and then packing for college. Now I sat at the old kitchen table with my mother and enjoyed her wonderful pancakes one last time before climbing into my jam-packed car.

As I sat there, a flood of emotions hit me. It was there I had sat as a five-year-old, laughing, clowning around, and spilling milk with my brothers. It was the same table where my grandfather sat, looking out through the window at us playing and giving us a smile and a wave of his hand. And it was one place I could sit with my mother day or night, and she would patiently listen to whatever "crisis" or problem I was having in grade school or high school.

Over the years, the chairs around the table began to empty. My grandfather passed away, leaving a huge, open spot. My older brother, Joe, got married and had a table of his own to sit at. My twin brother, Jeff, had already left for a different college. And now it was down to Mom and me, sitting at that table one last time.

I remember how well I thought she was handling that morning. No tears.

No dip in her always-present smile. Just that nonstop encouragement that calmed my fears and made me feel as if I wasn't driving 1,200 miles by myself or starting a whole new way of life; I was just heading off to class or down to Pete's Fish and Chips for a Coke.

I finished breakfast, hugged the best mom in the world, and confidently strode to my '64 forest green Volkswagen, every square inch crammed with "important stuff" for college. I fired up the engine, beeped the horn, and drove off into the sunrise with a wave and a smile.

I hadn't gone three miles down the road before I realized I'd forgotten my sunglasses.

In Arizona, when you drive off into the sunrise without sunglasses, you notice it. I'd left mine on my nightstand. I turned the car around, drove back into the driveway, and walked in to find my mother still sitting at the kitchen table, *crying.*

All morning, Mom had kept a stiff upper lip and managed to hold her emotions in check. Sure, she was seeing her last son leave home. But she felt that what he needed was confidence, not crying. Then I walked back in the door unexpectedly—and saw her sitting at the table.

That's all it took to open the floodgates. It was only the two of us who hugged, cried, and held each other, but suddenly the table was crowded with every family member who had gone on, and with hundreds of loving memories.

We finally did stop crying, and I drove to Texas to begin a new chapter of life. But I never had breakfast with Mom at that table again. It went in a garage sale while I was off at school (along with my baseball-card collection that could have paid for my college education today).

I can't tell you how many times I've wanted one more meal with all my family around the table. Grandma and Grandfather passing the food. My brothers and I laughing and cutting up, and Mom trying to keep three "starving" boys fed. But it won't happen again unless the Lord allows replays in heaven. (Isn't that a great thought?)

There are endings when a transition comes. And there's often a time of questioning as well.

2. The phase of questioning

As I write this chapter, it has been less than a year since I faced another last-time-at-the-table experience. For nearly ten years, I had the privilege of working alongside Gary and Norma Smalley and their wonderful staff of men and women like Terry Brown, Roger Gibson, Greg Smalley, Jim Brawner, Kari Sumney, Penny Blanchard, Penni DeOrtinzio, Beth Selby, and many others in Phoenix.

In June 1993, they moved the ministry of Today's Family to Branson, Missouri. Now, Branson is the exact center of the United States (in terms of population distribution) and an excellent place to raise families, be near Kamp Kanakuk, and expand a ministry. You can even hook record-breaking fish, catch a different country music show every night of the week, and go to Silver Dollar City to boot!

But when the moving van pulled out for Missouri, Cindy and I didn't follow it. Moving to Branson would have meant leaving our home state and church, our kids' school, my mother, and Cindy's parents and family. It seemed clear, after much prayer about what God wanted us to do, that He was telling us to stay in Arizona.

My ten years of ministry with Today's Family came to a close when those moving vans pulled out, and so began a new ministry called Encouraging Words. And while I feel we're doing exactly what the Lord wants us to do, that's not to say that there weren't times when I've questioned this new challenge.

Try building a counseling practice in mid-summer in Phoenix (when everyone suddenly leaves for Denver and San Diego). And as many readers who have started a new business know, billions of details and hundreds of dollars go into setting up an office, even with a staff of only one. (There are also some advantages to working alone. For example, I got to take myself out to lunch for both Secretaries' Day *and* Bosses' Day—and I had a great time at both parties!)

In a few short months, I've set up the ministry and launched a nationwide seminar on the Old Testament concept of "the blessing" (where I also teach about LifeMapping). With the encouragement and support of friends like Focus on the Family and Rapha Treatment Centers, I'm already booked nearly two years out at many of the top churches across the country. I'm busy writing children's books and relationship books like this one, and even my small counseling practice has filled to overflowing. (Of course, it's not August yet!)

But even that promising start doesn't mean questions don't crop up. And it doesn't mean that I don't think back to working and clowning around with

Gary, or about the fact that we could be fishing and working together in Missouri even today.

Since the day I left seminary and joined a ministry team, I've always had someone to grab for lunch. I've always been part of a team where something was happening to someone that would bring a smile or elicit a word of support in the halls. There has always been someone to double the victories and help share the sorrows—that is, until now.

In a few short months, I've gone from the center of a large beehive of activity and people to the incredibly quiet walls of a 12x12 office. I've gone from walking down to the yogurt shop with a work friend sometimes *twice* in one day, to eating lunch alone four or five days a week.

I'm not complaining. I feel God has blessed my family and new ministry in every way. But it's okay to question, too. That's a part of the transition process, and it may be the stage you're in right now.

I think of Kyle, whose wife left him two years ago, and he still can't piece together why. And of Lydia, who understood logically all the reasons for job cutbacks but still can't understand why she was the one cut.

You can truly believe, as I do, that you're right where God wants you. But there still may be that occasional "What if . . .?" Thankfully, there's a third step that helps in answering those questions. It's the step that risks moving on.

3. Taking the step to begin a new day

As I mentioned earlier, I teach a CrossTrainers Bible study for men every Tuesday morning at my home church. One morning, I was teaching on transitions. (Yes, all the men are guinea pigs for all my new messages and books. I just hope they don't *read* that they are!) We had been studying Dr. Gary Rosberg's excellent book *Let's Talk*, which discusses "closing the loop" on relationships. And for many of us, "closing the loop" involves coming full circle on a time of transition.

During the small-group time that day (we use a format of 20 minutes of singing and praise, 20 minutes of teaching, and 20 minutes of small-group discussion and prayer), a friend in my group told a helpful story.

Before their honeymoon in Hawaii, he and his wife-to-be decided to take scuba lessons together. That way, when they got to the islands, they could go out on a boat as a couple and enjoy diving amongst the coral and schools of beautifully colored fish.

They completed their lessons, had their wedding, and then flew to Hawaii. They chartered a boat along with some other would-be divers, and everything was going according to plan—until they actually got to the place where they were to enter the water.

The boat had stopped in the "transition" swells created where an underwater coral reef and the open sea meet. The boat jerked and swayed, and the uneven chop of the water made it difficult to get suited up and even to get safely over the side. The swells were so bad, my friend said, that he had to coax his new wife to climb into the water. Even when she got in, her eyes were still as big as saucers, and she refused to go under, instead bobbing up and down like a cork.

Afraid that she would be thrown back against the boat and hit her head, he finally grabbed her mouthpiece, prevailed upon her to put it in her mouth, and then pushed her underwater for the first time.

In the space of a few seconds and by dropping down a few feet, they experienced an incredible change. They went from chaos and churning waters to an incredible calm. No more whipping wind. No more pounding waves. Just placid waters and a peaceful quiet.

That's a great picture of this third element of transitions. Namely, when you take active steps in the face of transition and do something new and different, the waters often begin to grow quiet and a sense of calm enters your life again.

Back in July 1993, I was so frazzled and worn from my career transition that I wondered if I could ever make the change. But I'm thankful for five couples who make up the most supportive board any ministry could ever have. And most of all, I'm thankful for an incredibly supportive wife who kept putting the mouthpiece in my mouth—reminding me to breathe and encouraging me to enjoy the plunge. And it's amazing how the waters have changed.

From initial feelings of loneliness and being overwhelmed, I've grown to love the freedom to build and create a whole new ministry. And while the "transition waters" were a bit rough, now the seas have calmed, and I feel right in the center of where God wants me.

And that's my encouragement to you in this chapter. Perhaps you've got a number of cards on your LifeMap that represent major changes in core relationships, vocational shifts, or physical challenges. It's okay to question and, like Jesus, ask to put down some "cups" you've been handed; or, like Paul, to pray that those thorns be removed. But as we look to our Heavenly Father for strength, we'll also be able to take those first active steps in a new direction . . . and see the inner waters begin to calm down.

David is a man who went from successful entrepreneur to working for a huge company. He went from making instant decisions to waiting months before a single change he suggests is approved; from calling all the shots to waiting for someone else to make the call.

The waters have been rough in making that change. But the major thing that's helped him—and that's helped me in starting Encouraging Words—is looking at a God who never changes and trusting Him for the strength to make first steps.

David doesn't see his company changing much. The waters there are still choppy. But he can trust God, lean back in the water, and find an inner place of quiet.

The Strength to Accept Transitions

From the Old Testament to the New, God's Word highlights one transition after another in the lives of His people. Adam and Eve certainly made a major transition in leaving the garden. Abram trusted God as he left his homeland of Ur for the unknown. Peter went from a lionhearted supporter, to swearing he didn't even know Jesus, to a "rock" once again. The Scriptures are filled with people who faced all the transitions we do, and many who faced them well.

We've already looked at Joseph and the incredible transitions he went through—all those changes of geography, vocation, and core relationships without ever giving up trust in God or giving in to pessimism. And then there's the Lord Jesus Himself. If anyone modeled "closing the loop," it was Him. Just pick up your Bible and take a look in the Gospel of John, chapter 19. There you'll see three of His seven last words from the cross.

He had faced the great battle at Gethsemane. He had prepared the disciples at the Last Supper. He had already forgiven His executioners. And then on the cross, He even provided for His mother's care. ("Woman, behold, your son! . . . [Son,] behold, your mother!" [vv. 26-27].)

As the Lord prepared to make the unfathomable transition from the very source of life to taking death upon Himself for us, He cried out, "I am thirsty" (v. 28). That wasn't just a dying man's request for refreshment. Rather, He who was the "living waters" was now thirsting for the first time from eternity past for His Father's presence.

All that love, passion, and drama were then tied in a final knot when He cried out, "It is finished!" (v. 30).

That part of His work and life was done. The Son of God had died so that we who love Him would never have to taste spiritual death. The resurrection and His reign in heaven and on earth were still to come. But the ending of the cross had to take place before the new beginning at the empty tomb.

Without the ending of His life, there would be no newness of life. Without Good Friday, there would be no Easter. Unless a grain first falls to the ground and dies, there's no stalk of life-sustaining wheat. That ending of Jesus' life opened up a whole new beginning for each of us who will put our faith in Him alone as our Lord and Savior.

Let's face it, since the time of Abraham, God has called each of us to be "strangers and aliens." There isn't a one of us who can tear down his barns to build new ones and be certain the Lord won't call him home before the job is done. We're *all* in transition. We were born for transition, born to move from darkness to light; from slavery to sonship; from child to adult; from living to dying; from a decaying earth to our heavenly home.

Last Thoughts on Transitions

Let me close our look at this fourth element of LifeMapping with a couple of parting suggestions. First, as much as God allows, *anticipate transitions*.

I have a friend in the defense industry who lives in Southern California. Nearly eight years ago, he looked around and realized a change was coming; new defense contracts would not keep rolling in steadily. And with the world changing, his job security was becoming as unsettled as the rock plates beneath Los Angeles.

That's when he began thinking in earnest about a second career. Not that he wanted to make a change, nor that one was imminent. But as they teach you in the Marine Corps, when the tactical situation gets bad, you never retreat. You just advance to a fallback position to continue the fight.

"Just for fun," my friend took several aptitude tests, and he discovered he had some artistic talents. As an engineer, he had used those abilities to create circuit boards and information pathways. Now he began taking art lessons as a hobby to develop his talents.

Before long, his hobby grew into displaying his work at small art fairs. Then he had a small show that highlighted his pewter and bronze works. Next he storyboarded what it would take to start an art studio, involving his wife in the process as well.

By doing this contingency planning, they got a realistic look at where they would have to cut and what they could do if he lost his job one day (or simply decided to switch careers). Soon they began making financial sacrifices (including accelerating the payment of their mortgage) to put themselves in position to be free to move in whatever future direction God had for them.

Seven years later, my friend did lose his job, but not his bearings. By preparing well in advance for a "second-season" career, he and his wife were ready to get back in the game when many of his unprepared friends were still scrambling to find a new playing field.

Take time to look down the road five years and, should the Lord tarry, anticipate the transitions looming ahead. Doing so can be a great help when the "gate" opens and change is fast upon you.

Second, *don't be afraid to take that next step.* One of my favorite verses that I've read and reread during times of transition is Joshua 1:9: "Have I not commanded you? Be strong and courageous! Do not tremble or be dismayed, for the LORD your God is with you wherever you go."

Joshua was getting ready to take over the reins of Israel's leadership from Moses and guide the people in a new, challenging direction. And yet he didn't make that transition alone. He had a mighty God who loved him and would be with him every step of the way.

Focus on the Family has published a book by a wonderful person and friend, Tim Burke, called *Major League Dad.* You may know him from the Focus broadcasts he did with his wife, Christine, as a father who loved his spouse and children enough to give up a baseball career to spend time with them. The world knows him as an All-Star pitcher who could have been making millions instead of staying home with special-needs kids.

I had the chance to see Tim at a pro athletes' conference here in Phoenix recently. He looked great and was happy about life and his new book. And while Tim and I had the opportunity to talk only for a moment, I asked another active ballplayer how Tim was doing with the transition.

He had heard someone ask Tim if he missed baseball, especially with spring training about to begin. "You bet I miss it," Tim said, and then with a smile he added, "and I've never been happier."

That's making a transition well. Not easily. Not without cost. But in a God-honoring way that moves him forward. That's facing a major transition like Robert E. Lee, like Joseph, and like the Lord Jesus.

Transitions aren't easy, and it's all right to question. You bet I miss my grandparents and not having another chance to make things right with my father. You bet I'd turn back the clock if I could and take the lines of age and pain off my mother's face. You bet I miss hearing Gary say, "Let's go get a yogurt," instead of going by myself.

But I've never been happier. And I pray you haven't been, either.

The Next Step in the LifeMapping Process

We've taken a good deal of time to look at the past—four chapters, in fact, to look at your strengths, freeze points, flash points, and transitions. Now it's time to follow your LifeMap to a place where there are no footprints. It's the future, and we'll look at four things you can do in seeking to make it a truly better place.

PART 3:

. . . TO YOUR FUTURE

Image Management vs. Authentic Living

In our preview of the last four LifeMapping elements, I mentioned that you now face an inescapable Y in the road. Whether you've realized it before or not, the way you deal with your strengths and successes, freeze points and flash points, positive transitions and difficult trials, points you toward one of two roads.

If you take the high road, you're bound for *authentic living*. That's a road where you're able to look at your past honestly, learn from it, grieve over parts of it if needed, *but then move on in a healthy way*. It's a road that has to be chosen each day, but you can be all but certain you're on it *if* you're practicing three important life-style traits I'll describe in this chapter.

The other road is taken all too often. In fact, it has become a common Christian choice. It's a road I call *image management*, and while it was prevalent in the early church, it's epidemic today. It lures people by offering an imaginary way to live two lives, but it leaves you split off from yourself, a tragedy waiting to happen.

What exactly do I mean by image management and authentic living, and how can you capture this area on your LifeMap? Let's answer that question by looking first at an example of image management and the shimmering, deadly mirage it creates.

When Special Friends Go South

Have you ever found a kindred spirit who, from the first moment you met, bonded with you like a lifelong friend? That's what happened to Joan when she met a woman, Sara, who was to become one of her closest friends. She looked up to and greatly appreciated Sara. Unfortunately, Sara became one of the greatest examples of image management I've ever heard about.

Joan and Sara met at church, and from the moment they were introduced to each other, everything clicked. They discovered they both liked to read mysteries. They had grown up in towns only 20 miles apart, and their high schools enjoyed a friendly athletic rivalry. Now both were avid tennis players.

On a deeper level, both women had come from homes with an abusive father. Both were active in the church, and Sara was even a Bible teacher in the women's fellowship. Joan would sit spellbound as Sara taught, because Sara had such insight and great confidence in presenting God's Word.

As the months went by, the two women spent more and more time together. They shopped, played tennis, and lunched as a team. They and their husbands went camping several times a year. Sara became a special friend and a mentor to Joan. But all that time, Sara was immersed in image management.

Let me give you a definition of image management before you see it fleshed out in Sara's life: *Image management is the attempt to support a public self, without dealing with private self issues, that leads to increasing inner tension and, finally, a breakdown of values.*

You could say that's just a two-dollar definition of hypocrisy. But it involves the choice to have one life-style that others see while ignoring the smoldering fire of a private life that finally spells doom for that public image.

Joan will never forget the day she got the call from another church friend. Joan knew that other women made serious mistakes, but that would never happen with Sara. Yet the news was confirmed in the next morning's newspaper: Sara had embezzled thousands of dollars over a period of five years from the bank where she worked. She had also almost succeeded in framing an innocent co-worker for the crime.

Joan was crushed. Of all the Christian women she had met, Sara was literally the last one she would ever have expected to dishonor Christ. But now Sara faced the likelihood of going to prison.

What happened in Sara's life, and in the lives of many people like her? She had thrown all her efforts into building a *public self*. She put massive energy into creating an image, in this case a spiritual one. She wasn't just a nominal Christian; she appeared to be sold out. But it was only looks. The whole time, she had been pulling bricks out of the foundation of her life by refusing to honestly face problems in her *private world*. In fact, she never talked about them with anyone.

That's the problem with not facing the past—it's often a sure way of repeating it. Sara began supporting an image, not living authentically. And by trying to keep two worlds—public and private—*separate*, she ended up increasing the internal pressure of a duplicitous life until all the joy and spark were gone and only image management was left—the last thing before the fall.

"But that's just one woman's story," you might protest. "That doesn't mean image management is footloose in the Christian community."

Want to bet?

They Were Doing It All Right . . . Almost

In case you think that practicing image management is something reserved for the '90s, think again. Here are some people who had it down pat in the first century:

> To the angel of the church in Ephesus write: The One who holds the seven stars in His right hand, the One who walks among the seven golden lampstands, says this: "I know your deeds and your toil and perseverance, and that you cannot endure evil men, and you put to the test those who call themselves apostles, and they are not, and you found them to be false; and you have perseverance and have endured for My name's sake, and have not grown weary." (Rev. 2:1-3)

Let's stop there. Doesn't that sound like one squared-away group of believers? In fact, the Lord Jesus Himself ("the One who holds the seven stars") commended them seven times for their diligent work. (The number seven, biblically, is the number of completion.) They were All-Pros at doing things right—and at doing all the right things. But in the midst of all their "doing," they left one thing out.

"But I have this against you, that you have left your first love" (Rev. 2:4).

Bingo. Image management, pure and simple. Effort independent of honesty. Keeping the outside of the cup shiny and leaving the inside full of rot. And it's still an incredibly common Christian choice today.

How easy it is to do all the "right" things! Spend time with the kids. Take them to AWANA or the local youth program each week. Participate in a Sunday school class as well as church. Host a home fellowship. Be a part of visitation on Wednesday nights and the new members' class on Sunday afternoons. And add choir, MOPS, and Bible Study Fellowship just for good measure.

Do, do, do. And yet in all the doing of good, there's danger. Seriously. For effort without a right attitude can lead to callousness. And once you begin going through the motions, you're inching closer to simply maintaining an image.

What's the antidote?

We'll look at the far-better life-style choice, *authentic living*, shortly. But first, listen to Christ's challenge to that same group of "doers": "Remember therefore from where you have fallen, and repent and do the deeds you did at first; or else I am coming to you, and will remove your lampstand out of its place—unless you repent" (Rev. 2:5).

Did you catch the powerful three-point sermon in that single verse? First, "remember" from where you've fallen. Think back. Spend time in reflection—like what you've been asked to do in the first four elements of LifeMapping!

The first step to again move forward is what's been mentioned a dozen times already. It's to take an honest look back.

The second way out of image management is to "repent." Literally in the original Greek, it means to "turn around." Quit going through the motions and kidding yourself that you can have public and private selves that don't match up. Genuine repentance involves exchanging one way of life for another.

Then there's point three: "Do the deeds you did at first." Go back to basics. Get a clear, authentic plan for the future. That's the very thing we'll be doing in the final four parts of LifeMapping.

If you don't do those three things, there's an "or else." In this case, you stop being a light to others. "Or else I am coming to you, and I will remove your lampstand out of its place."

Like someone who has been stretching an extension cord until it's ready to pull out of the socket, if you don't turn around and begin walking in faith, you'll finally pull so far away from His strength that you lose your ability to shine God's light—and whatever position He's given you from which to share it.

Those are challenging thoughts, for I believe that all of us, to some degree, engage in image management. We give a smile to the postman who knocks at the door when a kid has just broken a vase and we're so mad we could scream. We tell the boss, "No problem; I'll do it," when what we want to say is, "You do it! You just gave me another project an hour ago!"

It's tough to live up to an inner code of honor that eliminates every vestige of image management. And sometimes there's nothing wrong with keeping your chin up when you really feel like crying. But like a tenacious weed, image management needs to be attacked at the root. How? By practicing *authentic living* and the three major life-style decisions it represents.

Just before we turn our eyes down that path, however, let's get one more clear look at the deceptive trail image management presents. Glance at the five questions below, and see if they look like life-style choices you're making consistently. If they do, you're in danger of being like Sara . . . and like an errant king named Saul.

Five Marks of an Image Manager

In the Old Testament, King Saul is a tragic figure. He was tall, dark, and handsome. He was also chosen by God when a stubborn people begged for a human ruler. But if Sara was a *practitioner* of image management, King Saul was a *grand champion*. Without a doubt, he would have had to answer yes to all five of the following questions. See if you do.

1. Are you great at beginning spiritual commitments but lousy at finishing them?

Saul was. In 1 Samuel 11:6, we read, "Then the Spirit of God came upon Saul mightily." In the Old Testament, the Holy Spirit didn't reside on just anyone. At that time in God's economy, the temple veil between God and humankind hadn't been ripped apart by Christ's death, nor had Pentecost happened, when the Spirit came and indwelled each believer. You can count on one hand the number of people God's Spirit "came upon" in the Old Testament, and it might surprise you to read that Saul was one of them.

Saul started with God's Spirit upon him. But he ended up seated in the slums by a witch, asking for her guidance. Later in 1 Samuel we read, "The LORD did not answer him [Saul]. . . . Then Saul said to his servants, 'Seek for me a woman who is a medium, that I may go to her and inquire of her' " (1 Sam. 28:6-7).

God allows even great saints to walk away from His Spirit. It happened to Saul. It happened to Sara. Fast starters . . . but 50-yard-dash runners in the marathon of life. How about you? Are you a great starter . . . and a poor finisher of spiritual commitments?

2. Does the fear of losing others' approval "force" you into increased compromise?

An image manager begins fighting desperately at times to keep one thing intact—not his integrity, but his image. (Sound uncomfortably like any public figures in our day?) When Saul saw his image with the people going south (with a mighty army coming down from the north to battle them), he rushed into a compromising position.

We read, "Now he waited seven days, according to the appointed time set by Samuel, but Samuel did not come to Gilgal; and the people were scattering from him. So Saul said, 'Bring to me the burnt offering and the peace offerings.' And he offered the burnt offering" (1 Sam. 13:8-9).

If your image is at stake, who cares if sacrifices are only for priests to conduct? If it'll keep your followers on board, the ends justify the means. Or at least if you're Saul, you may think so until you're finishing your sacrifice just as Samuel walks up.

What was Saul's excuse?

"Because I saw that the people were scattering from me, and that you did not come within the appointed days . . ." (1 Sam. 13:11).

In other words, "It's your fault I did this, Samuel!"

Saul continued, "So I forced myself and offered the burnt offering" (v. 12). "For the people, Samuel," he suggested, "not for me."

Really? That excuse didn't fly with Samuel, and it doesn't work for modern image managers, either. They may cut corners in everything from drinking and sex to ethics in business to keep their "in-crowd" status, but it's all image, and it's storing up judgment.

3. Does your fabricated image become more "real" than reality?

Saul simply didn't get it. In 1 Samuel 15, God gave him a specific, if terrible, order. He was to be the instrument of divine judgment and eliminate an entire tribe. Amalek was to be destroyed, and along with him all his cattle and sheep, plus every one of his people, young and old.

But Saul let Amalek and the best of his livestock live, and he saved much of the treasure and booty as well. What happened when Samuel confronted Saul over his disobedience?

" 'Blessed are you of the LORD!' " Saul said. " *'I have carried out the command of the LORD.'* But Samuel said, 'What then is this bleating of the sheep in my ears, and the lowing of the oxen which I hear?' "

And Saul's classic, image-driven response: "Then Saul said to Samuel, 'I *did* obey the voice of the LORD' " (vv. 13-14, 20, emphasis added).

There's no objective reality involved with image managers. They can become so good at being self-centered and deceptive that even doing something dead wrong can be grounds for celebrating doing something right. They may steal your car and run it into a pole—but walk away praising the Lord that they weren't scratched a bit though the car was totaled. "What was that pole doing there anyway?" they might say. "And why were your brakes so bad?"

4. Do you find that your repentance is sorrow over getting caught instead of over the act itself?

Time and again, as I've mentioned before, Saul was caught and corrected. But his repentance was always skin deep (and that's giving him a few folds). If you kick yourself for getting caught instead of mourning the loss of character involved, you may be practicing image management. Particularly if you answer yes to the last question.

5. Do you refuse the counsel of others or the chance to change?

Saul brushed off God's prophet when it came to his correction. He wouldn't listen to his son Jonathan, either, when he strayed into sin by attacking David.

He wouldn't listen to anyone who spoke God's word . . . but he did ask to speak to that witch.

If you find yourself increasingly defensive or drawing away from spiritual correction, watch out. That may be an attempt to prop up an empty image rather then hear God's clear direction through the advice and prompting of others.

There you have five marks of an image manager, yet none are behavior patterns you have to choose, especially if you'll do the opposite of what Saul did . . . and what *Success* magazine recently put on its front cover, "The Art of Deceit."

The Art of Deceit

A current book sweeping the Western business community makes *The Leadership Secrets of Attila the Hun* look like a grade-school catechism. It's a best-selling Chinese book called *Thick Face, Black Heart.*[1] It teaches deception, disguise, trickery, spying, and lying if necessary. Whatever it takes to win, and whatever image you need to wear to conquer, that's what counts. The greatest business "warrior" today (from the author's standpoint) is a stealthy, ruthless, "black hearted" person who turns truth into lies and lies into the truth. (Sounds like a book that has already been circulated in Congress, doesn't it?)

In the words of the book, you gain the upper hand by "pretending to be a pig in order to eat the tiger." In other words, if you have to undergo humiliation to overcome a foe (dressing like a pig), it's worth it if you can destroy your adversary.

Or consider, "If you kill the rooster, it will frighten your monkey." Years ago in China, when a monkey was disobedient, the trainer would kill a rooster in front of it. Witnessing the poor rooster's demise served as a powerful teacher. (I'm sure that's an understatement!)

What a thing to teach! To be two-faced is the mark of *wisdom?* To be cruel—if that's what it takes to win—is applauded? Sounds as though Judas would do well in such a climate, doesn't it? That "son of Satan" was certainly a *Thick Face, Black Hearted,* blatant image manager.

While some in the Chinese business world may embrace the idea of being two-faced, that's not God's mind-set. There is tremendous strength in becoming someone who follows the road to *authentic living* rather than image management.

To help you know if you're on that right road, the next section presents the three life-style choices that can help you write your own book. It's the one that I'm sure your God and family would rather your life inspire: *Honest Face, Pure Heart.*

The Antidote to Image Management: Authentic Living

Three life-style characteristics, working together, will develop authentic living and give you the strongest possible defense against image management.

1. Exercise the strength it takes to be humble.

First Peter 5:5 says, "God is opposed to the proud, but gives grace to the humble." You could always tell when Saul was around. But you couldn't tell him much. There was the time he gave a foolish order for his troops to take no nourishment on the field of battle and thus robbed God's people of a great victory. When his son and soldiers urged him to change his orders, he would have put Jonathan to death to maintain his right to be wrong if his troops hadn't intervened (see 1 Sam. 14:24-46).

If you're a person who's used to going first class, it can be easy to build up an arrogance that says, "I've got an image. You'd better recognize it and cater to it."

It's like the stuffy British waiter who was obviously unimpressed by the dignitary seated at his table. After this "important" man had endured what he felt was inattention and inferior service for his station in life, he called the waiter over and said, "See here, sir, *do you know who I am?*"

"No, sir," said the waiter coldly. "But I shall make inquiries and inform you directly."

If you're allowing pride in your talents, person, possessions, or position to creep in, you're walking toward image management. Humility can put you back on the right road, the one the Lord Jesus took. He held the power to calm the sea and raise the dead, but "although He existed in the form of God, . . . [He] emptied Himself . . . [and] humbled Himself by becoming obedient to the point of death, even death on a cross" (Phil. 2:6-8).

2. Commit yourself to a life of continual learning.

I remember one professor I had in my doctoral program who took the word *attitude* and pushed it about two miles to the extreme. What an incredible chip on his shoulder! He was convinced that since he had his Ph.D., he was as close to being a g-o-d as you could get.

One way he demonstrated this was to require an incredible amount of reading from those of us in his class. But I'll never forget someone asking him in all seriousness, "Sir, what books have you read recently that you've benefited from?"

He replied haughtily, "I haven't read a book since graduate school, and I won't. My own research and understanding are better than anything in print."

Not only was that a lack of humility, but it also displayed an attitude that says, "I've stopped learning. I've got it. That's all I need." And it's a sure way to begin having to defend your positions rather than expand your horizons.

Keep reading. Keep attending classes or workshops regularly. Keep learning and being teachable. It's a great way to keep the "little gray cells" from melting down, and it's a powerful hedge against letting image management creep up on you.

3. Finally, be willing to build your own accountability base.

I'm not going to go into detail on this antidote to image management here, because you'll find it to be a key part of the next chapter. But I'm convinced that accountability is at the heart of authentic relationships. (It's even encouraging to see that it is sneaking back into the workplace. See *The Oz Principle*, a best-selling book that's all about accountability.[2])

If you'll notice, this antidote isn't just the "idea" of accountability but a genuine accountability base *that you build yourself*. It's not something you figure will happen when your church's small-group ministry gets organized. Nor is it something that will "take some time" because you just moved a year ago and don't know anybody well enough.

If you want to avoid image management, you're going to have to build your own accountability group. (Again, more on that in the next chapter.) Such groups provide relationships that hold untold riches, but they're a lot like buried treasure. You have to actively seek them out; they don't usually dig themselves up and drop right into your lap.

Humility, teachability, and accountability. Those three life-style choices will help you avoid image management and keep going right down the middle of the road marked "authentic living."

> *By trying to keep two worlds—public and private—separate, you end up increasing the internal pressure of a duplicitous life until all the joy and spark are gone.*

Looking Over Your LifeMap

Take time now to go back over your LifeMap. Can you see a pattern or even some instances of where you chose image management over authentic living? I have at times. Here's that part of my LifeMap that I displayed earlier.

John Trent's LifeMap

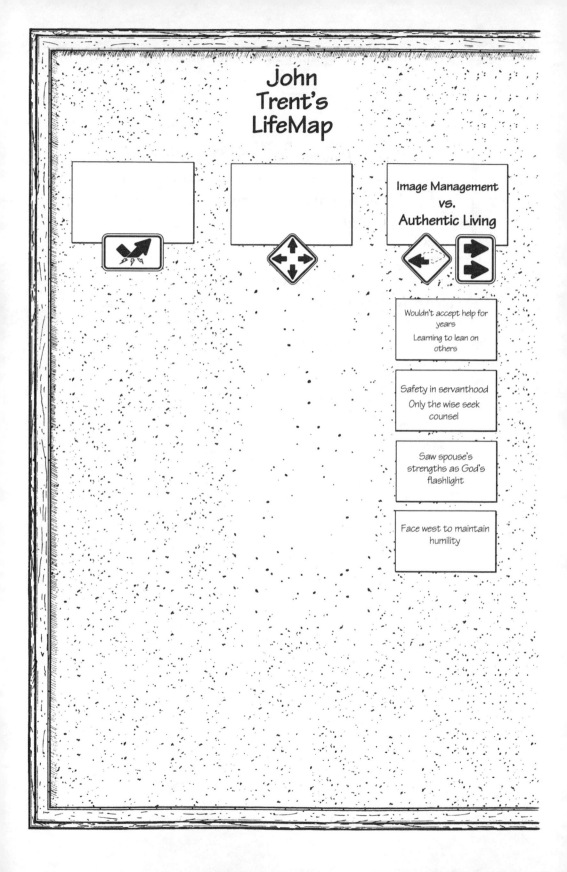

Image Management
vs.
Authentic Living

Wouldn't accept help for years
Learning to lean on others

Safety in servanthood
Only the wise seek counsel

Saw spouse's strengths as God's flashlight

Face west to maintain humility

For years in high school and on into college, I was so self-conscious and insecure about appearing weak that I did anything and everything I could that was "hard": football, wrestling, pole vaulting, baseball. Even in noncontact activities like music, I had to do something "challenging." I couldn't play just *any* instrument.

In eighth grade, I asked my music teacher what was the hardest instrument to play. Without hesitation, he said, "The bagpipes." That did it. I just "had" to take pipe lessons, and within three weeks I was. (What a mom!) For the next five years, I played in the Phoenix Scottish Pipe Band. (I still drag out my pipes occasionally and play "Highland Laddie" or "Amazing Grace" just to watch Cindy, the girls, and Cracker the dog run for cover!)

"Doing everything the hard way" and "not wanting to intrude on anyone" might look laudable on the surface. But refusing to ask for or accept help was linked to an image I was keeping up, not authentic living. It wasn't until I had to ask for help in college (in particular, one time when I became extremely ill, had no money, and had to rely on someone else to pick me up and pay for me to go to a doctor) that I let go of an image-driven weakness.

On the other side of the coin, my learning to appreciate Cindy's detail strengths has been a great help to our marriage. As I've said in other books, starting several years ago, Cindy and I made the decision to see an outstanding Christian counselor for six sessions every year as an enrichment experience. The first year we went in, I remember my good friend Dr. Bill Retts asking, "So what brings you two in?"

I answered, "Nothing! I'm sure you'll refund our money on the next five sessions after this morning."

But then Cindy pulled out her list!

While we could probably stand to go in twice as often, the bottom line is that if I go in for just six sessions a year, I'll still die long before I run out of issues to talk and learn about!

As for facing west to maintain humility, that's a reference to something I've done for years to keep achievements in perspective. In my early Christian walk, when I was tempted to pride over some ministry or personal accomplishment, all I had to do was "face west" toward Phoenix (where I grew up) and think back to my non-Christian past. (During those years, I always lived east of Phoenix.)

I didn't come to Christ until late in high school, and I had lived a less-than-honoring life-style before that time. In the Scriptures, Paul confessed that at times, he felt like "the least of the apostles" as he thought back to his years as Saul (1 Cor. 15:9). In the same way, "facing west" mentally helped to keep me humble and to make me thankful that God could forgive and use me in spite of my past.

You say you're committed to walking the road of authentic living? Great. Then it's time to turn the page and take another step in the right direction—namely, the sixth step in the LifeMapping process—storyboarding clear goals and directions for your most important relationships. That's the purpose of the next chapter, where you'll turn your storyboarding skills loose on a positive plan for your future.

Gaining a Clear Life Plan

Have you ever planned something and had it turn out much differently from what you expected? That shouldn't happen once you storyboard a clear plan for the major areas of your LifeMap. But that's exactly what did happen to me with some special plans I made for Cindy on our first wedding anniversary.

It was 1980, and our paper anniversary was coming up soon. Like any sensitive husband, I easily remembered our wedding date (though I have to give an assist to the fake silver serving plate we always used that had the date etched right on it).

But what to do to make that first anniversary special?

We were living in Dallas at the time, and I was a youth pastor at a fine church. Our salary as a first-year youth pastor ranged right between eking it out and scrambling to make ends meet, so there wasn't a lot left over for entertainment.

I was talking with a good friend who was a banker at the time, and he mentioned a wonderful restaurant he'd dined at, one I'd heard about but had never been to. It was the Petroleum Club in downtown Dallas, high atop the

Southland Life Building. And the more he talked, the more this sounded like just the place for our first anniversary. Then I asked him about the prices . . . and when he told me, I sounded as if they'd just turned off my iron lung.

Crestfallen, I headed back to work, trying to scale down my dinner plans from high atop the Southland Life Building to underneath the Golden Arches. Then suddenly an idea hit me. No . . . but *yes*. It *could work! It* would *work!* There was one place we had stashed away some money for something that really wasn't *that* big a deal.

I called my friend, who arranged everything for me. He got a friend who was a member of the Petroleum Club to sponsor me for dinner that night, and my surprise plans were beginning to take shape!

All I'd told Cindy about the evening was that we were going "somewhere incredibly special" and that she needed to wear something just a fraction less fancy than her wedding dress.

We drove downtown, went up the glass elevator and goggled at the magnificent view, and then walked into a truly five-star restaurant. They treated us as if we owned the place. We had *six* waiters come by our table (five of whom we didn't really need). Our name had been beautifully engraved on a match cover, strolling violinists roamed the aisles, and there was even someone who went around taking your picture. (I was sure we'd end up on the society page.)

The food was exquisite. We sat at a window table enjoying the fantastic view. Here I was with a beautiful wife who loved me, and she was all decked out in a gorgeous dress. I even had enough cash in my pocket to pay for everything, including the exorbitant tip and all the pictures I thought were free (or I wouldn't have had them take six).

As we drove home, you can imagine the glow cast over the evening. Candlelight dinner . . . beautiful setting . . . celebrating our love and anniversary. . . . Cindy laying her head on my shoulder as we went along. *Was this going to be a romantic evening or what?* Here's how it turned out to be "or what."

As we neared our home, my loving, practical, detailed, organized wife asked me a perfectly harmless question. "Sweetheart," she purred, "that was a *wonderful* dinner."

Sweetheart, I thought. *This is going to be a great evening.*

"But can I ask you something?" she said, almost whispering in my ear.

Ask me anything. I'm yours!

"Where did we get the money for that kind of dinner?"

Oh, no! Don't ask me that!

When a loving, detailed, organized, practical wife asks you a financial question—*and then you put in a long pause before you answer*—you can imagine what happened next.

"Honey, *where* did you get the money?"

Honey. It's gone from Sweetheart down to Honey.

"Jooohhhnnn!"

Not "John!"

With a loving, detailed, organized, practical wife, it doesn't do any good to lie. So as we pulled into our driveway, I turned to her, took her hands in mine, and said, "Honey, I don't know how to tell you this . . . *but we just ate our couch!*"

The only extra money we had at the time was the money we'd been saving toward a couch. But there was plenty of time to put that money away again! After all, it was our anniversary. Not only that, but I had liberated that money from the low-percentage-rate account it was languishing in and used it to help stimulate the Dallas economy.

Suffice it to say that none of those (and many other quickly-thought-up) explanations worked, and there was no "touchy the toes" that night!

Seriously, I'm thankful that God has given me a *forgiving,* loving, detailed, practical, organized wife who still loves me but still can't believe what I did more than 15 years ago. (And believe me, I only did it *once.*)

That's a dramatic example of planning something and having it go all wrong. What I'd like to do in this chapter is to help you look at your life and lay out plans, goals, and ideas that can help things go right.

LifeMapping and Time Management

There are countless good books that can help you with the specific details of time management. There's the Franklin System that's available nationwide; Time Systems out of Phoenix is the one I personally use. And then there's the Covey material that links goals with values and quadrants of time.

Our goal in this chapter isn't to try to build a weekly calendar. Rather, it's to get an overall plan that can become both a prayer guide and the means to an action plan. So while many of your storyboard cards may ideally end up on a "to do" sheet, think first of overall goals, and then of how to move them into action.

But how do you plan life goals? Pick out the key roles you play, and put each one on a topper card.

For example, let's say you're single, and as you look over your roles and responsibilities, your "life plan" headers look like this:

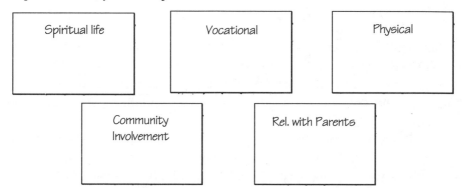

Whatever your toppers end up being to fit your particular situation, you use the same storyboarding technique you've used all along to fill out the subbers (namely, brainstorming and sharpening). And while you can get as detailed as you like, *here are four questions that can help you flesh out the subber cards under each header:*

1. What do I *need* to do in this area?
2. What do I *want* to do beyond the essentials?
3. How can I accomplish it?
4. Who am I encouraging to help keep me responsible for my goals?

With those four questions in mind, you can begin to fill in the subbers under each of your key personal and vocational roles, and you'll start to see a set of clear goals taking shape.

> *Confidence is a vital element of fleshing out a life plan.*

John Trent's LifeMap

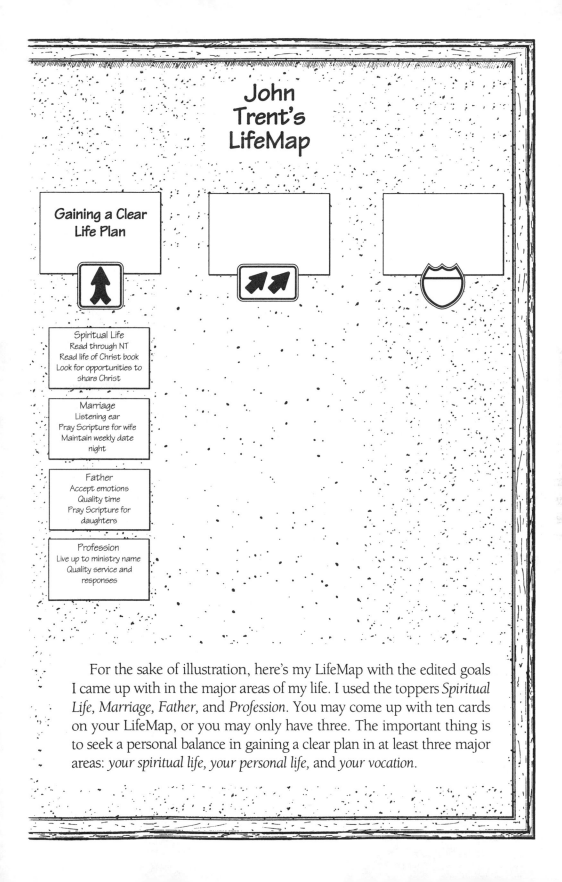

Gaining a Clear Life Plan

Spiritual Life
Read through NT
Read life of Christ book
Look for opportunities to share Christ

Marriage
Listening ear
Pray Scripture for wife
Maintain weekly date night

Father
Accept emotions
Quality time
Pray Scripture for daughters

Profession
Live up to ministry name
Quality service and responses

For the sake of illustration, here's my LifeMap with the edited goals I came up with in the major areas of my life. I used the toppers *Spiritual Life*, *Marriage*, *Father*, and *Profession*. You may come up with ten cards on your LifeMap, or you may only have three. The important thing is to seek a personal balance in gaining a clear plan in at least three major areas: *your spiritual life, your personal life,* and *your vocation.*

Under my LifeMap, I first storyboarded the topper "Spiritual Life." As I thought about the four leading questions above, I came up with the following abridged list.

Spiritual Life

"Read through the New Testament" means a daily plan of Bible reading that would take me through the New Testament twice in one year. This (along with prayers) answered the first question of what I needed to do to meet the basics of a growing spiritual life. Then, in regard to the second question about things I'd *like* to do, I determined that reading an outstanding book on the life of Christ (like those by my friends Max Lucado or Ken Gire) would be a positive goal. And finally, I listed "Look for opportunities to share Christ" as a further goal for maintaining a missions outlook wherever I am, at home or away.

Once I'd storyboarded this first topper, I just went across the row of toppers, filling out the subbers under each—with the following exception. *As I began to set my goals and plans as a husband and father, I storyboarded this part with Cindy's input and encouragement.* That way, I wasn't coming up with another "We ate the couch!" plan that sounded great to me but came far short of meeting her needs and reality.

Marriage

With Cindy, my goals were to maintain a listening ear (not a lecturing mouth), to take a section of Scripture and pray God's Word for her, to have regular dates with her to keep our relationship fresh, and to be accountable to my CrossTrainers' small group for all of the above (more on that later in this chapter).

What I mean by praying God's Word for her is to take actual Scriptures and personalize the passages by praying them specifically for Cindy. For example, "Lord, may You be my wife's shepherd. May You cause her to lie down in green pastures and give her rest this morning. May You guide her this day with Your rod and protect her with Your staff . . ." That's personalizing and praying Psalm 23 for her.

Several good books list many Scriptures already designed for you to personalize prayers based on the Scriptures for your loved ones, like the excellent *Praying God's Will for Your . . .* series of books by Lee Roberts. (There are volumes on praying for your wife, husband, son, or daughter.)[1]

Then Cindy helped me flesh out my goals as a father. As you'll notice, that list began with "accept emotions," and there's a specific reason for it.

Father

I grew up in a fairly unemotional home, with a mother who handled things calmly like the businesswoman she was and two brothers who were also pretty relaxed (except for the time my older brother accidentally shot me with the spear gun and things heated up pretty well). It only seems logical, therefore, that out of that masculine-oriented, relatively quiet background, the Lord would give me a wife, two daughters, and even a hyperactive female dog to share my life with! And while Cindy doesn't lean too far on the emotional side of things, both Kari and Laura are a bouquet of varied emotions.

I can't say as I've understood them all, or that I've always responded well to their laughter and tears, followed by intense times of reflection, then more laughter, more tears, and so on. But valuing them and their emotions is a major goal I have worked at to demonstrate my love. (For an excellent book on recognizing, understanding, and dealing with your child's varied emotions, see Norm Wright and Gary Oliver's book *Kids Have Feelings Too!*[2])

Along with understanding and accepting their emotions, I've had to work at dealing with my own. (Wright and Oliver have another book that's outstanding for men called *Men Have Feelings Too!*[3]) For example, for a time, whenever I'd get really upset with the kids over something they had done (like being "too emotional"), I'd point my finger at them just to "emphasize" my displeasure.

"Why are you being so angry with the kids?" Cindy would ask.

I'd always come back with the line, "I'm not angry. *I'm just being emphatic.*" (I made sure to *never* point at her when I was being emphatic!) Actually, I was frustrated, but I didn't recognize it as such.

But then Cindy came back with a piercing comment wrapped in a question: "Wasn't one of the cards on your LifeMap about listening and trying to understand the girls' feelings about things?"

Ouch.

It didn't take me long to realize that she was right and that things needed to change. If I wanted that card to stay up and have any credibility, I needed to get out of the habit of pointing my finger at them—and recognize and deal with the emotions I had when I was frustrated. So I gained a great deal from reading Gary Oliver's book, and then one evening, I called Kari and Laura into the living room and asked them to forgive me for the times when I'd gotten angry and pointed at them.

"To show you I'm serious about this," I went on, "anytime from now on that Dad gets angry and points at you, you will *instantly* get a $1 bill."

Instantly you could see their eyes open wide. "A *whole* dollar?" Laura asked.

"Yes," I said.

And then for the next four weeks, both kids did their best to provoke me to point at them!

To my discredit, I was well on my way to funding their college education at Harvard after the first two weeks. While I didn't keep an exact account, I must have shelled out close to $15 in "pointing fees." But it's now nearly two years later, and I'll bet I haven't lost $5 in that 24-month period.

That's not just because I got tired of reaching into my back pocket and emptying my wallet, either (though I have to admit that helped). Rather, I had that card on my LifeMap as the policeman, gently reminding me each time I looked at it that my kids are worth far more than finger pointing. And besides—I wanted to have the credibility to leave that card on my LifeMap!

The other cards in my "Father" area include "quality time" (defined very differently for each girl) and, as with Cindy, praying Scripture for their safety and spiritual and physical growth. And once again, I make myself accountable in this area to my small group.

Profession

Then finally, the last topper card relates to my profession. While this is the edited version of my LifeMap due to space limitations, two things remain prominently placed on my subber cards (besides making myself accountable once more).

First, I want to live up to the name of my ministry, Encouraging Words, when I'm talking and dealing with all people. Second, I want to build quality service and a response system that honors each person who attends a seminar or contacts my office by mail or phone.

I can't say I've mastered this last card yet in beginning a brand-new ministry with a one-person staff. Since I'm the shipping department one day, the counseling department the next, and the correspondence department on day three, I sometimes have to keep people waiting for a letter or phone call much longer than I'd like. But I'm working on this card. My board and I are praying for funding for that first staff person to help with correspondence and seminar details, and I've been seeking counsel from other ministries on how to set up quality systems that can best meet the needs of those who come to a seminar, write, or call.

In brief, then, by developing the subbers under those four topper cards, I came up with this abridged version of my LifeMap. I realize that your headers might look very different, and your list of subbers could easily be much longer underneath. But regardless, *now is a great time to put down the book, head to your storyboard corner, and use brainstorming and sharpening to flesh out those key elements of your life.*

Three Words to Guide Your Goal-setting Process

As you do this part of your LifeMap, keep in mind the following three words. They will help you to create a plan that's realistic and practical.

Credibility

As you sit down individually or with your spouse or a small group to gain a clear life plan, it's important to commit yourself to credibility. If you have your *American Heritage Dictionary* handy, you'll see *credibility* is made up of two words—*credit* and *ability*. In other words, credibility means that God and others can take your words and actions *right to the bank*. So if you put up a card like "Accept emotions" under your "Parent" card as I did, you need to be willing to walk the walk, not just talk the talk. And you gain credibility by working consistently toward making what's on your cards a vital, everyday part of your life.

Confidence

While you may not think of confidence as being an important part of fleshing out a life plan, it's actually a vital element. First of all, lean on Proverbs 3:26, "The LORD will be your confidence." If you take the time to carefully and prayerfully storyboard goals in each major area of your life—goals that honor Christ and help you love Him and others more effectively—you can lean on

Him for strength to help make those plans a reality. And then keep Hebrews 10:35-36 in mind: "Therefore, do not throw away your confidence, which has a great reward. For you have need of endurance, so that when you have done the will of God, you may receive what was promised."

Confidence in a God-honoring plan can also give you endurance to stay the course and keep moving forward—all the way to the promise of love, peace, and joy that comes from loving and serving Christ. And finally, you'll see your confidence increase the more you base your life plan on the Word of God.

I've always been thankful for my four years at Dallas Theological Seminary, but I didn't realize until a few years ago one important side benefit of its intense instruction in the Scriptures (like requiring students to take both Hebrew and Greek, the original languages of the Old and New Testaments). What does learning God's Word have to do with confidence?

In a study done of several different seminaries, each of which represented different schools of theology and thought, one thing stood out loud and clear. When it came to the area of personal and relational confidence, the Dallas students scored right at the top. That wasn't out of arrogance but because of the focus on the Scriptures as the solid basis for their faith and lives. And that confidence translated into high levels of direction and a clearer sense of mission.

You'll never go wrong if you tie your life plans in to God's Word. It will give you a sense of mission, strength, and confidence that can keep you going during those times when you need endurance.

Communication

Credibility and confidence are good starters, but to pull off your life plan, you'll also need to communicate it to your spouse, your children if they're old enough, and special friends who can hold you accountable. In other words, don't be the kind of person who works out a life plan and then walks in the door and announces, "Honey, guess where we're moving tomorrow?"

Sitting down with your spouse as a couple to come up with a life plan is very important. Additionally, discussing it with others adds to the commitment and confidence to make it a reality.

Credibility, confidence, and communication centered on a clear plan—

that's what you can think about now as you list the major areas of your life and then begin storyboarding positive details under each one. But without someone to help hold you accountable when you're finished, your chances of seeing your plan come off your LifeMap and into real life decrease dramatically. Below are just a few reasons I believe loving accountability is so important.

Accountability: Holding Up Each Other's Arms

In July 1993, I had the privilege, along with some 54,000 other men, to take part in the Promise Keepers national conference in Boulder, Colorado. Talk about incredibly inspiring! To sing "How Great Thou Art!" with 54,000 men, arm in arm and hearts knit together, is as close as I'll get to a heavenly choir until I actually arrive there.

Promise Keepers operates by a simple set of principles. Men need a relationship with their Heavenly Father through our Lord Jesus Christ. And men need each other. That's not a complicated formula, but it's incredibly powerful. And like no one else on a national level, Promise Keepers has tapped the collective hearts of many men who were looking for some way to band together and make a public stand for the Lord.

I'm thankful for Promise Keepers and the challenge and high calling it issues at its national and now also regional conferences. But I'm grateful, too, for what I've learned from a group out of Des Moines, Iowa, called CrossTrainers. The one-two punch of the once-a-year national gathering of Promise Keepers, linked with the weekly gathering of a CrossTrainers chapter, is an almost unbeatable combination. It gives you the motivation of joining a great army and the encouragement of being in a small group.

It has been my privilege to lead a CrossTrainers chapter at my home church (something you can start at your church as well).[*] And each week, I get to see men break into small groups, link arms, and help support each other in the goal of maintaining and developing their storyboarded life goals. *In fact, each man in my CrossTrainers group has completed a LifeMap, discussed his goals with his spouse or a close friend if single, and is having his small group hold him accountable for what he has written down—including me.*

That's where I see a key part of the LifeMapping process becoming reality in your life and mine. Whether the accountability comes from your spouse, a close friend, a neighbor, or a small group like a CrossTrainers chapter or a women's Bible study, discussing your LifeMap with others is a powerful way of committing yourself to positive change.

I'll admit that when I first showed others my LifeMap, some things weren't easy to talk about. Those cards on your LifeMap can be very personal, and I'm not suggesting you pass them out at a movie theater to total strangers. But in the safety of a supportive friend or group of people you know, trust, and love, showing your LifeMap can make your goals more real and tangible.

Final Thoughts on Life Planning and Goal-setting

Let me say again that this chapter and this element of the LifeMapping process aren't meant to take the place of some of the highly tuned time-management tools on the market. What we're after here is more of a broad brushstroke that can at least get you started in the planning process—and in setting up a target that you can ask God to help you hit. But there is one final application that I highly recommend. Namely, once you have your plan in place, sit down at least once a year for a time of review and refocusing.

With the flash points and transitions we've already talked about that spring up in our lives, your LifeMap may look very different a year from now. That's why it's important to be flexible and to consistently evaluate and fine-tune the process. At a minimum, link a yearly physical exam with your review of your LifeMap. That way, you've got a built-in reminder to check up on your physical, relational, and spiritual health.

For all of us, planning can be much different from putting something into practice. And in the seventh and eighth elements of LifeMapping that follow, you'll discover two crucial tools to help take all your writing and turn it into reality.

The first is a key element called *learned hopefulness*. It can help you put away the natural tendency to fall back into negative patterns and past hurts. The second, called *memorial markers*, can give you a tangible target to help keep you moving toward that positive future you've just outlined.

Learned Hopefulness

As we get ready to talk about the seventh key element of LifeMapping, a concept called *learned hopefulness*, just picture the scene in the following hypothetical story and see if you can relate to the dilemma this man finds himself in.

On the Way to LAX

It's just another red-eye flight between Los Angeles International (LAX) and Dallas. The 737 hurtles through the lower stratosphere at 600 miles per hour. Seven and a half miles below, lonely lights glimmer on a carpet of black felt. A few quiet conversations and the low whine of the massive Pratt & Whitney engines below the wings weave a sleepy background hum.

The man in seat 8-A is oblivious to all that. His name is Ed, and he's eagerly turning the pages of a Louis L'Amour novel. As he pushes the button and leans back farther in his seat, he lets his mind slip into the time of the Wild West.

For just a moment, it's him in the scene . . . rolling out of his blankets under desert stars the size of dishpans. He pulls on his boots after first giving them a shake to dislodge itinerant scorpions or tarantulas. Shoulders broadened by his skill with an ax, and with a waist kept trim by the constant work and slim rations on the trail, he looks even taller than his six feet, two inches when he stands. On catlike feet, he walks over to stoke the embers of last night's fire and then dips a blackened coffee pot in the nearby spring. Rolling a cigarette and murmuring a greeting to his horse—a sturdy, line-backed dun—he scans a slowly graying horizon.

Then he straps on the pistol. It's a battle-worn but sturdy Colt Dragoon .45 that he carried through the War Between the States . . . and that has carried him through many a shoot-out since.

A few miles away, in the town of Salt Flats, he expects to encounter a round-faced, black-suited banker. That man conspired with a greedy rancher to seize the land of his army buddy—and then had him dry-gulched from ambush, leaving a grieving widow and an orphan son behind. He may also run into the weak, slack-jawed sheriff who looked the other way. And there's always the chance he may happen upon the quiet man, the soft-voiced man with the tied-down guns. He's a man with vacant gray eyes, a casual walk, an ironic smile, and a hand as fast as blurred lightning. It may be today, it may be tomorrow, but they will meet.

With his Henry repeating rifle tucked in the boot of his saddle, the reassuring weight of his Colt on his hip, and the reins hanging loosely in work-hardened fists, he will ride into town.

And he will make a difference.

He will back away from no fight. He will face the injustice. He will square his shoulders, look evil in the eye, and put a bloody end to it if need be—or die in the attempt. And when the matter is done, he will ride back to his small rawhide outfit in the foothills.

With his own two hands, he will shape his home out of native stone. With his own two hands, he will break a string of wild mustangs, build his herd, and carve out his own piece of the American West. And when the time is right, those same two hands will reach out to the prettiest girl in the county. No word will pass between them; just an understanding look will tell them that no love could be stronger and that the next generation of tall, proud men to ride the range will be the fruit of their marriage.

Ed closes the book, shuts his eyes, and for a suspended moment of time feels good about his dream. But suddenly, the flight attendant's voice breaks in, telling the passengers to put their seats forward for landing and rudely reminding him that things aren't nearly so satisfying in his own piece of the American West.

Sure he filled out his LifeMap, but so much has happened between then and now. All those days at the office and then crawling into bed with a bitterly unhappy wife at night. His teenagers, hardly more than indifferent strangers these days, will be gone before he gets up. He, in turn, will be gone when they get home. The marriage? It's taking on water, and sometimes it's hard to keep bailing. At the office, that golden opportunity seems near—yet somehow just out of reach.

Staring out the small window at the cold, empty daybreak, his stomach tightens as the ground rushes up to meet the plane. *If I'd only lived in the Old West,* he reflects, *things would have been different.* He'd have been able to use his two strong arms, a rugged horse, a ready rifle, and a firmly set jaw to face anything and anyone. But now . . . well, there doesn't seem much he can do or say to change anything.

In fact, if the truth be known, he thinks as he waits for the plane to pull into its gate, *I may have a plan for my life, but there's no way I can make it come true.*

It's Only a (True) Story

I hope that story doesn't ring close to true in your life, but let's face it, it could. For as you've taken time to work through, reflect on, and create your LifeMap to this point, there may be a nagging concern in the back of your mind. Namely, like other "paper plans" you've given time to before, everything seems to just sit there on the page until the next consultant comes in with a new plan.

Perhaps you're like our friend in the story above, and you've run into the harsh realities that your marriage, children, and work don't seem to fit neatly within a 3x5 card. Your spouse isn't interested in helping you create your LifeMap, and there seems little hope that that will change anytime soon. So why not just put this plan with all the others that haven't really brought real improvement?

If that's your perspective on where you've come so far, you'll love this aspect of LifeMapping. That's because it's all about a biblical method of facing the inevitable barriers that stand between any plan and positive change—and it's about how to move beyond them, in some cases for the first time.

With that in mind, let me introduce you to two concepts you'll soon become familiar with. One is a positive tool I'll seek to have you put into practice called *learned hopefulness*. The other is the dark side of that same concept that others have called *learned helplessness*.

The best way I can illustrate those concepts is with the abbreviated story of my friend Dave Dravecky. He has already been through a lifetime's worth of challenges and changes.

When your LifeMap seems to fall apart

It took only a split second on that cool, August night in Montreal's Olympic Stadium. Sixty feet, six inches straight out from home plate, Dave Dravecky's future snapped in the midst of a pitch. In the instant it took for his arm to break, all his comeback dreams, all his carefully laid plans were shattered. With a "crack" that could be heard by those in the upper deck, a Cinderella story ended like a nightmare.[1]

In the weeks that followed, the decisions were agonizing; the prayers, real; the surgery, radical. And while the doctors assured him that the cancer was gone, so was his arm. It wasn't just part of his arm, either, but the entire arm and most of his shoulder.

Dave had to take many difficult first steps following his surgery:

The first time he forced himself to stand in front of the mirror and look at the hole where his arm had been.

The first time of struggling to get a shirt buttoned with one hand.

The first time he stared at his shoelaces and wondered how in the world he was going to tie them.

And always there was the phantom pain that felt as if his fingertips were on fire—when there were no fingers there to feel anything.

I had the privilege of dining with Dave Dravecky and his exceptional wife, Jan, on the eve of another first for Dave. The next morning, he was to face a horde of anxious television talk-show hosts and newspaper reporters who had descended on Orlando for his first public interview since the operation.

The interviews would go incredibly well. His words conveyed to millions of viewers were a crystal-clear testimony of his undaunted courage and his unshakable faith in Jesus Christ. But the night before, at the intimate author dinner that Focus on the Family always hosts at the Christian booksellers' convention, we got to hear about an even more touching first . . . and indirectly learned a great deal about learned hopefulness.

Dave had taken facing live cameras and national media attention in stride in his years as a successful baseball star. Much more difficult for him was the prospect of how his two children would react to seeing him for the first time with no left arm.

The day Daddy came home

Dave and Jan had decided not to have the kids come to the hospital during his short stay there after the amputation. Instead, the day Dave came home, they brought each child into a room, one by one, to see Daddy.

Their son, Jonathan, was the first to come in. An energetic nine-year-old at the time who loved baseball and his father, he walked all around the room, looking at Dad from all angles without saying a word.

Finally, Dave said to him, "Well, do you want to see my scar?"

"Yeah!" Jonathan said, his eyes lighting up.

Carefully removing the bandages, Dave showed him the massive job of suturing that had been done on his shoulder.

"Wow, Dad!" Jonathan said. "Wait right here. Don't move a muscle. I'll be right back, I promise. Don't go *anywhere*."

Several minutes went by before Jonathan came back in the room and said, "Dad, I've got some of my friends outside. Can they come in and see your scar, too?"

Any doubts Dave might have had about his son's being distant or uncomfortable around him were dispelled as he became the best "show and tell" object on the block!

Young boys take scars as a badge of courage. But would the same thing happen with their daughter, Tiffany? Or would an empty sleeve put a barrier between the two of them?

Their precious daughter had waited patiently outside for her turn to see Daddy. When it finally came, she ran to him. And when she reached him, he was able to do something he hadn't done for weeks with his painful, cancerous arm in a sling—give her a big hug.

"Well, what do *you* think?" he asked with his irrepressible smile.

"Daddy," she said, "I'm glad they took your arm off."

"You are?" he asked, slightly taken off guard. "How come?"

"Because now you can hug me again."

As traumatic as his experience was in many ways, Dave Dravecky wasn't broken by what happened to him. Shaken, yes. Set back. Honest about his struggles. But not shattered.

He would never climb a mound again as a professional baseball pitcher, never again put his rally cap on in the dugout or get another strikeout to go in his record book. In an instant, his status as a pro pitcher dropped totally out of the box scores. But that didn't finish Dave Dravecky. It just moved him into a different league.

In the Official Scorer's book of life—the one that tracks each of us daily as a spouse, a parent, and a godly man or woman—he pitched a winning game. He may have switched positions from a ballplayer to a spectator, but as a person, he made it to the All-Star game.

Only Two Choices

Like Dave Dravecky, you have only two choices when you face challenges to your neatly-laid-out LifeMap. Those two options are very different. And the choice you make will radically affect the way you treat others, how highly you value yourself, and even your personal health.

What are your options?

Dave Dravecky illustrates one choice you can make—to confidently and positively face the future. I call that learned hopefulness, the seventh element of the LifeMapping process.

What comes from the Dravecky school of facing the future? Try an honest optimism that leads to action, not denial. It spurs you to make a clear plan, keeps a tremendous, lifelong challenge before you, and draws out your best efforts at commitment and self-control. But learned hopefulness is not your only option.

Many of us regularly make a choice to view what's ahead in a way that almost guarantees a losing season. And it's usually made when we wait until we get a wake-up call from life before we face the future. Consider these examples:

- A 64-year-old major airline captain suddenly realizes his scheduling supervisor is counting down the flights until he (the captain) is forced to retire.
- The rumor that a number of long-term employees are being laid off shoots through your department so fast that even a Star Wars defense couldn't stop it.
- Your parents notify you that after graduation, your subsidized life-style is going to change radically.
- The ultrasound confirms that it's not just twins coming in six months but *triplets.*

When a changing future can't be avoided, too many of us swerve away from hopefulness and crash headlong into a self-erected barrier called *learned helplessness.* And instead of sticking to our LifeMap plans and moving forward, we let a hurdle stop us from moving forward.

What is learned helplessness? See if you can identify it in the letter that follows.

> I'm 34 years old, and I've been married three times. (Dr. Trent, it's not my fault; I always seem to pick losers.) My problem is my hair . . . or lack of it.
>
> I know that many men feel there's nothing wrong with being bald, but I do. I started losing my hair when I was in high school, and I've tried *everything* I know since then to stop what's happening to me or to reverse it.
>
> I know that my first wife left me because of my hair. My latest wife even told me straight out that I was obsessed with my hair and that was why she was leaving.
>
> *My lack of hair is ruining my life.* I know it's the reason I'm not making sales like I used to. . . . I can tell that people just look at me differently. . . .
>
> When I was 18, I had hair implants put in, and then again at 21. I even went to a well-known plastic surgeon recently and offered to pay him in advance for transplanting whatever skin I needed to fix my head.
>
> All he did was insult me by saying that I shouldn't waste my

money on scalp surgery—the money I spent on my head should go into seeing a psychiatrist!

I'm sure that doctor wasn't a Christian. That's why I'm writing you to ask your advice.

When it comes to facing the future, that man has a major problem. In his mind (or actually on top of his mind) is something that will forever keep him from finishing first in life—or even coming in a strong second. He couldn't picture a successful future for himself without thick, curly locks of hair. And by picking out something in his life that he was powerless to change and making it the source of all his problems, he was directly limiting his entire future.

What that man and many like him have chosen is a life based on learned helplessness, which results when you convince yourself you're missing something in the present that holds the key to your future. Recall the man in our opening story who wished he could escape back into the Wild West, where he thought he could be powerful and manly. Then his LifeMap would work. But he lives in the 1990s and can never go back . . . or move forward.

Where does such thinking come from? Usually, some trauma in the past has convinced the pessimist that "fate" has already dealt him a losing hand and he's powerless to draw any more cards.

How common is this problem? Epidemic.

Now, the problem isn't usually something as noticeably vain as our hair. For most men at least, the difference between a good haircut and a bad one is about a week. And the rest of us are thankful for whatever hair we have left and whatever color it's becoming!

But take a long look in the mirror and ask yourself if you've defined your future according to any of the following:

"If I had married _____, things would have been different."

"If I had chosen college instead of my trade, I wouldn't be in the situation I'm in now."

"If my parents had stayed together . . ."

"If my pastor hadn't fallen . . ."

"If my coach had just played me . . ."

"If my company hadn't transferred me . . ."

"If my father had just given me the breaks he gave my brother . . ."

Learned Helplessness: Following a Map to Disaster

Learned helplessness is a *practiced* way of viewing the future that keeps you dependent on the past. It almost assures that all your plans aren't worth the paper they're penned on, and it can strike a devastating blow to your sense of self-worth and, in turn, to your most meaningful relationships.

If you actually "learn" how to be helpless, how does it happen? What starts you down that increasingly bumpy road? In most cases, it begins with some painful, inescapable situation.

When there's no hope of escape

Back in the 1970s, at the University of Pennsylvania, a surprising observation was made concerning animals. It came from a study that would have animal rights activists up in arms today.[2]

For several weeks, researchers repeatedly placed different dogs in what came to be called a "shuttle box." It was a long, narrow, wooden box with a wire-grill floor that was divided into two compartments.

> *Learned helplessness is a practiced way of viewing the future that keeps you dependent on the past.*

A dog was placed in the first section of the box and then given a painful but not harmful shock. By jumping over the small barrier in front of it to the other section of the box, the animal could escape the shock.

As you might expect, the dogs in the study quickly learned to jump over the barrier and avoid the shock. Small dogs, large dogs, even cats and mice did this. They all reacted the same when put in the shuttle box. When a painful problem presented itself (i.e., the shock), they took speedy action to change their situation and move away from it. But then one day, their "successful" experiment came to a screeching halt.

In another, unrelated experiment, dogs were bound fast in a body harness. Totally unable to move, they were delivered 64, five-second shocks over a 60-minute period. Their responses recorded and the experiment concluded, the next day they, too, were put in a shuttle box.

The shock came on in the box . . . and whereas all the dogs before them had jumped to the safety of the other side, these dogs did *nothing*. They just hunkered down, sat still, and endured the pain.

After repeated shocks, the animals might wander across the barrier, ending the shocks. But they didn't learn anything. The next time they were put in the box, they would again sit still without moving.

A normal dog would whine, bark, or in other ways express its displeasure. What's more, it would actively make some movement to avoid the shock. But these animals did not. They were passive, almost stoic in the way they sat and endured pain.

Physically, the animals had not been harmed. They were fully capable of taking action to get away from the pain. But mentally, that small barrier between them and freedom became Mount Everest.

What conclusion was drawn from those and related studies? Namely, that *uncontrollable negative experiences can freeze up an animal on the inside, making it passive, pessimistic, and withdrawn.*

There's a real danger in jumping from animal behavior to the exceedingly more complex reasoning of human beings. But the comparisons are striking.

Experiencing a major trauma—from losing a spouse, to losing a job, to losing your parents' blessing—affects a person deeply. For some of us, such an event not only marks our past, but it also immobilizes us as we face the future. Instead of actively believing we have the inner resources and determination to solve our problems, we can become passive, dependent, and depressed with the first barrier that goes up. In short, we learn that in the face of pain, escape is hopeless. And what's more, we internalize three terrible perspectives on the future.

1. Effort doesn't match achievement.

If you practice learned helplessness, there is the feeling that no matter what you do, your efforts won't match your achievement. Unfortunately, in our fallen world, sometimes that statement rings true. Take Roger, for example.

Over five years, he worked his way up from bagging groceries to ordering them as assistant manager. He put in countless weekends and unquestioned overtime, and he always gave an accurate accounting at closing time. If anyone deserved the promotion to store manager at the new "mega" store about to open, it was Roger. And that's just what he was verbally promised.

Roger's diligent work stood out to be counted, but he never counted on what happened. The absentee owner decided his nephew was cut out for leadership. And with no notice to Roger's superiors, and no experience on the nephew's part, that unqualified man was given the position.

What about Roger? He was given the grand opportunity to move to the new store and *train* the person who would be sitting in the glass office where he should have sat.

That was nine years ago, and Roger has never been the same since. After two bitter years of enduring emotional pain every day, he left the grocery business for an unsuccessful run at college. After failing at that—and finally his marriage—his life slowed down to a crawl. He's in construction now, but every rent payment is a struggle, and every suggestion to open a door of change is slammed shut.

"Why try?" is Roger's attitude. After all, it's the "breaks" that make you, not back-breaking work. He already tried that and got nothing but shocked. He learned the hard way that effort doesn't equal achievement.

In our fallen world, there's enough truth in that perspective to make some of us accept it as absolute fact. For example, we consistently witness it in the world of sports. Consider the case of two catches, one that was made and one that wasn't.

Jackie Smith was a football tight end who ranked with the best in the NFL for more than a dozen years. Several times All-Pro, he was the career reception leader for the St. Louis Cardinals before he was traded. His efforts over more than a decade inched him toward the Hall of Fame—until one play was run.

It was Super Bowl Sunday, January 1976, and his new team, the Dallas Cowboys, was marching for the winning touchdown against the upstart Pittsburgh Steelers. With his patented moves, Jackie Smith broke free from the defensive coverage and stood wide open in the end zone.

Roger Staubach, the Cowboys' All-Pro quarterback, threw a soft spiral that flew right toward Smith's numbers and those sure-grip hands. But this time, his hands became boards.

The ball bounced off his hands, onto the turf, and the Cowboys lost their chance to score. They would go on to lose the game as well. Jackie Smith spent 12 years as a player, with miles of reception yardage, a room full of awards . . . and one dropped pass.

On a radio talk show I heard *nearly 20 years after that game*, Smith was *still* having to defend what happened on that one play. All his years of achievement were forgotten.

The second catch involved another receiver, an overachiever named Phil McConkey with the New York Giants. He played less than half as long as Jackie Smith (and often as a backup). But he had one terrific game—in a later Super Bowl—and he made one spectacular catch.

What was McConkey's fate? Front-cover notice on *Sports Illustrated* and lasting adulation from the fans for whom "the catch" was a key to a Super Bowl victory.

Is the fate of those two men fair? In many cases in our society, effort *isn't* rewarded as much as achievement. But taking a shortcut to fame or fortune (or a degree or position) doesn't carve out the inner depth and maturity that consistency does. While McConkey may get more credit, there's no question who was the better career receiver.

You can see the same thing in two doctors who carry the same two letters behind their names: M.D. There's a huge difference between the head surgeon at the hospital who has performed 500 heart surgeries and the newly commissioned resident who has assisted on five.

Would you stay on a plane if the flight attendant announced as you taxied away from the gate, "Serving you today is Captain Johnson. Now, this is the first flight that he's ever piloted, and he's never actually *landed* a plane this size. But he's done great at video games that simulate flight, and we're sure he can get us off the ground and land us safely"?

Effort does bring inner rewards, even if there's no outward recognition or achievement. Unfortunately, the pain of not seeing your efforts rewarded can convince you that it's pure chance that counts, not persistence. And if that is the case, what's the use of genuine effort?

You may not see instant changes if you begin to develop and put into practice what you've learned in the LifeMapping process. But by dealing with your past in a positive way and then gaining a clear, accountable plan for the future, you *are* making strides even if things around you don't change instantly.

The pain of not seeing effort bring achievement can bend your LifeMap and lead you toward learned helplessness. Then it's a short step down the road to the next harmful attitude.

2. Someone has stolen the only key to genuine change.

Most people who are lost on the road to learned helplessness often feel that not only does fate rule them, but it's also a *cruel* fate that puts the single key they need to be happy just out of reach.

The story I told earlier of the man who lost his hair is one example of this mindset. Another is Brian, who was the older of two brothers. If Dad should have bonded with anyone, he figured, it should have been him, not his younger brother. He wore his heart out to please his father. But no matter how far he stretched toward him, he could never reach the arms of acceptance he wanted so much. Instead, he had grown up watching his younger brother and father bond ever closer together.

In a climate of unfair comparison and favoritism, Brian made a subtle but terribly damaging decision. Deep inside, he equated what he was missing with what he could never become—*younger*. And because he focused on something that could never happen as his sole key to happiness in the future, he became a committed pessimist . . . and eventually sank into clinical depression.

In studies of pessimists, they persistently look *backward*.[3] For example, pessimists consistently grow up wanting to be younger, like Brian; optimists grow up looking forward and wishing they were older. By never being able to "forget what lies behind," pessimists stay stuck in their pain rather than "pushing forward" to a positive future.

If you feel your effort doesn't match your achievement and that the only key to happiness is forever out of reach, you're also likely to hold a third perspective that can kill the most positive LifeMap.

3. I'm all alone in my pain.

During the experiments that first showed learned helplessness, the dogs who had experienced the repeated shocks were verbally, even physically, encouraged to jump the barrier, but they didn't. While the shock was going on, it was as if they drew so far into an inner, protective shell that they were oblivious to outside encouragement.

I've seen the same type of behavior in countless men and women with whom I've counseled. Pam was one of them. She grew up on an Indian reservation, where her father pastored a mission church. When it came to discipline, her father wasn't just strict—he was severe.

One Sunday when she was nine years old, for example, she was sitting next to a friend at the back of the church, whispering about something they were going to do after the service. In the middle of his sermon, her father called out Pam's name, and he ordered her to come up front. Before the entire congregation, he laid into her about how disrespectful and dishonoring she was being in church. And then he took her outside (but in full view of the congregation from the windows) and gave her an embarrassing and humiliating whipping that she has never forgotten.

Many years later, when Pam's marriage began crumbling, her pain called forth echos from the past. Wrapped in the powerlessness she felt as a child, she grew almost comatose when it came to listening to her husband's complaints or to any counsel.

Many men and women who have gone through some kind of trauma see a painful situation coming and beat a hasty, inner retreat. Instead of being open to counsel or hearing others cry for help, they pull further and further inside, isolating themselves more and more and cutting themselves off from genuine help—and from a successful future.

Such a deep sense of impenetrable loneliness can lead to disaster. Among those who share that mind-set are compulsive gamblers, sexaholics, alcoholics, and child abusers. Convinced deep inside that there is no escape from their pain, they abuse a drug or behavior to somehow deaden the pain. But they only compound it in the process and get further mired in their problems as a result.

The book of Proverbs has much to say about the "sluggard" and the "fool," both models for learned helplessness. One of the verses that applies shows the foolishness of inner isolation: "He who separates himself [from God and others] seeks his own desire, he quarrels against all sound wisdom" (Prov. 18:1). And the final result of having no future: "The sluggard buries his hand in the dish, and will not even bring it back to his mouth" (Prov. 19:24).

Have you given over your future to some unpredictable fate, not to consistent effort? Does some missing "key" keep the door locked to change in your life? Are you hard of hearing when it comes to accepting or even asking for sound counsel?

If you answer yes, you're right where the enemy wants you. Instead of following a LifeMap headed toward fullness of life in Christ, you're following a dead-end trail toward fractured relationships and an unfulfilled life.

But there is hope. If you can learn to be helpless, you can also learn to reverse the process. It happens over time, not overnight. But your LifeMap doesn't have to be just window dressing or something reserved for those "motivated" others. In the next chapter, you can learn to practice learned hopefulness and see it help you over those barriers that currently hold you back from real change.

$\mathcal{P}$racticing Learned Hopefulness

We've talked at length about learned helplessness. Now let's get a clear picture of its opposite—the seventh element of the LifeMapping process, learned hopefulness.

In even the most painful past or present situation, you still face a choice. Even if you're helpless to change your immediate circumstances, you *can* choose to make inner alterations to your character. And one of the most important ways to keep your LifeMap on track, even amidst future trials or transitions, is to practice learned hopefulness.

Before we define and elaborate on this important element of LifeMapping, let's look at someone who practiced it. In the next two paragraphs that summarize years of courage and unbridled optimism, see if you can pick out who I'm writing about. One hint: You saw him in the 1992 presidential campaign.

Over My Dead Body

Two years in solitary confinement. Leg irons shackled around his ankles 15 hours a day. No light in his cell except for that single bulb that came on at dark and stayed on until daybreak.

After more than 300 brutal interrogations, having his already-broken leg deliberately snapped, being beaten in the face with a fan belt until he went into convulsions, and repeatedly being shown pictures of Jane Fonda leading protesters back home while he was denied letters from his wife—*all that and he was only halfway through his 2,714 days in captivity.*

If anyone should have been a candidate for learned helplessness, it was Commander James Stockdale (now Admiral Stockdale, retired). Yet as the senior American officer at the infamous "Hanoi Hilton," he never gave up and never gave in to the enemy's demands that he be used for propaganda purposes.

In the hands of his brutally cruel North Vietnamese captors, he had no power to change his circumstances. But he maintained—actually *increased*—his personal resolve to the point that it was unbreakable. When they threatened to kill him if he didn't give in to their demands for phony confessions and publicity photos, his reply was, "Over my dead body will I be used. Over my dead body will I let my fellow prisoners down."

Admiral Stockdale was Ross Perot's pick for the position of vice president in the 1992 election, and he was a man of unbridled optimism and unflinching courage. But if his strength seems like something you and I could never reach, let me tell you another story about someone who had to develop learned hopefulness the hard way. Maybe you can relate to his story a little more easily.

Fourth Down . . . and a Future to Go

Football middle linebackers have a look about them. Maybe it's their eyes that are always darting back and forth. Perhaps it's their inner intensity or their ability to intimidate everyone—even waitresses who are hustling to bring them coffee.

All through college, David was at the center of his college team's defense. They played an attacking, punishing style that had taken them to two bowl games and pounded opponents each Saturday. David was as powerful as they come on the playing field. But in one play during the preseason of his senior year, David's knee was shattered, and along with it his football career. For the first time in his life, he seemed powerless to control his situation.

Imagine what it's like to have a LifeMap whose goal cards read "Play pro ball," "Work toward All-Pro," and "Use my income from the NFL to help ministries and others." Then imagine taking them down and putting up "No goals," "No direction," "No income."

When I met David, he was recuperating from knee surgery and facing the fact that he would never play football again. His anticipated livelihood gone and his options uncertain, he had turned his frustration inward and was fighting a losing season within himself. That's when we had a long talk and I told him much of what I'd like to present to you now.

In the last chapter, we saw how learned helplessness follows three downward steps. Like that twisted counterpart, learned hopefulness is also built on three important steps. But these three uplifting steps can spell the beginning of a special future—even if you feel you're at the end of the line.

1. Learned hopefulness starts with commitment.

That day, as I sat for hours talking with David, three things stood out. All three of them were steps David had taken to become a successful football player, and now those same qualities could help him take hold of learned hopefulness.

One thing quickly became obvious. Years before, David had made a *commitment* that he was going to be an outstanding football player. That commitment took him through the two-a-day practices during training camp, the unreasonable coaches, and the occasional crushing defeats.

He had demonstrated that he could plan a life's direction and head full-speed toward it. He had trouble seeing it in the midst of his trial, but he had already demonstrated the inner strength to develop learned hopefulness—a commitment to move forward toward reachable goals.

2. Learned hopefulness is maintained through self-control.

Once David made the commitment to become a football star, he linked it with tremendous self-control. While other teens were getting summer jobs, sitting as lifeguards around the pool, he was driving steel on a construction crew. When average people still had their heads on their pillows, he was pounding the pavement and running wind-sprints. His commitment gave him the discipline to make sacrifices . . . all because they pointed toward an ultimate end.

3. *Learned hopefulness centers on a significant challenge.*

Each college football season, a clear-cut challenge was put before David: to be the best at his position and to help his team win the conference championship and a major bowl game.

With loads of eager teams and coaches and benches filled with talent, that was an enormous challenge. And for year after year since high school, that challenge gave him a reason to face the future. But David's commitment, self-control, and challenge all evaporated in that single play when his knee was blown out . . . or did they?

Actually, those important habits of the heart hadn't been lost; they just moved behind a cloud. For as David and I talked that day, it was as if the clouds lifted and he saw again what it would take to be successful, this time outside football.

What David learned that day is what I want to show you in this chapter. Namely, when it comes to getting over barriers to positive change, you need the same three things he practiced.

Commitment

If your future seems bleak, the first thing to do is to go back to your commitments. David was already a Christian, and it was right there that we started as I asked him three questions.

"Do you want your life to count for Jesus Christ?" I inquired first.

"Absolutely," he said.

No matter how your circumstances change, your commitment to Christ can be that essential anchor in the storm. And because He is your solid rock, you may be lashed by the storm, but you won't be washed away.

Next I asked, "One day, do you want to be a husband and the kind of parent God would have you be?"

Again, the answer was a resounding yes.

Finally I asked him, "Are you willing to do whatever it takes to be the man God wants you to be?"

"Sure," he said. "It's just that I don't know who He wants me to be now that I'm not a football player!" His LifeMap had totally changed . . . or had it?

A first key to sorting out the confusion came with the commitment he had made to Christ as a *person*, not just a football player. More specifically, he wanted to be the best, most-growing person he could be. Once he had re-affirmed his commitment to those goals, it was time to draw on the second factor that could help him move over his huge barrier.

Self-control

It may surprise you, but for men and women I see in counseling, *the degree of self-control they have is in direct proportion to their feelings of self-worth.*

In times of transition, when our LifeMaps get challenged or blasted, we often lose the emotional energy to discipline our attitudes and appetites. We "reward" ourselves with junk food instead of exercise; we let five hours a night go by before we finally stumble over and turn off the television; then we procrastinate on what we need to do at work the next day.

> *In times of transition, we often lose the emotional energy to discipline our attitudes and appetites.*

Self-control is a daily decision to make A-priority items those we work on first. (And opening the mail or watching soaps on TV should go down near Z on anyone's list.) As author Richard Foster put it, self-discipline is simply doing what we need to do when we need to do it.

A Clear Challenge

It's true that the biggest challenge on David's LifeMap disappeared in seconds. But that didn't mean he couldn't look at his God-given strengths and abilities, gain counsel from others, and begin to design and head toward another challenge. That's what another man named Don had to do, and he did it very successfully.

Don had built his life around his family. All three boys had been athletes, both in high school and college. He had coached their Little League teams. Even in the changeable Seattle weather, he had watched every game and many practices as the years went by.

He was as supportive as a father could be—and as lost as a man could be when his sons outgrew sports. In tears, he admitted to his middle son, "I've got to find a purpose beyond you boys. I've been so wrapped up in your sports, I've lost any other direction."

I'm thankful I can say that Don did find a new purpose when his sons left home. Today he's still working with young men, teaching, coaching, encouraging, and loving them. But many of the boys he works with now have never known a father's love. They're part of a voluntary inner-city program that puts kids at a study table after school with a snack and tutors to help them. Only when the boys have put in their study time are they free to join in the basketball and baseball games that Don oversees. His three days a week volunteering with this ministry have him continue to use his coaching and encouraging strengths, and they've made a world of difference in those kids' lives and his own.

When our children leave home, we complete a major project, or we graduate from school, many of us lose the major challenge that has kept us going. And that nagging sense of uselessness and purposelessness can tear us down and even destroy our health.

How clear is your purpose in life? If your LifeMap has been rearranged by a forced job change or a core-relationship change, it may be time to redraw the future toward other places where God can use you.

With David, it was clear that after football, he needed a new goal and mission. We talked about his strengths as a person, about what gave him the most fulfillment in life and what he most enjoyed doing. Interestingly, all the feedback I received had to do with solving problems and practicing analytical strengths.

Math was his favorite subject in school. Calling the signals on defense became just another problem-solving exercise. Even helping classmates or someone he was dating work through difficult problems gave him joy and a sense, like Eric Liddle's, that his strengths were bringing him fulfillment and giving God pleasure.

I asked David if helping people solve problems that were crippling them was a big enough goal to last a lifetime. "You bet!" he said. With all the problems people get themselves in, it certainly seemed like a mission with a future! But how, specifically, would he help them?

As we talked further about what problems he saw that most distressed him in people and that he'd most like to solve, he jumped on one aspect—helping people with physical problems. Again, there seemed to be enough people struggling in this area to command his attention until the rapture. David especially thought of older football players who had become so crippled later in life that they could hardly walk.

The more we talked, the more excited he became about the idea that he could begin to make a difference in the lives of people who were hurting physically—the freedom it would give them and the way it would reduce stress in their marriages. We both grew excited as we pictured him as a physical or occupational therapist or in some other capacity where he could help hurting people. But then we hit a potential problem: David had no formal training in a health-related career.

Here's where many people get bogged down. They make the commitment to go forward the best they can. But then they let the "realities" of additional schooling or training derail their dreams.

As David and I continued talking, we saw that even though his formal education and former vocation hadn't directly prepared him for his mission, they *had* indirectly. The hours of discipline on the practice field all stressed "doing things right" in the game; the college courses in communication would help him motivate others and explain clearly what they needed to do to get better. Even his summer job of laying steel stressed the need for patience and for building slowly and well if you wanted something done right. All those were factors he would need when working with hurting people.

David went away convinced that he had a new mission to fulfill and confident that he now had a LifeMap that could get him there.

Did David's story end there? No. His readjusted LifeMap took him to a Southern California school where he began studying to become an occupational therapist. And while he took almost five years to complete what's normally a two-and-a-half-year program, he finally graduated and landed a job with a sports injury clinic, where he is now making a difference.

Because he maintained a LifeMap that kept the end in view, he didn't mind having to cook pizzas for a short time to pay for his extra classes. For in the process of being a pizza cook, he knew he was learning something that could help him be a better therapist one day. That might involve "coffee cup" counseling with another employee God brought alongside or learning more about business accounting from the owner.

Suddenly, setbacks and delays were easier to deal with because even in the detours, there were important things to be learned. And the learning didn't happen only at work. With his commitment to Christ and a vocational direction in clear view, he was very aware that if he was going to teach others patience, self-control, and good health habits, he had to demonstrate them himself.

David's story isn't an exception. It actually points out a rule we all need to follow. Namely, as believers, we don't have the option to traffic in learned helplessness.

Learned hopefulness focuses on our strengths, looks at changes as coming from the hands of a sovereign yet loving God, and brings out the best in us through heightened commitment and self-control. It also puts before us that third essential component we must have to be motivated to move forward— a significant challenge.

Are you tired of "paper plans" that never pay off? Has learned helplessness held you back? Then remember the biblical antidote of commitment, self-control, and gaining a significant challenge. There's one more thing that will be a great help, too—it's the eighth element of LifeMapping called *memorial markers*.

" 'For I know the plans that I have for you,' declares the LORD,
'plans . . . to give you a future and a hope' " (Jer. 29:11).

Memorial Markers

As our look at LifeMapping nears an end, it's my hope that you are more aware of where you've come from, more certain about where you're going, and more confident that the Lord Jesus has been with you through every freeze point, every flash point, every twist and transition of your life. It's my hope, too, that you've got a positive future you can prayerfully pursue, surrounded by the commitment and conviction to practice learned hopefulness.

But there's one final element of LifeMapping that needs to be explored. If learned hopefulness can help you deal with problems that seem to throw you off course, memorial markers can add an incredibly powerful way to record and maintain gains in your life.

But what exactly do I mean by a memorial marker? Actually, it's a concept as old as the Exodus.

Joshua's First Day on the Job

"Let this be a sign among you, so that when your children ask later, saying, 'What do these stones mean to you?' then you shall say to them, 'Because the waters of the Jordan were cut off before the ark of the covenant of the LORD; when it crossed the Jordan, the waters of the Jordan were cut off.' So these stones shall become a memorial to the sons of Israel forever" (Josh. 4:6-7).

Do you have a good first-day-on-the-job story? Joshua certainly did. The LORD woke him with the challenge to lead the entire nation of Israel across the Jordan River at flood stage—*without getting wet.* The catch wasn't for Joshua to build a bridge but to trust in the same God who had once before parted the waters for Israel to pass through.

Actually, Joshua was getting a second chance to follow a LifeMap that had been handed to Moses and the rest of his generation. If you'll recall, Moses called on Pharaoh to "let my people go." Finally, after a series of plagues, they did escape from Egypt. But as they came to the Red Sea, Pharaoh's heart hardened again, and he raced after the fleeing Israelites to kill them. That was not to be, and in one of the greatest miracles recorded in the Scriptures, Almighty God parted that sea to let His people go free, then crashed the water down on top of the pursuing Egyptians.

Can you imagine the incredible sight those people saw that day? God's power miraculously intervened to save them. And later, they would see God's power to sustain them with water and with manna to eat.

But even a steady dose of miracles didn't increase those people's faith. Remember their response to the report of the 12 spies who had gone ahead to scope out the Promised Land. Ten of the spies (I dare you to remember any of their names) brought back a bad report of giants in the land and an unconquerable enemy dead ahead. Only two of the 12—Joshua and Caleb (lots of people name their kids after them)—remembered a God who could destroy an army of Egyptians complete with iron chariots and who would fight for them now.

But the pessimism of the ten spies would prevail. And in God's judgment on their lack of faith, all the people of that generation except Joshua and Caleb would die without entering the Promised Land. Now it was time for a second chance at God's first choice.

Joshua had already been in the Promised Land once, and he didn't hesitate at all to go back. This time, however, there were a few more lunches to pack than 12. The Ark of the Covenant went ahead of him, and then the entire nation followed. As the robes of the priests dipped in the Jordan, the waters of that flooded river stood up above and below them—an incredible miracle no less marvelous than that first parting years before.

That's the story of what happened when Joshua entered the land. Let me make two applications, and then we'll look at what happened *next* that involves memorial markers.

Don't Be Too Hard on Those Early Israelites

First, it's easy to judge those "faithless" Israelites who froze up instead of following Moses, Joshua, Caleb, and God into the Promised Land. But recall from the last chapter how a painful, inescapable situation produces a condition of helplessness in an animal or person.

Where had the nation of Israel just come from? Slavery—*painful, inescapable*, brutal slavery. Little or no straw to make their bricks. A life where they learned that nothing they could do would free them, and nothing they could say ever counted. That's a climate where a feeling of helplessness would develop easily.

But that all changed when Moses brought back the power and love of a mighty God. The people now had every reason to hope. But when the trials came, where did they want to head? Forward toward God and learned hopefulness? No, they wanted to go backward toward Egypt and again take their fill of leeks and garlic. In fact, several times they begged Moses to let them go back to Egypt and slavery instead of moving forward to the Promised Land.

Second, can you better understand now why the transition going on in Russia is bitter and intense for so many? And why so many "old style" hardliners are calling for people to "go back" into Communism—even though it is a failed, corrupt, killing system? They've come from generations of "helplessness," and it can be an addictive, pernicious pattern.

Without a doubt, people can be swayed from their hope. Just ask the people of Israel who never got to go into the Promised Land. Or ask Peter, who denied Christ three times after swearing he would die first.

But people can come back. Peter, indeed, turned back into that rock Jesus had pictured him to be, and the next generation of Israelites didn't complain—they got up and moved out when Joshua said, "Let's go!"

One major difference between the two partings

There are many similarities between the parting of the Red Sea and the parting of the Jordan. Both sealed a man in the leadership role God had given him with all the people. Both were mighty demonstrations that God's power was with Moses and Joshua from the first day of their ministries. But there was one difference, and you saw it in the verses quoted at the start of this chapter.

Namely, *after Joshua had gone through the waters, God had him go back.* Actually, God had him send 12 men back to the Jordan, and this time they were to pick up 12 stones from the middle of the dry riverbed as a testimony of God's power and purpose.

Those stones would become a memorial marker—a clear picture that would remind young and old that yes, indeed, God had worked in a mighty way that day and was working in their lives still.

That's a great story, but what does it have to do with LifeMapping? *Plenty!*

So far, you've pinned up cards that represent strengths, successes, and acceptance levels. You've pictured freeze points, flash points, and untied transitions. You've dealt with image management issues, forged goals for the major areas of your life, and even been challenged to keep commitment, self-control, and your clear plan ahead of you by practicing learned hopefulness.

But one thing is missing. *It's a tangible reminder of the process you've been through.* It's a memorial marker that can give you a picture of all you can become. It's something that has proved a great help to Jim and Susan, the couple whose story started this book.

The Real Thing

That opening story was a dramatic instance of a man who took image management to new heights. By not telling his wife that he'd been married before, their trust level instantly went from rock solid to rubble when she learned the truth. Restoring their relationship took time, lots of counseling, and, finally, Susan's willingness to forgive. But they got through the storm together with a LifeMap that had changed for all the right reasons.

When the time came for their last counseling appointment, I had something wrapped up to give them. I passed it across the table to them, and they opened it with questioning looks. Once the package was open, they had even more questions.

Inside the package was a nice oak frame and nonglare glass covering two matted dollar bills. At least they *looked* like dollar bills. But upon closer examination, Jim and Susan saw that the top bill was actually a counterfeit (one I'd ripped off from my kids' playroom), while the bottom bill was the real thing. And the reason for the difference wasn't just that I'm cheap.

Do you get the picture and see how those two bills might be a memorial marker for them?

What was the main problem they had when they first came in? It was Jim's being a "phony." That's why the top dollar bill was a counterfeit. It looked good from a distance, but you couldn't cash it in, even on a toy. That bill was a picture of what Jim had been.

The crisp, fresh-from-the-mint bill on the bottom was the real thing, however. The "real thing" was what Jim wanted so much to be and what Susan struggled so hard to believe he could become.

Those dollar bills were like 12 stones from a river. They pictured where they had been, what God had done for them, and what He promised to do in their future. That picture still hangs in their home today.

All kinds of objects, pictures, or even animals or plants might serve as your memorial markers. (For a list of more possibilities, turn to Appendix A.) One of my favorites is made up of three handwritten letters that I carry everywhere I go.

Three Letters of Love

If you run into me at a conference or at the airport sometime and I've got my organizer with me, you have permission to ask to see those three letters. Two of them wouldn't win any art contests, but they're invaluable to me nonetheless. One is from my precious older daughter, Kari, and the other is from my precious younger daughter, Laura. They're letters of love, signed and colored as only kids can do. They help me remember that my family ministry begins with loving my own family first and then seeking to help others.

The third letter I carry isn't from Cindy, though I take her picture with me everywhere. (You also have permission to ask to see it as my proof that I married above myself!) That third letter is from my Great Uncle Max.

I haven't always been the greatest of grandnephews to him, but for more than 20 years, he's been the closest thing I've had to a loving dad. We didn't meet until I was in college, and we built a steady, growing relationship over the years. I sat with him at the hospital for two days straight when his wife was run over by a wrecker and lived to tell about it. I flew to his bedside when she passed away a number of years later with Alzheimer's.

Between those times of trial, Uncle Max loved me, grudgingly adopted me, and most of all let me adopt him. He looked so much like my father (all the Trents have that "look"), but I could laugh with him, cry with him, and even give him a hug—things I could never do with my own father.

As his health was failing, Uncle Max sent me a letter, asking if I would hang on to his living will should the worst happen. And while it was a sad note citing the realities of his advancing years (86 at the time of writing), it contains one line that has caused me to carry it every day since.

For a young boy who always wanted a father, who grew up with a LifeMap that had a missing place where that significant person should have been, what Uncle Max said in that letter brought tears to my eyes and a sense of closure to my heart. "Thank you, John," he wrote with a shaky hand on paper that's now worn with creases. "You have helped me so much in the past, and I am sure you will continue to do so."

And then he added the words, "*Because you are my son.* Affectionately, Max."

I had grown up with a hole in my heart, but finally I had a father who loved me and was proud to call me "son."

In addition to those three letters I carry, I keep a piece of Colorado granite on my office bookshelf. It's not large or impressive. If you turn it over, all you'll see is a handwritten date: June 12, 1967. That's the day I was at Young Life's SilverCliff ranch in Colorado and made a major commitment of my life to serve the Lord. I've carried that rock from office to office ever since, and it's still a reminder to me of my calling and commitment.

(For the story of my "Hospital bracelet" memorial marker, see "A Final Challenge to Each Reader" at the back of this book.)

I don't know what your memorial markers will be as you look over your LifeMap. Perhaps you'll pick a sturdy mantel clock that pictures a stable past and a precision-crafted future. It might be a ceramic rose that forever blooms now that you know Jesus, the rose of Sharon. It might be that bookmark your son made at camp that says "World's Best Mom. I love you, Jimmy."

Whatever your memorial marker turns out to be, I'd love to know. In fact, I'd love to hear from you regarding what you learned about this whole process of seeing highlights of your life in full picture form.

We've looked at the "whys" and "how to's" of LifeMapping, and we've now seen in detail the eight elements that can capture your life story. But while this book is coming to a close, it wouldn't be complete if we didn't know the ending. To learn that, turn the page to our last chapter—a few pages that tell "the rest of the story" of LifeMapping and of someone who is the Author of Happy Endings.

Walking with the Author of Happy Endings

As you've gone through this book and recorded your life story, perhaps you've found yourself walking on a path you would rather not travel. It may be a road twisted by detours, covered with icy confusion, and headed toward a dead end of despair.

If your LifeMap reflects the deepest hurts and most profound losses, is it *really* possible to do what was promised in the first chapter, *to rewrite your life story?* Even now, with all the insights into your strengths and a "highlight film" of your life before you, is that enough to sponge away the hurt and get you on track toward a positive future?

That depends on who's walking beside you.

On the Road to Fulfillment

If anyone seemed to be on a short road to ruin, it was that shattered group of Jesus' followers after His crucifixion. A few had watched their Master be arrested and led away at Gethsemane. Many more had witnessed His being paraded through the streets of Jerusalem, carrying His own cross. Some had even stood by and watched the One they called the Messiah suffer, die, and be buried.

By the next morning, whatever dreams their LifeMaps might have held seemed all but destroyed. Their plans were thwarted. Their hopes had turned to dust.

That was the situation two of Jesus' followers found themselves in on Easter morning, in the midst of a seven-mile walk to the town of Emmaus. The road looked darker and bleaker with each step as they recounted all that had happened—until someone unexpected joined them on their journey.

We don't know at what point Jesus joined those two. But we are sure of one thing, and it's something you can be sure of as well. When they began to walk with the Author of Happy Endings, their journey turned from frustration to fulfillment. From confusion to clarity. From questioning to quickened hearts and renewed resolve.

The scriptural account of that journey is recorded below. It may take you a minute to read through the whole story, but don't miss the message it has for you on your journey through life.

> Now that same day two of them were going to a village called Emmaus, about seven miles from Jerusalem. They were talking with each other about everything that had happened. As they talked and discussed these things with each other, Jesus himself came up and walked along with them; but they were kept from recognizing him.
>
> He asked them, "What are you discussing together as you walk along?"
>
> They stood still, their faces downcast. One of them, named Cleopas, asked him, "Are you only a visitor to Jerusalem and do not know the things that have happened there in these days?"
>
> "What things?" he asked.
>
> "About Jesus of Nazareth," they replied. "He was a prophet, powerful in word and deed before God and all the people. The chief priests and our rulers handed him over to be sentenced to death, and they crucified him; but we had hoped that he was the one who was going to redeem Israel. And what is more, it is the

third day since all this took place. In addition, some of our women amazed us. They went to the tomb early this morning but didn't find his body. They came and told us that they had seen a vision of angels, who said he was alive. Then some of our companions went to the tomb and found it just as the women had said, but him they did not see."

He said to them, "How foolish you are, and how slow of heart to believe all that the prophets have spoken! Did not the Christ have to suffer these things and then enter his glory?" And beginning with Moses and all the Prophets, he explained to them what was said in all the Scriptures concerning himself.

As they approached the village to which they were going, Jesus acted as if he were going farther. But they urged him strongly, "Stay with us, for it is nearly evening; the day is almost over." So he went in to stay with them.

When he was at the table with them, he took bread, gave thanks, broke it and began to give it to them. Then their eyes were opened and they recognized him, and he disappeared from their sight. They asked each other, "Were not our hearts burning within us while he talked with us on the road and opened the Scriptures to us?"

They got up and returned at once to Jerusalem. There they found the Eleven and those with them, assembled together. . . . While they were still talking . . . Jesus himself stood among them and said to them, "Peace be with you." (Luke 24:13-33, 36, NIV)

It's amazing how God's Word, clearly explained and carefully laid out, has the power to sweep away the storm clouds and usher in calm and peace. That's what happened in the hearts of Cleopas and his unnamed friend, and that's what can happen deep inside you as well.

If you're a Christian, you've got a tremendous advantage. In fact, you've got something far more helpful than a "map." You've got *Someone* who can be your personal guide—someone who can help you turn the corner on untied transitions, steer through emotional freeze points, and avoid altogether that road called *image management*.

Now that you can see your life story, you can also have your "eyes opened" to see the One who walks beside you. He's not detached and remote even from the darkest point on your LifeMap. He's not a "high priest who cannot sympathize with our weaknesses, but one who has been tempted in all things as we are, yet without sin" (Heb. 4:15).

This Someone has been down the road we walk. He's the only one who has even gone *around* the last corner and come back from the dead to stand beside us. To lead us. To shepherd us. To love us each step of the way until we're safely home with Him in heaven.

Therefore, let's take one final look at a LifeMap. This map recounts a measure of our Lord's life—not every event, but a few selected high points that show how you can pick up any topper card on your own LifeMap and see that He has been there first. What encouragement you can gain as you look at the life of Christ to see that He knows your trials, can feel your transitions, and sets before you clear goals and the strength to reach them!

Far from trying to squeeze the King of Glory into a box, I pray this look at our Lord will deepen your love for and awe of Him. He is big enough to speak all creation into being, yet He humbled Himself so much that He fit into a manger in Bethlehem.

There's another reason this look is necessary as well. Namely, as you've taken time to map out the direction your life has gone and is now pointed, *you're not the only one watching the outcome.*

Playing Before a Crowd

Therefore, since we are surrounded by such a great cloud of witnesses, let us throw off everything that hinders and the sin that so easily entangles, and let us run with perseverance the race marked out for us. Let us fix our eyes on Jesus, the author and perfecter of our faith, who for the joy set before him endured the cross, scorning its shame, and sat down at the right hand of the throne of God. Consider him who endured such opposition from sinful men, so that you will not grow weary and lose heart. (Heb. 12:1-3, NIV)

You've laid out your LifeMap to help you "run the race." But now fix your eyes on the One who has finished ahead of you and who won something worth much more than a gold medal: God's blessing. In doing so, perhaps you can gain a deeper measure of endurance to keep you from growing weary as you move toward the prize. (And for extra credit and great personal benefit, why not take this brief picture of our Lord's story and flesh it out with your own study and thoughts?)

Looking Up to His LifeMap

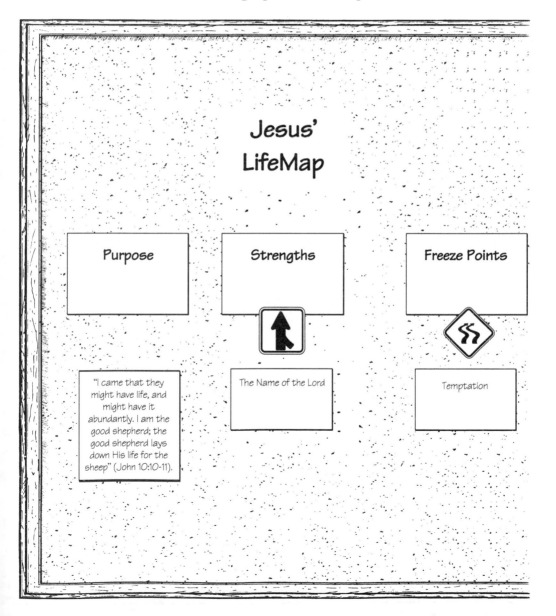

Jesus' LifeMap

Purpose	Strengths	Freeze Points

"I came that they might have life, and might have it abundantly. I am the good shepherd; the good shepherd lays down His life for the sheep" (John 10:10-11).

The Name of the Lord

Temptation

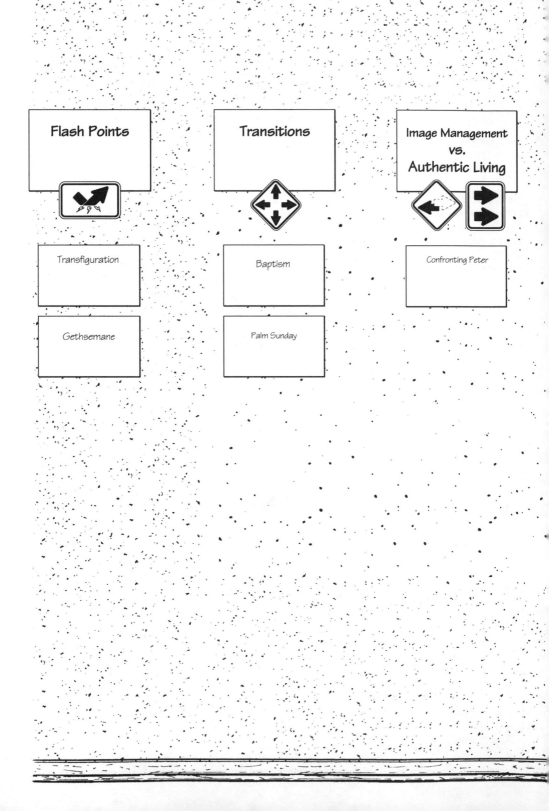

Flash Points

Transitions

Image Management
vs.
Authentic Living

Transfiguration

Baptism

Confronting Peter

Gethsemane

Palm Sunday

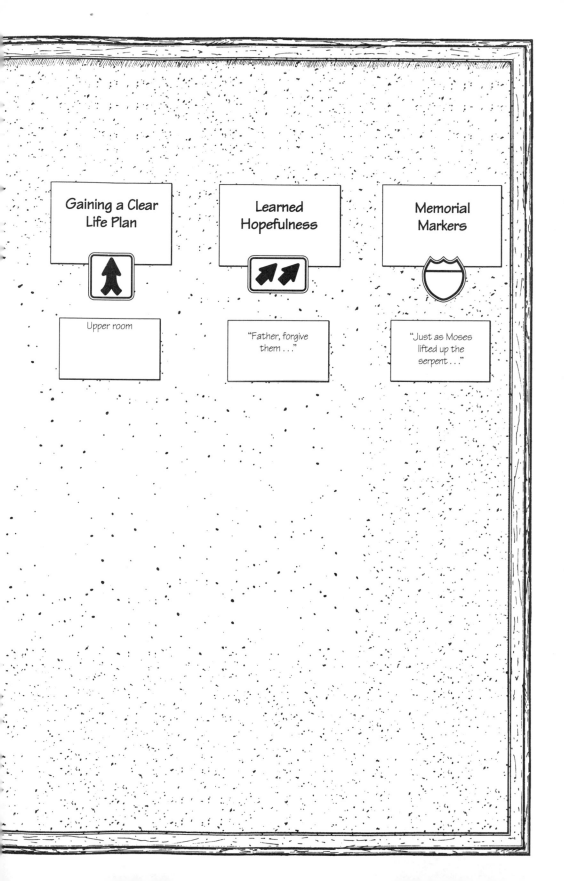

Gaining a Clear Life Plan

Upper room

Learned Hopefulness

"Father, forgive them . . ."

Memorial Markers

"Just as Moses lifted up the serpent . . ."

Strengths: there's power in the name

Many of us may have struggled to fill in the "strengths" section of our LifeMaps, but if we tried to catalogue all our Lord's strengths, we'd stuff the Library of Congress! In a focused way, however, the Scriptures picture His strengths in the names He carries.

In Hebrew culture, people's names stood for all they were and could become. So when the book of Philippians tells us that Jesus inherited "the name which is above every name" (Phil. 2:9), it's a reference to the fullness of deity that dwelled in Him.

God's name was so sacred, so holy, that it wasn't even revealed to His people until Moses asked, "Suppose I go to the Israelites and say to them, 'The God of your fathers has sent me to you,' and they ask me, 'What is his name?' Then what shall I tell them?"

God answered Moses, "I AM WHO I AM. This is what you are to say to the Israelites: 'I AM has sent me to you' " (Exod. 3:13-14, NIV).

Centuries later, Jesus would echo those same words and claim the same name that God revealed to Moses. When confronted by a group of angry Jewish leaders who challenged His authority, He said to them, "Truly, truly, I say to you, before Abraham was born, I AM" (John 8:58).

The Jews who heard Him knew exactly what He had just claimed. That's why their response was to pick up stones to kill Him—the penalty for someone claiming he was God.

But Jesus wasn't speaking blasphemy or laying claim to a title He didn't own. He carried the name above every name with all its authority. And God's name is captured in several different Hebrew words that act like a prism, shedding different-colored lights that reflect shades of His strengths.

For example, Jesus carries the name *Elohim*, the "strong and mighty," the Creator of the world; *Elyon*, the God worthy of reverence and worship; and *Adonai*, the owner and ruler of all men. He bears the authority of *El-Shaddai*, the ultimate source of blessing and comfort for the people of God; *Jehovah*, the unchangeable; and *Jehovah of Hosts*, the Lord and Master of even the angelic hosts.

There were many times, from His first miracles to Palm Sunday, when Jesus heard people celebrate His strengths. But He didn't rely on their opinions of His strengths for His acceptance level. At His baptism, none other than the Lord of heaven Himself celebrated His Son's obedience with the thundering words, "This is My beloved Son, in whom I am well-pleased" (Matt. 3:17).

While Jesus was born fully man, He was also fully God, a mystery unfathomable this side of heaven, but a reflection of the legion of strengths He carried within Him to build up and bless others.

And just think—the God of unsurpassed strengths finds and invests tremendous value in *you*. He saved you with His blood, sealed you with His Holy Spirit, and will stand next to you one day when you approach the Father's throne! And that's just one part of His LifeMap.

Emotional freeze points: the scorching winds of trial and temptation

The Lord's unbridled strengths abounded from all eternity past, yet He voluntarily laid aside His place in heaven to be born a man and step into our world. In so doing, He subjected Himself to all we face—including times of trial that could easily have caused emotional freeze points.

For example, even before He faced the daily abuse and hatred thrown at Him from the Pharisees and Sadducees, there were the 40 days and nights He spent facing the hot winds of death in the desert (see Matt. 4:1-11). Week after week, He was exposed to the bitter heat by day, the numbing cold at night, and the constant battle to fight off His physical hunger and not succumb to Satan's wiles.

John Milton, in his classic *Paradise Regained,* expressed the purpose of this time of testing in the following words, as though spoken by God the Father:

> But first I mean
> To exercise Him in the wilderness;
> There He shall first lay down the rudiments
> Of His great warfare, ere I send Him forth
> To conquer Sin and Death the two grand foes,
> By Humiliation and Strong Sufferance.[1]

During this trying time, Jesus faced a decathlon of multisided appeals to the lust of the flesh, the lust of the eyes, and the boastful pride of life presented by Satan himself, who wanted Him to choose second best.

Any of us would likely have come away from such a jarring experience with a numbing inner layer of hurt, compromise, or pain. But by basing His strength on the Word of God, and by leaning on the Holy Spirit (see Luke 4:1), Jesus emerged from that time of temptation triumphant.

What an example our Lord was of handling potential freeze points! We can also learn from how He treated possible flash points.

Individual flash points: the glory of the transfiguration and the agony of Gethsemane

Jesus certainly encountered pivotal events that marked nearly instantaneous changes. For example, one literal flash point happened at the Mount of Transfiguration. There, before the awestruck eyes of Peter, James, and John, Jesus went through a "metamorphosis" in which He put back on, for just a moment, the glory He had shared with His Father in heaven (see Matt. 17:1ff).

We're told that "His face shone like the sun, and his garments became as white as light" (the same picture we see of the resurrected Christ in Rev. 1:14ff).

Before taking His friends up the mountain, Jesus had just predicted His own death (see Matt. 16:21ff). Now those men who would most need that picture were given a glimpse of the glory He would once again display after the resurrection.

If that flash point displayed His glory and might *externally*, at Gethsemane an *internal* flash point took place. Knowing all, including the horrible death that awaited Him, Jesus took the same small group of disciples to a quiet garden on His last night before the Crucifixion. There He fell before the Father and honestly poured out His desire to avoid the pain—but not if it meant sidestepping God's will.

We read that Jesus was so distraught, He was "pain-wrapped"—in agony over what lay ahead. But even with precious little help from His friends, He battled through the pain and cinched up His faith even tighter. In fact, it was He who woke up the sleeping disciples and stood ready to meet His betrayer!

Christ won the war for our salvation at Calvary, but He had already won a hard-fought victory at Gethsemane. Those few hours of wrestling with that last, heavy calling marked Him with a confidence that would never dip or wane through His final hours. He would face all death could throw at Him in strength, and in His final breath He completed His work in the prophetic words "It is finished."

Besides facing situations that could easily have caused freeze points and even several flash-point occurrences, Jesus went through some incredible transitions.

Transitions: beginnings and endings

You're in the midst of a time of tremendous change? Jesus knows what that's like. Paul recounted the greatest transition in all of eternity in the book of Philippians:

> Although He [Christ Jesus] existed in the form of God, [He] did not regard equality with God a thing to be grasped, but emptied Himself, taking the form of a bond-servant, and being made in the likeness of men. And being found in appearance as a man, He humbled Himself by becoming obedient to the point of death, even death on a cross. Therefore also God highly exalted Him. (2:6-9a)

Jesus went from His place at the right hand of the Father, to a humble birth, to the humiliation of death on a cross, to once again being seated on heaven's throne. What a staggering exchange, and what a towering love for us that prompted it!

While the fact that God became human is the ultimate transition, Jesus went through the everyday transitions we face as well. For example, He went from a boy under authority to His earthly parents to an independent adult.

In one story of His early life, He stayed behind at the temple to learn from the teachers without Joseph and Mary's knowing it. But when they came back and found Him, He willingly went home with them, and "He continued in subjection to them" (see Luke 2:41-52).

Later, at the first event to which Jesus took His disciples, His mother would call on Him to do something about the diminishing wine supply at a wedding. There, instead of bending to her authority, He clearly established a boundary that marked Him as set apart from her control. He told her, "Woman, what do I have to do with you?" (John 2:4). He wasn't condemning her but decreeing His authority and independence. In this case, He would perform the miracle of changing water to wine, but He was following His heavenly Father's guidance, not His mother's command (see John 2:1-12).

Like any of us who have grown up, Jesus went through the transition from child to adult. But He didn't experience only chronological transitions.

Let's return to that incredible scene at the baptism of Jesus, where the entire Trinity burst into sight. There was Jesus, the Son, fulfilling all righteousness in humbling Himself to be baptized. Then as He came up out of the water, the Holy Spirit in the form of a dove descended on Him. And finally, the Father's voice boomed from the heavens, "This is My beloved Son, in whom I am well-pleased" (Matt. 3:17).

What a time of commissioning and declaration . . . and transition! From that point on, Jesus would move from a private world into His public ministry. And as if to demonstrate what a powerful shift had taken place, no sooner had God identified Him as His Son than Jesus was led into the wilderness to be tempted by Satan. (While God the Father had just said, "You are My Son," Satan immediately questioned God's Word in asking Jesus, "If you are *really* God's Son . . .")

From that time of testing forward, Jesus would be walking into the wind as He took confident steps toward the cross.

From child to adult, from private to public ministry, Jesus faced many of the same transitions we do. *And more.* Which of us has had to face the incredible reversal of public opinion that took place over a week? In four days, Jesus would go from hearing adoring crowds and rousing cheers and having palm branches spread before Him, to chants of "Crucify Him! Crucify Him!" jeers, slaps, being spit upon, and having His own palms pierced with nails. Mind-boggling transitions!

Jesus faced transitions more wonderful and terrible than anything in our life stories, but that doesn't minimize those major and minor shifts in our lives. He faced them, too, without compromise or sin, and He can help us get through them as well.

Scripture provides many other helpful examples of the first four elements of LifeMapping. It also records a number of events that illustrate the next four elements. For example, consider the issue of image management versus authentic living.

Image management or authentic living: Peter's confession and chastisement

In a short story of Jesus' dealing with Peter, we can see in two different ways the Lord's complete commitment to authentic living and His unyielding avoidance of image management.

At the time, rumors were flying everywhere in Judea and beyond about who this Jesus was. Healer. Magician. Demon. Deliverer. Resurrected prophet. But "Jesus would not entrust himself to them" (John 2:24, NIV)—or, in modern vernacular, to any public opinion poll or "spin doctor."

When Jesus asked His disciples, "Who do people say that the Son of Man is?" they gave Him a multiple-choice list of His fans' and foes' descriptions. But when He asked Peter, that humble fisherman bluntly said the same thing the angels had echoed: "Thou art the Christ, the Son of the living God" (Matt. 16:16).

Jesus blessed Peter for that declaration of faith, and He went on record as saying He would build His church on it—not because Peter had the right "spin" on who He was, but because Peter had spoken God's truth: "Blessed are you, Simon Barjona, because flesh and blood did not reveal this to you, but My Father who is in heaven" (Matt. 16:17).

Jesus would only commit His "image" to God's Word. That's why He turned so quickly from blessing Peter to blasting him.

After Peter's great declaration, the disciples were ready for lesson two. They knew He accepted the title of God's only Son. Now they needed to know specifically why the Son of Man had come.

Jesus began telling them that as God's Son, His purpose was to suffer and die and be raised on the third day. But Peter "took Him aside and began to rebuke Him, saying, 'God forbid it, Lord! This shall never happen to You' " (Matt. 16:22).

The disciples had plans to break the Roman yoke that bound the people of Israel. But Jesus wasn't interested in breaking anything less than the bond of sin and death that had captured every person. Turning on Peter, Jesus said, "Get behind Me, Satan! You are a stumbling block to Me; for you are not setting your mind on God's interests, but man's" (Matt. 16:23).

Try to put into modern perspective what Peter did in confronting Jesus. Whatever your political persuasion, you have to concede that in 1992, then-Governor Clinton's campaign managers did a superb job of managing and "spinning" their candidate's strengths and weaknesses.

Numerous published accounts reveal that they ran each day of the campaign from a "war room," seeking to position their man one day to take advantage of a positive story, working the next to turn away a negative story before it caused real damage. By managing Clinton's image on an immediate, reactive basis, they could quickly catch which way the political winds were drifting and craft a message to appeal to whatever group he was before.

While that type of strategy might win political elections (and Republicans use it, too), it was the antithesis of Jesus' management style.

In the example above, Peter pulled his candidate aside and rebuked Him for taking an unpopular stance, one that would surely cost Him public opinion "votes." All that talk of going to the cross and saying His disciples had to take up their cross daily and follow Him, too, was politically incorrect. To bring up the cross back then—the hated symbol of Roman oppression—was far worse than telling a *New York Times* reporter today, "We're committed to nuking the whales, putting corporal punishment and public prayer back in our schools, and calling homosexual conduct a sin!"

When Peter tried to put a new "spin" on Jesus' teaching, however, He didn't hesitate a second. "Get behind Me, Satan," He shot out. It was the strongest of language, and it was meant to stop any attempt by Peter to block Him from following God's Word and will.

Jesus would never have been elected to public office in His day or any other. He made far too many ethical demands on Himself and His followers, and He linked far too many promises of rewards with a person's faith and responsibility. He sought to make people authentic, truthful, and without guile. Everything He stood for fought against the image management that determines political fortunes today.

Following Jesus will clearly steer us straight toward authentic, guilt-free living. And if we look to Him, we'll also see that He operated from the basis of a clear, unwavering plan.

Gaining a clear life plan: from the Suffering Servant to the upper room

The plan from which Jesus operated was God's unchanging design. In John 14:24, Jesus said of His message, "The word which you hear is not Mine, but the Father's who sent Me." And in Matthew 5:17 He said, "Do not think that I came to abolish the Law or the Prophets; I did not come to abolish, but to fulfill."

Jesus would never waver from that will of the Father that had existed for all eternity past. As a child, He amazed the scholars with His questions when

He sat with them in the temple. In Capernaum, He amazed the Pharisees with His knowledge of God's Word and "teaching [of] them as one having authority" (Mark 1:22).

He lived God's Word. He breathed it. He would never compromise it. He had a clear plan for His birth and death that existed from all time (see Gen. 3 and God's promise to Adam and Eve that a Messiah would come). And that plan would take Him to the cross.

Look at the prophetic description of the horror of crucifixion penned by the prophet Isaiah. What makes this description even more incredible is that it was written hundreds of years before crucifixion was even *invented* by the Phoenicians. Isaiah 53:5 says, "But He was pierced through for our transgressions, He was crushed for our iniquities; the chastening for our well-being fell upon Him, and by His scourging we are healed."

Jesus also had a clear plan for His disciples when He called them away from their nets: "I will make you fishers of men" (Matt. 4:19). And He had a clear plan for them once He was gone: "Do not let your hearts be troubled. Trust in God; trust also in me. In my Father's house are many rooms; if it were not so, I would have told you. I am going there to prepare a place for you. And if I go and prepare a place for you, I will come back and take you to be with me that you also may be where I am" (John 14:1-3, NIV).

If you've ever felt that your life was out of control or operating on everyone's schedule but your own, a look at Jesus can be a big help. He based His life on a clear plan from start to finish, centering it on God's Word. He was also the premier example of someone who practiced learned hopefulness.

Learned hopefulness: "Father, forgive them."

Picture the scene. The Lord had been up all night. He was shoved through dark alleys and paraded through rocky streets on His way from unjust trials to a hill of crucifixion. If anyone should have been "helpless" in that circumstance, it was Him. But read again the crucifixion passages, and look at the incredible power and hope that jump off the page. No one took His life from Jesus. He voluntarily, purposefully laid it down.

Instead of hating, He prayed "Father, forgive them" for the soldiers who nailed Him to the tree.

When He could have been concerned only about the terrible agony He was suffering, He looked down at His mother and took care of her well-being: "Woman, behold your son. Son, behold your mother."

He cried out, "I am thirsty," not just because of His parched throat, but also in fulfillment of a well-known prophecy in the Psalms of what the suffering-servant Messiah would do (see Ps. 69:21; John 19:28-30).

And finally, He completed His work with the words "*It* is finished"—not "*I* am finished."

Where would such confidence come from on a deadly Friday?

From the assurance of a hope-filled Sunday three days hence—a day when the Father had promised to raise Him from the dead.

Jesus knew that there was no avoiding the cross, no covering it up or hanging anything less on it than a sinless offering. But that knowledge didn't make Him helpless or hopeless. Rather, He so loved us and was so certain of God's power to raise Him that He could face Gethsemane and not flinch from completing His purpose.

His hope lay beyond the pain in His immediate future to His place in heaven. As such, He could face the crown of thorns, the scorn, the horrible execution, and three days in a borrowed tomb—all because He had a sure "future and a hope." And because of Him, we do, too.

The next time something happens that makes you feel hopeless, think of Christ's LifeMap. His appearance before an unjust court was unfair. His being turned over for execution made escape seem impossible. And being laid in a tomb when dead left His disciples hopeless. But no matter what happens outside us, from defamation of character to an unfair death, we can carry hope inside because we're under the loving care and guidance of the God of Easter morning.

We've focused much of our examination of Christ's life on His birth and death. We could also have looked at His miracles and parables, His quiet times with the Father, and His preaching to the multitudes. But as we close our study of Jesus' LifeMap, let's take one last look at His death and at the incredible memorial marker it leaves us.

Memorial markers: "Just as Moses lifted up the serpent . . ."

Without a doubt, all of history past and future meets at one place—the foot of the cross. And while the Lord's strong faith didn't need a tangible reminder to keep His Father's reality and presence in mind, He certainly provided *us* with the most precious memorial marker of all.

Ask 100 Bible-believing Christians if they know John 3:16, and 97 will sing out, "For God so loved the world that He gave His only begotten Son, that whoever believes in Him should not perish, but have eternal life." But ask that same group to quote John *3:14*, and the smile will drop off 99 of their faces. Only one will be able to speak out.

> *The God of unsurpassed strengths finds and invests tremendous value in* **you**.

When Jesus was teaching the religious leader Nicodemus about who He was and what it took to be saved, He called that Old Testament scholar's attention back to a pivotal "picture" in the book of Numbers: "Just as Moses lifted up the snake in the desert, so the Son of Man must be lifted up, that everyone who believes in him may have eternal life" (John 3:14-15, NIV).

Snake? What snake?

In Numbers 21:4-5, the people of Israel were once again complaining. This time, it was over a menu with too-few choices and a land with far too little water to drink. In fact, the people were so upset, they cried to go back to Egypt, the land from which God had delivered them.

"Go back to the evils of Egypt?"

When Almighty God heard their complaints, He brought the evil of Egypt to them. They had escaped from a poisonous place, and as a vivid reminder, He sent among them "fiery serpents," the very symbol of Egypt! (Pharaoh's headdress, for example, carried a replica of a viper. If they wanted Egypt, they got it!)

The snake pictured in Numbers was considered by most experts to be the horned viper, which, like a sidewinder, would burrow under the sand in the middle of a pathway. Thus hidden, it would strike viciously at anything that passed. Within half an hour, the bite was fatal. And it didn't take many minutes before the people began running to Moses with pleas for forgiveness and his intercession with the Lord on their behalf.

Moses did talk to God, and He told him to make a bronze serpent and place it up on a tall pole, a tribal standard like those used to gather bands of people together when it came time to move the nation. Now when people were bitten by a snake, they had a choice. They could look up at that snake placed high on the standard and be healed—or they could think that was too easy or too foolish a recommendation from Dr. Moses and die from lack of faith (see Num. 21:4-9).

Can you see now the memorial marker Jesus referred to when He talked about His coming death? "As Moses lifted up the serpent in the wilderness, even so must the Son of Man be lifted up; that whoever believes may in Him have eternal life" (John 3:14-15).

Only after Jesus had put the cross in its historical perspective did John 3:16—and the rest of the story—come: "For God so loved the world, that He gave His only begotten Son, that whoever believes in Him should not perish, but have eternal life."

Just as with the Israelites of old, there was now only one place the Jews (and all others) could look to keep from perishing. Any who would look up to Jesus on the cross in faith and accept God's gift of His Son as payment for their sin would escape the penalty of sin and be "born again," as Jesus instructed Nicodemus.

What a memorial marker!

That empty cross that hangs on our church walls and as jewelry around many necks once lay in full measure on Jesus' back. It's a symbol that reminds us of an Old Testament picture of a snake lifted high on a standard. And what was true then is true now. All who are wise enough to look up in faith will be saved. But for any who seek to cure the snakebite of sin by themselves or who look up to anyone or anything besides Jesus, "The wages of sin is death" (Rom. 6:23).

How about you? Have you looked in faith to Jesus? There's no escaping it; we're all snakebit. As the Bible says, "For all have sinned and fall short of the glory of God" (Rom. 3:23).

But there is a way of escape for you and me—today, if you've never done it—by looking in faith to the free gift of God, "eternal life in Christ Jesus our Lord" (Rom. 6:23).

Joining His Followers in Living for Him

That brief sketch of the most precious and powerful life ever lived is the last LifeMap we'll look at, but it should be the first one put before you each day. In fact, if you could just take out your LifeMap and then overlay it with our Lord's attitudes, actions, and decisions, you would be like Him. *And you can!*

The Word that became flesh has given us His Word today, found in the Bible. That living, inspired, inerrant Word of God can be used by the Holy Spirit to keep you on track toward a positive future. It can also pull you out of any freeze points you may have faced and from any future wanderings into image management.

It's my prayer that you have gained much in reading this book. I hope that as you practice storyboarding, it will revolutionize your communication and reduce your stress level. By "looking back," I pray that you've gained insights into the freeze points, flash points, and untied transitions that can keep you from being your best at home, in ministry, and in your job. I would be thrilled if the work you do in storyboarding a clear life plan and then reinforcing it with learned hopefulness will make your future a brighter place.

But while I sincerely wish the best for you personally and in your most important relationships as you apply LifeMapping, I would be ecstatic if something even greater happened. Namely, I hope that as a result of reading this book, you took that first look of faith to Jesus Christ as your Savior and Lord (if you had never done so before). I guarantee that by accepting Jesus' shed blood on the cross as payment in full for your sin, and by basing your LifeMap on His, you'll discover more love, joy, and peace than you ever thought possible. And what's more, from the day you become a new creation in Him, He'll begin guiding your LifeMap so that at last, it leads you into the arms of a loving God and your reserved place in His heaven.

May the Lord bless you and keep you. And may this year be the most encouraging, hope-filled one ever as you walk alongside the Author of Happy Endings.

A Final Challenge to Each Reader

You've done it! You've completed the book and your LifeMap as well. *What now?* Look closely at your individual cards to see any patterns or recurring issues or goals that capture the landscape of your life. Now may be a particularly good time to do that—*before a "wake-up call" forces you to look at or shuffle the cards the way one did to me!*

An Unwanted Memorial Marker

With this book only a few weeks away from going to the press, God gave me a vivid reminder that the various cards under my LifeMap represent much more than just an academic exercise. They tell a story I needed to look at, and they point to several immediate changes I needed to make.

On a Sunday morning, I was getting ready to preach at a large church in Orlando, Florida. The day before, Gary Smalley and I had finished the biggest "Love Is a Decision" seminar we'd ever done (some 3,600 people). I had stayed over to preach at the church's jam-packed Sunday-morning service. Afterward, I planned to race to the airport, fly all day to San Antonio, Texas, and speak that night to more than 1,500 people at one of my "Blessing" seminars.

231

That morning, however, as I got up to speak, I felt shaky and light-headed. By the end of the sermon, I was so dizzy that if I hadn't had the pulpit to hold onto, I'm certain I would have fallen down right in the midst of their televised service! Thankfully, just as I closed my message, the pastor came up to give an invitation.

"With every eye closed and head bowed," he began. I bowed out, staggered down the stairs, and stumbled to my rental car outside.

I was fighting to get my breath, and my chest was hurting. The fresh air helped, and finally I was able to drive to the airport. I had never experienced anything like that, but I figured that a few hours of sleep on the plane would cure me.

They didn't.

I arrived in San Antonio weak and still shaky, only to discover that the seminar started one hour earlier than I had thought. I had no time to rest. In fact, the conference directors were at the airport to pick me up so we could race to the church to be on time. During the three hours of the conference, I felt what little strength I had draining away like air out of a punctured balloon. It was difficult to talk; I felt as if I were speaking in a slow-motion movie.

By sitting on a stool in the last session, I managed somehow to get through the evening. Finally, the conference ended, and people were filing out when two old friends from Dallas, Logan and Lisa Ware, came up to say hello.

"Do you remember us?" they asked.

"Absolutely," I replied. "And Logan, you've got to get me to the doctor— *right now!*"

What a greeting after not seeing them in more than ten years!

I'm thankful that Logan immediately took over and drove me to a doctor who had been alerted and was on call at a local hospital. I was so dizzy and weak that I had to lean on Logan to keep from falling as I walked into the hospital. I was struggling for breath, my whole body felt numb, and I figured I was probably having a heart attack.

The doctor took one look at me and thought the same thing. He raced me to the emergency ward and immediately began the process of doing EKGs and blood tests to see what was happening.

I was admitted to the hospital that night, and the next day, after numerous tests and what seemed like pints of blood being taken, the doctor and his colleagues came to two conclusions. First, I'm happy to say, they felt I hadn't had a heart attack. But second, they concluded that an artery under my heart had "spasmed" due to allergies and exhaustion, and that had caused the heart symptoms.

As I lay in that hospital room, far from my wife and children and not sure if I'd had a heart attack or if one was coming, you can bet my LifeMap came to mind! (So, too, did all the mental pictures I had of my father lying in intensive care when he had his heart attacks. I remembered helping him put the oxygen tubes around his ears just as I had to do now, and the way he winced, as I did, when they shoved in the IV needle.)

Two cards in particular came to my mind that night and the next day. One is in the section "Image Management vs. Authentic Living" and reads, "Wouldn't accept help for years." The other is under "Emotional Freeze Points" and reads, "Unwilling to let others truly get close." In many ways, I realized those cards weren't just a picture of the past. They represented a problem I still needed to deal with today—namely, an unwillingness to ask for help, even if it was killing me.

Growing up, I tried desperately to please a father who couldn't be pleased. As a result, I convinced myself that I wouldn't show any sign of weakness and developed an "I can do it myself; I don't need anybody" attitude. I wasn't about to ask for help or let anyone close to me know that I was struggling and felt overwhelmed.

What a revelation!

As I mentioned in the chapter on untied transitions, I began a new ministry in 1993 when Gary Smalley moved to Missouri. I joked about how I was taking myself out for Secretary's Day and mentioned how many details and plates I was having to spin. What a wake-up call when I found myself flat on my back with a heart monitor strapped on, listening to an outstanding Christian doctor tell me I was being crushed by trying to carry the ministry all alone!

"You need to let others know when you're worn out and need help," the doctor said. "You can't do it all alone!"

Where had I heard that before?

As I write this, it has been several weeks since I flew home and began the process of reviewing my LifeMap. And while it has always been more than just an academic exercise for me, *it has never been this urgent.*

Already, I've started to make changes—adding some cards and taking down far more. I've cut back on a great deal of my speaking, and I've also resigned from several responsibilities I carried at my home church. Additionally, I'm getting the word out to friends across the country who want to help my ministry that I just can't do it alone. I've got to hire a secretary who can help with the correspondence, calls, and conference details that have become overwhelming for this one person.

Most of all, I've met with my board and my wife to confess my sin of "trying to carry it all" the way Moses did. Both Cindy and members of my board had acted like Jethro, Moses' father-in-law, *before* my hospitalization, calling on me to divide the workload or be crushed by it. It's not easy to admit I can't do everything by myself. But I know now that I can't. And *wow*, did the Lord ever give me a vivid picture of how the demands of this ministry have to be shifted to Him and others, not carried alone in silence.

He also gave me a graphic new memorial marker. It consists of the two hospital bands Dr. Steven VanCleave cut off my wrist when I was released. One sits framed and on my desk, and the other I carry in my billfold as a reminder to slow down and to ask others for help.

It's amazing how God has used every book I've written in a dramatic way in my own life. *The Blessing* helped me deal with issues concerning my father. *The Two Sides of Love* moved Cindy and me closer in our marriage than ever before. Now *LifeMapping* comes when I'm in the midst of major changes and redirection in my ministry, and it gives me a tool to not only encourage others, but also to be helped tremendously myself.

I pray that it doesn't take a few days in the hospital to convince you that the issues and cards on your LifeMap are real. They're an important reflection of who you are. And for me, they're a convicting reminder of what I need to do now to make sure I'm around to minister to my family and others for as long as God will allow.

May the Lord bless you as you look across the landscape of your life and see His presence in your experience. My prayers and wishes for God's best go with you, and thank you for your prayers for me and my family as well.

$\mathcal{N}$otes

CHAPTER ONE

1. For example, see D.K. Snyder and R. M. Wills, "Behavioral Versus Insight-oriented Marital Therapy: Effects on Individual and Interpersonal Functioning," *Journal of Consulting and Clinical Psychology* 57(1): pp. 39-46; and Michele Weiner-Davis, *Divorce Busting* (New York: Simon & Schuster, 1993), pp. 77ff.

2. Gary Smalley and John Trent, *The Language of Love* (Colorado Springs, Colo.: Focus on the Family, 1988, 1991).

CHAPTER TWO

1. The complete version of Dickens's *A Christmas Carol* is available from Tor Books (New York, 1988).

2. Viktor E. Frankl, *Man's Search for Meaning* (New York: Simon & Schuster, 1984), p. 81.

3. Ibid., p. 83.

CHAPTER FOUR

1. Many good books describe Da Vinci's art and "graphic design" approach. One such book is Jack Wasserman, *Leonardo da Vinci* (New York: Harry N. Abrams, 1984), p. 8.

2. Bob Thomas, *Disney's Art of Animation* (New York: Welcome Enterprises, 1991), p. 15.
3. Ibid., p. 190.
4. My thanks to Lieutenant Commander George Wilson (USN, retired) and to Ensign William D. Hunter (USN, retired) for telling me their stories of using storyboarding to develop naval ships during World War II and beyond.

CHAPTER FIVE

1. R. Karasek and T. Theorell, *Healthy Work* (New York: Basic Books, 1990), pp. 19-21.
2. Two good books on assessing your spiritual giftedness, which would be a very positive addition to your LifeMap, are Rick Yohn, *Discover Your Spiritual Gift and Use It!* (Wheaton, Ill.: Tyndale, 1974) and C. Peter Wagner, *Your Spiritual Gifts Can Help Your Church Now* (Ventura, Calif.: Regal, 1979).
3. Donald Clifton and Paula Nelson, *Soar with Your Strengths* (New York: Delacorte, 1992), p. 23.
4. Ibid., pp. 19-20.
5. Adapted from the wonderful story recounted by Jack Canfield and Mark Victor Hansen in *Chicken Soup for the Soul* (Deerfield Beach, Fla.: Health Communications, 1993), pp. 125-28.

CHAPTER SIX

1. If you want to find an excellent Christian counselor in your area, the outstanding professionals at Rapha Treatment Centers can help. They've been invaluable to me in launching Encouraging Words, and they offer a nationwide counseling assessment and referral number: 1-800-383-HOPE.
2. Christopher Peterson and Lisa Bossio, *Health and Optimism* (New York: The Free Press, 1991), p. 2; see table 1-1, "Historical Perspective on Optimism Versus Pessimism."
3. C. Peterson, M. Seligman, and G. Vaillant, "Pessimistic Explanatory Style Is a Risk Factor for Physical Illness," *Journal of Personality and Social Psychology*, 55 (1988), pp. 23-27.
4. C. Peterson, D. Colvin, and E. Lin, "Explanatory Style and Helplessness," unpublished manuscript, University of Michigan, reported in Peterson and Bossio, *Health and Optimism*, p. 34.

5. H. Eyseneck, "Personality and Stress as Causal Factors in Cancer and Coronary Heart Disease," in M.P. Janisse, ed., *Individual Differences, Stress, and Health Psychology* (New York: Springer-Verlag, 1988), pp. 121-27.

6. R. Desowitz, *The Thorn in the Starfish* (New York: Norton, 1987), p. 91.

7. John Gottman, *Why Marriages Succeed or Fail* (New York: Simon & Schuster, 1994), p. 20.

8. Forgiveness can be difficult when you're hurting. For a good book to help speed the healing process, see Charles Stanley, *The Gift of Forgiveness* (Nashville: Thomas Nelson, 1987).

CHAPTER SEVEN

1. "Personal Glimpses," *Reader's Digest*, May 1992, p. 87.

2. Peter W. Bernstein, "Unforgettable Dr. Seuss, " *Reader's Digest*, April 1992, pp. 60-64.

CHAPTER EIGHT

1. M. Parker, W. Achenbaum, G. Fuller, and W. Fay, quoting from J. William Jones, "Personal Reminiscences, Anecdotes, and Letters of General Robert E. Lee," in Douglas S. Freeman, *Robert E. Lee,* vol. IV (New York: Scribner's, 1948), p. 206.

2. For a more complete account of that experience with my father and the lessons God taught me in the process, see Gary Smalley and John Trent, *The Gift of the Blessing* (Nashville: Thomas Nelson, 1993). See especially chapter 11, "When You Know You'll Never Receive a Parent's Blessing."

3. For a helpful look at what do when a pastor or church leader does fall (and how to help prevent it), see the excellent book by Dr. Ted Kitchens, *Aftershock, What to Do When Leaders (and others) Fail You* (Portland, Ore.: Multnomah, 1992).

CHAPTER NINE

1. Duncan Maxwell Anderson, "The Art of Deceit: From China, Principles of Strategy and Deception for Entrepreneurs," *Success,* March 1994, pp. 49-51.

2. Roger Connors, Thom Smith, and Craig Hickman, *The Oz Principle* (New York: Prentice Hall, 1994).

CHAPTER TEN

1. All the books in this series are published by Thomas Nelson.

2. H. Norman Wright and Gary Oliver, *Kids Have Feelings Too!* (Wheaton, Ill.: Victor Books, 1993).

3. H. Norman Wright and Gary Oliver, *Men Have Feelings Too!* (Wheaton, Ill.: Victor Books, 1993).

4. For information on starting a *CrossTrainers* chapter in your community, call Tom Vander Well at the CrossTrainers' office: 515-225-0034.

CHAPTER ELEVEN

1. For the Draveckys' inspiring story, see their outstanding book (written with Ken Gire), *When You Can't Come Back* (New York: Harper Collins/Zondervan, 1992).

2. Christopher Peterson and Lisa Bossio, *Health and Optimism* (New York: The Free Press, 1991), p. 91; Martin Seligman, *Learned Optimism* (New York: Pocket, 1990), p. 69.

3. Peterson and Bossio, *Health and Optimism*, p. 77.

CHAPTER FOURTEEN

1. Merritt Y. Hughes, ed. *John Milton, Complete Poems and Major Prose,* vol. I (New York: The Odyssey Press, 1974), p. 155.

23 Memorial Markers Others Have Used

Over the years, as I've worked with couples and singles, I've collected a number of their everyday memorial markers. If the concept of memorial markers is new to you, take time to read through the following descriptions for ideas that can easily be within your reach. These real-life suggestions may help you think of something that makes your commitment, goal, or desire for change more concrete.

1. "Our memorial marker is a ceramic inkwell with a long quill pen. We bought this together and leave it sitting out on the desk in our bedroom. Each day when we see it, it reminds us that, by God's grace, we're able to write a new page in our life story."

2. "For my marker, I splurged and bought a real nice, wooden duck decoy. What it represents to me is a rough piece of wood that a skilled hand lovingly carved and painted until it looks as if it could come alive. That's what the Lord has done for me . . . cutting away the rough edges and

bringing me to life. I leave it sitting out at work, and it's a great reminder of who He's helping me to become."

3. My good friend (and Focus author) Tim Kimmel has a wonderful memorial marker I explain with his permission. On top of his rolltop desk, he has two small pictures that sit on opposite sides of a large picture of his wife and children. The picture on the left is a photo of the hospital where Tim was born. The one on the right is a photo of the Kimmel family cemetery plot, where Tim will one day be laid to rest. In between where he came from and where he'll end up is that photo of Darcy, his wife, and their four children. This display graphically reminds him of where he came from, where he's heading, and what's important while he's alive.

4. "It's a small thing, but our memorial marker is a wooden clothespin with the words *God's love* handwritten on it. It's a reminder that no matter how hectic things get, His love is what holds everything together for us."

5. "My husband and I brought back a fairly large piece of coral from our once-in-a-lifetime trip to Hawaii. The marker reminds us of our commitment to take 'five-minute vacations' from our hectic schedules."

6. "Jayne and I have an unusual memorial marker that means the world to us. Two years ago, I was between jobs, and our savings had been totally depleted. We were facing the certain loss of our home. That's when an unmarked envelope came with two months' house payment inside. That literally made the difference between us keeping or losing our house. We feel certain it was someone from our church, but we still don't know for sure today. We framed that envelope as a reminder of how faithful God has been to us."

7. "My memorial marker is a small, antique, red wagon that I've turned into a coffee table in my home. It's not pretty anymore, but it's sturdy and reliable and gaining more value as an antique every day. And by the way, I'm a senior citizen. That wagon reminds me of my continued worth to God and others as I get older."

8. "The marker I use is something I know meant the world to my grand-father. It's his old, folding carpenter's ruler, all scratched and weather-beaten. I keep it on top of my desk as a reminder of the godly heritage he left me. He always walked the straight and narrow, and it's a reminder to me to be a man of integrity."

9. "I decided to carry a pocket watch instead of a wristwatch to remind me of my commitment to my God and family. I had engraved on the outside my wife and son's initials, plus my favorite verses, Joshua 1:8-9. It's a hassle sometimes to have to reach into my pocket to look for the time, but it always reminds me of what's most important to me when I do."

10. "Our memorial marker has to do with adding more 'softness' to the way we treat each other. We each bought one of those extra-soft teddy bears as softness reminders. Not only have they worked, but having stuffed animals on my bed makes me feel like a kid again!"

11. "I have a fishing lure hanging in my sewing room, framed in a shadow box. While I don't fish, it's a reminder of all the times my father spent with me when I was young, fishing. It makes me think of the time he gave up for me and of how I want to be there for my children."

12. "We went through the terrible experience of a two-year-long lawsuit. There were days when we not only wanted to give up, but we questioned God as well. We found our memorial marker at the mall after a really tough day. We were walking through a shop when my husband and I both saw a ceramic bulldog dressed up to look like Winston Churchill. When we both stopped laughing, we bought it, and it was a great reminder to us to have the tenacity of a bulldog to get through that lawsuit—and we did!"

13. "While nobody else would pick out my memorial marker, I see it every time I pull open the bathroom medicine chest. There, amidst my shaver and various sprays, is a bottle of Old Spice aftershave. It's empty except for its lingering smell. But it was my father's last bottle of aftershave, and it makes me think of him. I keep it to remind me that I'm building memories for my kids every day."

14. "After learning about LifeMapping and memorial markers, I thought of something I needed to change, and I ran into a picture of my commitment at the mall. I was going by a knife shop and saw a beautiful pocketknife with a carved handle. Now I carry a constant reminder to 'cut out' one particular negative pattern from the past."

15. "My marker is a miniature brass telescope. It reminds me to focus attention on important issues like my relationship with Christ and my family. You'd be surprised how many people ask about it as it lies on my desk, and I get to cement my commitment all over again in telling them!"

16. "My grandmother's wire-rimmed glasses are what I use to remind me of my commitment to be more like Christ. She had blue, piercing eyes that her glasses didn't dim a bit, and she was a model of someone committed to God's service. Just having them on my dresser at home is a reminder to be like her and to be all I can become for the Lord."

17. "While it's nothing spectacular, our memorial marker is a large sea shell we picked up on a trip to Hawaii several years ago. It's one of those fluted shells, where you can put it up to your ear and still 'hear' the ocean's roar. This reminds us that our children will remember—and be able to play back—the words we say to them. Years from now, we want the sound others hear coming from their lives to be a pleasing sound and memory."

18. "It's shut down now, but I used to live near an iron smelter. My marker is a 5x7 picture that sits on my desk of that old plant running at full steam, with the sparks and red glow of molten iron being poured out. It's my desire that God purify and melt away the impurities in my life as well, so that I can be someone who supports others and stands the test of time."

19. "At our wedding, a wealthy friend of my father's gave us a genuine Waterford crystal paperweight. For a long time, we just put it away because our house was mostly antiques. But after learning about memorial markers, we took it out to remind us to treat each other and the children as *extremely valuable . . .* and *very fragile.*"

20. "After your conference where you talked about LifeMapping, my husband came up with our memorial marker. He's in land development and often commissions an aerial photograph to be taken of a tract of land he's considering purchasing. We talked about it, and he had a pilot go up and take an aerial view of our neighborhood! That's our reminder that we need to think and pray not just for our house, but for our neighbors and community around us as well."

21. "I was driving past my old neighborhood several months ago when I saw my memorial marker. Due to redistricting, the area getting older, and fewer people having kids in that section of town, they tore down my old grade school. I stopped the car while they were demolishing it, went over, and picked up a brick. To everyone else it's just an old brick, but to me, it's a reminder that I'm from the 'old school,' where commitment, honor, and love meant something. It's also a reminder that if I let anger or dishonor enter my home, it can tear my home down the way my school was torn down."

22. "I come from a family where favoritism was practiced. I know what it's like to feel left out, and that's why I chose a small brass measuring scale like the legal scales you see. I bought two small weights that weigh the same and put them on each side of the scale so they're balanced there. That's a picture to me of my goal in blessing my children—to keep things in balance as much as I can so my kids don't feel the way I did."

23. "My memorial marker is a small piece of rusted iron I picked up. I've struggled with anger a lot, and I'm finally committed to getting the help and support I need to control it. That rusted iron is a reminder that anger can rust what's precious to me (like my marriage) if I don't get help."

*T*ripling Your Task Effectiveness at Home and at Work

Nearly 15 years ago, the seminar leader who taught me storyboarding said, "Without question, this method will triple the effectiveness of the meetings you have and cut their time in half!" When I heard that, my ears perked up! Like many of you, life seemed to be one nonstop meeting, leaving little time to actually get important tasks done.

In this book, I've stressed the use of storyboarding to help draw out and create a "high point" picture of your life story. But as I mentioned, you can also use it for any number of tasks both at work and at home. In this appendix, I've provided three additional storyboards that show how you can use the tool for such personal applications.

First, you'll see how a couple storyboarded their move, gaining a clear plan for a transition that can be incredibly frustrating. That's the same thing Cindy and I did when we moved from Dallas to Phoenix. The storyboard had us so well organized that the night before the movers came, we were packed and swimming at the Summit Hotel, ready to meet them at the house the next morning.

The second storyboard refers to the couple mentioned in chapter 2 who turned storyboarding loose on their Christmas holiday and reduced their stress dramatically. By working together to get all the component parts of their hectic schedule in front of them, they could shift certain things, eliminate others, and emphasize still other aspects of the holidays. Instead of feeling crushed by the horde of details, once they got them up and saw them, they took control of many variables. That way the negatives were cut down, and they had a wonderful time celebrating the birth of our Lord.

The third storyboard shows how a big project—in this case a reunion for more than 40 families—was planned. While such a storyboard could go into more detail, the edited version that's here will show you how the people pulled off a wonderful family time without a hitch.

Finally, you'll see how one church used storyboarding to design a successful camping experience for 200 families. That's just one of many church activities that could be planned more efficiently with this great tool.

The storyboards in this appendix are just four of hundreds of examples I could give. You could turn storyboarding loose in your place of ministry to plan a preaching schedule for the year, to develop an outreach program for the church, or to design a parenting or new believers' class.

Likewise, you could use it at work to help you write your job description (but don't be surprised when you do this for the first time and have 14 major topper cards). Or you could storyboard a team project—anything from developing quality systems to designing an advertising campaign.

As you can see, storyboarding has endless applications. After you've tried it, please write and tell me how you used it. I'll compile a list of creative ideas for inclusion in a later edition of this book. You can reach me at Encouraging Words, 12629 N. Tatum Blvd., Suite 208, Phoenix, AZ 85032.

Sample Storyboards

Moving

Purpose Steve/Jane	Company/ Personal Steve	Packing Material Jane	Boxing Items Jane	Packing Team Steve	Moving Van Steve
To follow God's calling	Do-it-yourself moving van	Tape gun & tape	Small boxes	Friends from church	Size
To begin grad school	Ck. prices on moving co.	White packing paper	Medium boxes	Friends from work	Number of days allowed
To live in Phoenix		Bubble wrap for dishes	Large boxes	Professional packers	
		Blankets	Wardrobe boxes		
		Rope	Mirror boxes		
		Peanuts	Mattress boxes		

Auto Steve	Trip Route /Misc. Steve/Jane	Fun on the Road Jane	Estimated Trip Costs Steve	Unpacking Team Steve	Receipts Jane
Check tires	Buy map	Games in the car	Auto fuel costs	Friend in Phoenix	Jane will hold receipts
Change oil/fluids	Route trip	Go to Six Flags	Van rental costs		
New wiper blades	Estimate travel time		Moving van est. fuel costs		
Check fan belts	Make hotel reservations		MV insurance costs		
			Estimate fun costs		
			Hotel costs		
			Food costs		

Christmas Holiday

Purpose

To celebrate Christ's birth

To show my family love

To create memories for the family

To communicate with friends

Church Services

Christmas Eve services

Regular Sunday services

"Events"

Lighting of the downtown lights

The living Christmas tree

Office party

Home fellowship white elephant party

Sunday school party

Kids' parties

Family Memories

Decorating together

Daily Advent calendar

Cut a tree this year

Singing around the tree

Travel north to play in the snow

Home Decorating	Gifts (Family)	Gifts (Others)
Buy the tree	Matthew	Grandparents
December 3 decorating day	Hannah	Parents
Buy some extra lights	Bethany	High's family gift draw
	Robin	Steger's family gift draw
	Greg	Robin's friends
		Greg's friends

Family Reunion

Purpose	Date	Place	Family Olympics	Food
To have fun	August 18-24	Stutts Ranch	3-leg race	Giant sub sandwich
To see relatives		Hyatt Hotel	Life Saver pass	Fried fish/chicken
To renew relationships		Motel 6	Leg sit	Lasagna
To strengthen the bond		Greenway Baptist Church	Potato-sack race	(Lunches) on your own
			Piggyback races	Pancakes
			Tug of war	Breakfast tacos
			Egg-on-the-spoon race	Cereal
			Puggy Bunny	
			Hippity-hop race (under 5)	

Sat. Night Sharing	Sunday Devotions	Family Picture	Cook/Clean Teams
Mom Stutts	Singing (Richard)	Time	Red
Mom Miller	Devotional (Darrell)	Place	Green
		Professional	Purple
			Blue

Family Camp
First Baptist Church

Purpose

To encourage growth in Christ

To create stronger family relationships

To stimulate the building of friendships between families

To learn principles on becoming a better parent

To have FUN!

Site Selection/ Facilities

Sleeping for 200 families

Gymnasium

Outdoor sports

Camp prepares the food

Water sports

Theme

Parenting

Family relationships

"The Blessing"

Trusting Christ

Promotion

Develop materials: posters/brochures

Coordinate pulpit announcements

Promote in adult classes

Write drama for Sunday morning worship

Have speaker come early and speak at service

Family Activities	Registration	Closing/ Follow-up
Volleyball	At church	Special drama
Horseback riding	At camp	Honest & open sharing at campfire
Lake day		Family dedication (written covenant)
Arts and crafts		Small groups back home for adults
Olympics		Small groups back home for youth

More Family-Strengthening Tools From John Trent, Ph.D.
Uncover the keys to a more satisfying life. These valuable resources offer
encouragement and practical advice for enriching your relationships with
your spouse, children, friends, and colleagues.

LifeMapping (SoundWritings)

Break free of the past and move toward a brighter future with *LifeMapping*—
also available on tape. Convenient to listen to while driving, walking, jogging, or
running errands. Two audiocassettes. 180 minutes.

The Hidden Value of a Man

John Trent and Gary Smalley reveal why men are often successful in their
professional lives but powerless in showing affection to their families. This popular
book will help you step back and take an honest inventory of your relationships and
realize the importance of showing respect to those nearest the heart.

The Two Sides of Love

Discover what it takes to make a commitment *really* last. Trent and Smalley present
the key to healthy, fulfilling relationships—balancing love's hard and soft sides. This
best-seller can help you develop a unique closeness with the people you care about
most. Also available in paperback with study guide.

The Language of Love

Couples often struggle for years to achieve a deep level of intimacy, but they miss
the mark due to poor communication skills. In this widely acclaimed paperback,
Trent and Smalley reveal dynamic ways to maximize insight, intimacy, and understanding in our marriages, families, friendships, and professions. Study guide
included.

These titles are available at your local Christian bookstore.

For information about John Trent's seminars or other resources offered by the Encouraging Words ministry, write to John at the following address:

John Trent
Encouraging Words
12629 N. Tatum Blvd.
Suite 208
Phoenix, AZ 85032